Coaching Myths

D0525087

Coaching Myths

Fifteen **Wrong** *Ideas in Youth Sports*

RICK ALBRECHT

McFarland & Company, Inc., Publishers
Jefferson, North Carolina, and London

LIBRARY OF CONGRESS CATALOGUING-IN-PUBLICATION DATA

Albrecht, Rick, 1952–
    Coaching myths : fifteen wrong ideas in youth sports /
Rick Albrecht.
        p.   cm.
    Includes bibliographical references and index.

    ISBN 978-0-7864-7369-4
    softcover : acid free paper ∞

    1. Sports for children — Coaching.   2. Coaching (Athletics)
I. Title.
GV709.24.A54 2013
796.083 — dc23   2013007515

BRITISH LIBRARY CATALOGUING DATA ARE AVAILABLE

Cover photograph © 2013 Photodisc/Thinkstock

Manufactured in the United States of America

*McFarland & Company, Inc., Publishers
    Box 611, Jefferson, North Carolina 28640
        www.mcfarlandpub.com*

Acknowledgments

As is the case with nearly every acknowledgments section of nearly every book published, I must begin by stating that it would be impossible to list all the individuals who provided me with guidance, reassurance, suggestions, and support while I was writing this book. I will therefore only mention two groups of people without whom this task would never have been undertaken, let alone, completed. First, are the hundreds of students enrolled in my classes at Grand Valley State University who read, reread, edited, discussed, and greatly improved each successive draft. Second, are my many mentors and colleagues at the Institute for the Study of Youth Sports at Michigan State University who were there at the beginning of this rewarding journey into the world of coaching education.

Table of Contents

Preface: Rethinking the Way We Coach

"In the beginner's mind there are many possibilities, but in the expert's there are few."
— Soto Zen master Shunryu Suzuki[1]

"It's what you learn AFTER you know it ALL that counts."
— Sign prominently displayed in
Coach John Wooden's office[2]

The responsibilities and demands placed on youth sport, interscholastic, and intercollegiate coaches are frequently underestimated. As coaches, we are not only expected to teach motor skills to young athletes but to do so in an environment that is conducive to the ethical, emotional, social, and physical well-being of each and every one of our athletes. Tasks as important as these cannot be accomplished in a haphazard fashion. They require deliberate and conscious thought. As illustrated by the two quotes at the top of this page — one based on ancient wisdom, the other on years of practical coaching experience at the highest level — the more we think we know about coaching (or anything else for that matter), the less likely we are to learn new and better ways of being a coach. Simply put, to improve ourselves and our athletes, we have to stop coaching out of habit and challenge ourselves to rethink the way we do the little things.

If we have any desire of becoming effective coaches, the first question we have to answer is also the most obvious — "Why do I want to be a coach?" Although the question may be obvious, its answer very often is not. When I ask students in my coaching education classes this question I generally get one response — "Because I like sports." Liking sports (or at least a given sport) is indeed a prerequisite for coaching — necessary yes, but hardly sufficient. How does "liking sports" make you different from just about everyone else you know? Your dentist probably likes sports. Your accountant

1

probably likes sports. Your plumber probably likes sports. But why have you decided to be a coach instead of a dentist, accountant, or plumber? Believe it or not, I've had a couple students actually admit that they were training to be coaches "Because I can't do anything else." Although I appreciate their candor, I can't say that I'm comforted by the fact there are people out there who choose to become coaches simply because they can't (or don't think they can) do anything else.

The first step in improving ourselves as coaches requires us to do pretty much what we tell our athletes to do — take a good, hard look at ourselves and assess our strengths and weaknesses. Needless to say, this can sometimes be an uncomfortable experience for those of us who are more accustomed to scrutinizing the performances of others. The following questions might help you get started. Simply take a couple minutes to reflect on the following questions every day:

- What went well in practice today?
- What didn't go so well today?
- Where does the athlete or team still need to improve?
- What can I do to make myself a better coach for this team?
- Is there anything I can do that would make me a more effective teacher?
- Did my players have fun today?
- Did I have fun today?
- Did I send an unmistakable message to my players that I really love being their coach?

How Do We Learn to Be Coaches?

If you're like most of us, you've had very little formal training to be a coach. Although more and more colleges and universities are offering degrees and certificates in coaching, most of us developed our coaching philosophies, ethics, strategies, tactics, practice plans, and even our pep talks by watching other coaches. Those of us who were athletes got our first taste of what coaching was all about by watching the way our own coaches conducted practices and executed game plans. In fact, much of the practical education we received came from working long hours of "apprenticeship"— as volunteers and assistants — under the tutelage of more experienced coaches. Even now we often find ourselves coming away from a coaching clinic or televised game with an idea from a well-known coach. The way we learn our coaching style from others reminds me of something I saw as a child.

When I was a young boy, the circus came to town. As was customary when the circus visited a small town like ours, they publicized their arrival by parading their animals, clowns, and acrobats down Main Street. The thing I remember most about these parades was the way they had trained the massive elephants to walk in a straight line. To keep these powerful, sensitive, and intelligent beasts from going off on their own, the elephants had been trained — from the time they were small and vulnerable — to feel most secure and safe when they had their trunks intertwined with the tail of the elephant in front of them. The handlers merely had to make certain the lead elephant (usually one so old and weak it was unlikely to present a challenge) went where they wanted. By habit, all the others would mindlessly follow along, comforted by the sense that they were linked to their herd. Might they have been happier going in another direction? Might they have found more food, shade, or water just by veering a bit to their right or left? Perhaps, but it really doesn't matter because none of the elephants ever attempted to go anywhere other than where those before them had gone.

And so it often is with coaches. We feel comfortable simply copying what we've seen other successful coaches do. But like the elephants on parade, we sacrifice the possibility of improving ourselves in order to maintain our sense of security. This is far more than my personal observation. Research supports the fact that coaches often base their approach to coaching on their experiences as an athlete, and by working with experienced coaches (Lemyre, Trudel, and Durand-Bush 2007).

There's little doubt that we all learn valuable lessons from watching the mistakes and successes of others. In fact, it is so common psychologists even have a term for it — vicarious learning. We need to keep in mind, however, that it's not sufficient to simply be as good as our coaches and teachers — it's our job to be *better* than our coaches. And that requires abandoning our herd mentality.

Our understanding of what makes for good coaching is constantly changing and coaches in the Twenty-first Century can't afford to limit themselves by mimicking what others — or they — have done in the past. A striking example of how the coaching profession has changed can be seen in an ESPN documentary from a few years back, *The Junction Boys*. The movie — based on a book by the same name (Dent 1999) — depicts the appalling way legendary football coach Paul "Bear" Bryant physically and mentally "conditioned" (some would say "tortured") his Texas A&M players at training camp prior to the 1954 football season. His long and harsh physical practices that went on for 10 days in the 100 degree Texas heat, his withholding of water, and his failure to provide proper medical care might have been an accepted way to "toughen up" players at the time but would likely result in a coach today being sued — or perhaps even being sent to prison if they followed the lead of this celebrated and successful coach.[3]

How This Book — and the Greatest Coaches Ever — Can Help You Be a Better Coach

This book contains no special magic. In fact, the only thing "special" about it at all is that it will allow you to systematically examine some of the most commonly held myths we, as coaches, tend to pass on from one generation to the next.

Although the information in each chapter is based on the most current scientific evidence available (please notice all the scientific references that are given), each is written in the everyday language of coaches and covers the topics that we all deal with on a daily basis. As a way of demonstrating the practical significance of each chapter, you will see that each myth or misconception is introduced with a quote from a famous and successful coach. We'll see that these icons of coaching often break with tradition and discover for themselves that much of what passes for "conventional wisdom" are little more than myths, misconceptions, and mistakes that are mindlessly passed on from generation to generation. The coaches who will provide the keynote quote for the chapters are:

• Bill Walsh: Elected to the Pro Football Hall of Fame in 1993, Coach Walsh took a floundering San Francisco 49ers team to three Super Bowl championships and established the foundation for his successor, George Seifert, to win two more. His innovative "West Coast Offense" and superior leadership style changed the way professional football was played.

• Tom Izzo: Considered one of today's premier college coaches, Coach Izzo has guided his Michigan State University men's basketball teams to seven Big Ten Championships, six NCAA Final Four appearances, and an NCAA Championship in 2000. His success at the helm of the Spartans led ESPN basketball guru Andy Katz to declare that MSU was the top college basketball team in the country during the decade between 1998 and 2007 (Katz 2007).

• Mike Krzyzewski: "Coach K" has won more NCAA Division I Men's Basketball games than any coach in history. In his 37 years as a head coach at Army and Duke his teams have won 927 games, made 11 NCAA Final Four appearances, and won four NCAA Division I Championships.

Krzyzewski also served as the head coach of the gold medal-winning USA Olympic Basketball team in 2008 and 2012.

• C. Vivian Stringer: The first coach in the history of college basketball to lead three different teams to the NCAA Women's Basketball Final Four, Coach Stringer is the third winningest coach in women's college basketball and has been named the Naismith College Coach of the Year (1992). She was inducted into the Basketball Hall of Fame in 2009.

• Joe Torre: During every one of the 12 years he was manager of the New York Yankees, Torre led his team into post-season competition. During his tenure the Yankees won six American League pennants and four World Series championships. In 2008 he became the manager of the Los Angeles Dodgers and promptly took his new team to two consecutive post-season appearances. In total, Torre won 2,326 Major League games as a manager.

• Dean Smith: When he retired as the head men's basketball coach at the University of North Carolina in 1997, Coach Smith had accumulated more NCAA college basketball victories than any coach in the history of the game. During his 36 years at the helm of the Tar Heel program his teams won 30 Atlantic Coast Conference regular season and tournament championships, went to 11 NCAA Final Fours and won the NCAA Men's Basketball Championship in 1982 and 1993. Coach Smith's coaching accomplishments were acknowledged by his induction into the Basketball Hall of Fame in 1983 and the College Basketball Hall of Fame in 2006.

• Tony Dungy: Considered one of the true gentlemen in pro football (Chandler 2011), Coach Dungy led the Tampa Bay Buccaneers and the Indianapolis Colts to 11 post-season appearances in his 13 years as a head coach. In 2007, the protégé of four-time Super Bowl champion coach Chuck Noll, won his own Super Bowl championship with the Indianapolis Colts and became the first African American head coach to win an NFL championship.

• Tom Landry: A true legend in professional football, the stoic Tom Landry served as head coach of the Dallas Cowboys for 29 years. During that time his teams had 20 consecutive winning seasons, won five NFC Championships and two Super Bowls (1971 and 1977). In 1990 Landry's lifetime of accomplishment earned him a spot in the Pro Football Hall of Fame.

• Pete Carroll: Currently the head coach of the Seattle Seahawks, and formerly the top man with the New York Jets and the New England Patriots, Coach Carroll is probably best known for his accomplishments while the head coach of the University of Southern California (USC) Trojan football team from 2001 to 2009. He took the Trojans to a bowl game in each of his nine years as head coach and seven straight years led his teams to top four finishes in the Associated Press poll — including a ranking of #1 in the nation for 33 consecutive weeks. Carroll's Trojans also won back-to-back National Championships in 2003 and 2004.

• Dan Bylsma: As the youngest coach in the NHL at the time, Coach Bylsma took his Pittsburgh Penguins to the 2009 Stanley Cup championship just four months after being named the team's head coach. In his first 25 games that year, he guided his team to an 18-3-4 record — the second best start by a new coach in league history. The following year Bylsma was presented the Jack Adams Award as the NHL's most outstanding coach.

• Jason Garrett: While serving as offensive coordinator and assistant head coach of the Dallas Cowboys, Jason Garrett became one of the most sought-after young coaches in the NFL. In 2011, he was named the eighth head coach of the Cowboys.

It is no coincidence that I also rely heavily on the words of Coach Wooden throughout the book. Over the years his wisdom about coaching (and life) has inspired millions of coaches — and a far greater number of non-coaches. I had the honor of meeting this man I consider the greatest coach — and teacher — of all time when he visited Kalamazoo, Michigan, to support the Western Michigan University basketball program (he had become friends with the then Bronco head coach Steve Hawkins years earlier when Hawkins served as his "driver" at basketball camps). During our brief one-on-one chat, Coach Wooden was, as you might expect, the most gracious and generous man I had ever met. But it was what happened after our meeting that made me fully understand the tremendous impact Coach Wooden has had. This elderly gentleman (he was 95 at the time) never coached a local team, had no affiliation with nearby schools, and had coached his final college game long before many of the 3,000 people in attendance were even born. But there they were. Folks from 9 to 90, men, women, boys, and girls of every race and ethnicity showed up that evening simply to hear what this man had to say. Coach Wooden epitomizes the way we should all coach. He serves as my role model and I hope he will be yours too.

If some of the information presented in this book makes you uncomfortable — that's exactly the way it should be. You might even disagree so much with certain parts of the book that you'll find yourself trying to dismiss or deny its truth. That's perfectly normal. Whenever we're confronted by a whole new way of thinking it makes us uncomfortable. Just keep in mind that this book is based on our best understanding of coaching theory — at least today. Perhaps fifty years from now someone will have to write another book debunking the myths put forth in this one. Until then, the information in this book presents the most scientifically based way to help you become a better coach.

"Mastering the Xs and Os Will Make You a Successful Coach"

People matter most—more than equipment ... or Xs and Os. People are at the heart of achieving organizational greatness.
—Coach Bill Walsh[1]

Have you ever noticed that, when left to their own devices, our athletes will generally choose to practice the skills they are good at while purposely avoiding the skills they really need to improve and therefore *should* be practicing? (Don't worry, in the Myth No. 2 chapter we'll discuss ways we can help them make better decisions). It's a frustrating three-step cycle that results in little overall improvement in performance as depicted in Figure 1.1.

Although most of us can easily recognize these unproductive behaviors in our athletes, it is much harder for us to accept the fact that we are engaging in the same self-limiting behaviors nearly every time we attend a coaching clinic or study a diagram in a coaching magazine. As coaches, we absolutely *love* our Xs and Os. We attend clinics and workshops in the hope of stumbling across a new drill, a new strategy, a new technique, a new tactic, a new offense, or a new defense that might give us a competitive advantage. We scour the coaching literature for any "gadget," "gimmick," "trick," or "wrinkle" we can add to our already overflowing arsenal of surefire "gotchas."

Organizers of coaching clinics and producers of coaching materials understand perfectly well that coaches are primarily interested in Xs and Os and, like all good entrepreneurs, they make a living giving their customers what they want. In just the past month for example, I attended two coaching education meetings. At least a dozen times the organizers of these two sessions stressed the importance of "luring the coaches in" to our educational program by offering, as bait, what the coaches want most — Xs and Os. As a result, an endless line of "successful" coaches are paraded before us and

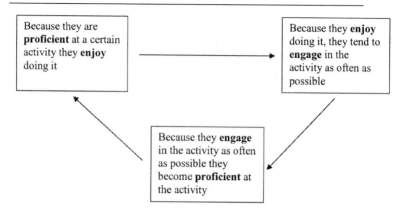

Of course the reverse is also true:

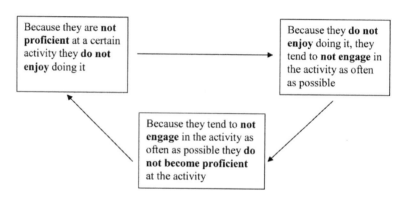

Figure 1.1: Cycle of Practice Preferences Resulting in Little Improvement in Perform-ance.

we sit mesmerized by their every word — resolute in our belief that whatever it was that worked for them will work equally well for us.

Now there's nothing wrong with whiling away the hours rubbing elbows with the "rich and famous" of the coaching profession or listening to their often cited (and perhaps somewhat embellished) "war stories." Nothing wrong, that is, unless we have fooled ourselves into believing that we are acquiring privileged information that will somehow help us become a better coach. The unfortunate truth is it usually won't — for a variety of reasons. Two of these reasons, in particular, deserve special mention. First, as you can well imagine, it's often impossible for us to reproduce the exact conditions that allowed these techniques to work in the first place. Second, we coaches — like many professionals — tend to overestimate the overall contribution technical expertise has on our success.

You Coach Under Very Different Conditions

Let's begin by examining why "your mileage may vary" when attempting to implement techniques that apparently worked so well for some of the "big-name" coaches in your sport. One reason is that these coaches rarely tell us about the successes they had when they were coaching at *our* level (many of them, in fact, never coached at our level at all). Instead, they entertain us with colorful anecdotes about what worked for them when they were coaching elite college, professional, or Olympic athletes. Although we typically find their stories interesting enough, the question we should be asking is whether or not these experiences are relevant to our particular coaching situation. Specifically, it might help if we ask ourselves five simple questions to determine the degree to which their athletes and situations are similar to ours and thus, the extent to which we might expect their positive experiences to transfer to our team and to our athletes:

Question #1: Do my athletes possess the same level of physical, perceptual, and cognitive development?

Physical development. What might be a perfectly appropriate skill or tactic for an elite adult athlete might be horribly inappropriate when used with less mature or less skilled athletes. For example, knowing how the San Antonio Spurs successfully break a full court press or the weight training regime employed by the Oakland Raiders will provide us with little useful information if we are coaching junior high school basketball or "pee-wee" football. Not only are our athletes often physically incapable of performing these skills (imagine most seventh graders throwing a length-of-the-court overhand "baseball" pass to an open cutter under the basket) they can often do more harm than good to a physically immature body (much of any weight training resembling that employed by an NFL team would obviously be inappropriate for youth sport football players).

I am reminded of the hundreds of youth baseball coaching clinics I presented while working at the Institute for the Study of Youth Sports at Michigan State University. Hardly a clinic went by where a coach — driven by a burning desire to dominate the rest of the league — didn't ask me how to best teach the mechanics of throwing a "curve," "slider," "slurve," "split-fingered fastball," or "sinker" to his 11-year-old pitcher (not surprisingly, the boy was often the coach's son). Even if such a pitch could be mastered, the irreparable damage it might cause to a youngster's undeveloped joints, tendons, ligaments, and muscles renders the question ludicrous. Despite its inappropriateness, coaches constantly clamored for this information and, if I had favored them with these demonstrations, they would have no doubt rewarded me with hours of undivided attention (not to mention better speaker evaluation ratings).

Perceptual development. Sport performances require athletes to take in and process tremendous amounts of rapidly changing information about themselves and their environment. Imagine how much sensory input needs to be analyzed in a fraction of a second just to catch a "routine" fly ball. Similarly, consider the body-hand-foot-eye coordination needed to successfully execute an overhand serve of a tennis ball, head a soccer ball past an opposing goaltender, do a forward roll on a balance beam, make an accurate bounce-pass to a running teammate, or use a crooked stick to flip a sliding piece of rubber between defenders, while balancing on two thin metal blades on a surface of ice. As coaches we need to understand that young children don't have the ability to process complex sensory information as efficiently as adults. For example, most of us have watched baseball and softball coaches hitting towering fly balls to their young outfielders. Now, here's something to think about. How many of those long fly balls were actually caught? It's easy to think that most of the balls were simply missed because the young players lacked the skills needed to make these catches and, given the demands of the game, this may seem like a perfectly reasonable expenditure of practice time. Perfectly reasonable that is, until you consider the fact that the outfielders needed far more than ball-catching repetitions. Until their eyes reach adult proportions; young children generally lack the visual capability (technically called "dynamic visual acuity") to track the flight of a long, arching fly ball (Morris 1977; Sanderson and Whiting 1974; 1978). Oops. At a minimum, having them try to catch these long fly balls is a total waste of valuable practice time. But even far more damage could have been done. First, having the ball players try to perform a task they simply can't do only leads to frustration and a sense of incompetence. The come away with the misimpression that they're just not very good at this game. Second, and this should be of greater concern, having the outfielders attempt this drill puts them in danger of sustaining a serious injury. Having our athletes engage in an activity where they could easily get hit in the head with a long fly ball — just because they can't see it properly, is a risk we should never ask them to take. As coaches, we need to educate ourselves regarding the perceptual abilities (and inabilities) of our athletes. Listening to a well-known baseball manager tell us how the New York Yankees have designed their practice in a way that their minor league outfielders catch 100 fly balls a day has little significance for us if we are coaching six-year-old T-ballers. We have to recognize that drills that work with adults may be a waste of time when employed with our younger athletes. In fact, they may be worse than a waste of time because asking our athletes to engage in drills that are impossible for them to complete successfully may negatively impact their self-confidence for, and enjoyment of, the game.

Cognitive development. We've all seen coaches (some of us may even be one of these coaches) who, after reading way too many coaching magazines, pull out their trusty clipboard and proceed to scribble and scratch a series of plays for a bunch of high schoolers (each play with its own intricate sequence of "checkoffs" and contingencies) that are so confusing and complex they would probably reduce a theoretical physicist to tears. These coaches then have the audacity to be furious when the youngsters are unable to remember and execute every zig and zag correctly — so much so, in fact, that they often feel justified imposing harsh punishments on their team (yelling, screaming, push-ups, sprints, etc.) to ensure that the players will "do a better job of thinking" the next time (we'll have a complete discussion of the misuse of punishment in the Myth No. 9 chapter). Young athletes simply don't have the capacity to cognitively process this level of complex information. As coaches we often feel compelled to learn more minutia about our sport than we'll ever need to know — and certainly far more than we should ever try to teach our athletes. When working with young or inexperienced athletes, a polite variation of the old "KISS" principle (let's change the traditional "Keep It Simple Stupid" to "Keep It Short and Simple") will likely produce the results you are looking for.

It's absolutely essential for us to remember that the youngsters we work with are not merely pint-sized adults. There are real, qualitative differences in the way their bodies work, the way they take in and use sensory information, and the way they engage in complex thought processes. Simply put, just because a tactic or strategy has been shown to work with a select group of adults, there is no reason for us to expect similar results with the children many of us coach.

Question #2: Do my athletes have the same levels of commitment, motivation, and desire to excel athletically?

When famous coaches tell us about their successful experiences, we must constantly remind ourselves that they have been interacting with a very talented group of adults (or near-adults) who, after many years of personal sacrifice — and incalculable outlays of blood, sweat, and tears — have risen through the ranks to become "elite athletes." Athletes with lower levels of drive and desire rarely survive to participate at such lofty levels of competition. Too many of the coaches who write articles for coaching magazines and give presentations at coaching conferences and clinics work with people who have already achieved their life-long goal of "making a living" as an athlete (by receiving lucrative college scholarships, endorsements, sponsorships, contracts, etc.). It's unusual for our athletes to possess this same level of dedication. Our athletes are often just being introduced to their sport and frankly, don't yet know if they even like it or not. The extent to which our young athletes — who generally participate in sports to be with their friends and have fun — differ in regard to the drive, desire, and dedication exhibited by elite athletes will impact the success we will have using the same motivational techniques used by elite-level coaches.

Question #3: Do my athletes have the same time and energy to devote to their sport?

Another way in which our athletes may differ significantly from those depicted in the old coaches' stories is in regard to the time and energy they have available to commit to their sport (see the Myth No. 12 chapter for a discussion of the pros and cons of early specialization in one sport). When we were kids, most of us were allowed to grow up slowly. Sure we were involved in a lot of activities over the years, but nothing like children today experience. Dozens of books have recently been published with revealing titles such as *The Hurried Child* (Elkind 2001), *The Over-Scheduled Child* (Rosenfeld and Wise 2000), *Reclaiming Childhood* (Crain 2003), and *Under Pressure: Rescuing Our Children from the Culture of Hyper-Parenting* (Honore 2008) each bearing witness to the hectic pace at which kids today are being propelled through childhood. Many children now ricochet continually between school activities — and music lessons — and art class — and soccer practice — and choir rehearsal — and part-time jobs — and religious instruction — and math tutoring — and driver's training — and ... well, you get the idea. Now think about how much time athletes competing at the collegiate, professional, or Olympic level can devote to working on their sport skills. One indication comes from research done by the National Collegiate Athletic Association (NCAA) which found that during the season, college student-athletes generally spend between 35 and 45 hours per week on athletic activities. Even in the off-season, about 75 percent of these athletes indicated they spent this much or more time in athletic training or competitions (NCAA 2009). Considering the fact that many skills take thousands, if not tens of thousands of repetitions to master, it is little wonder that coaches working with these athletes who have almost unlimited practice time experience success where we often fail (Ericsson, Krampe, and Tesch-Romer 1993; Ericsson, Nandagopal, and Roring 2009).

Question #4: Do I have access to the same support staff?

When evaluating the success of well-known coaches we should not overlook the fact that, unlike most of us, these coaches have a cadre of full and part-time support staff working around the clock to assure their success. Assistant coaches, equipment managers, field crews, athletic trainers, team physicians, sport nutritionists, physical therapists, sport psychologists, secretaries, personal assistants, personnel managers, academic counselors, publicists, promotions directors, chiropractors, the occasional masseuse, and a litany of other specialists are standing "at the ready" to help the coach execute the game plan. We, on the other hand, often have to rely on the generous support of our spouse, an occasional volunteer parent, and a local seven-year-old kid with broken glasses and no front teeth who we euphemistically — but obviously to his great delight — refer to as our "team manager." Why we expect that simply following a famous coach's lead will help us conjure up the same results — when we are operating at such a distinct disadvantage — has always been a great mystery.

Question #5: Do I have access to the same facilities, equipment, and funding?

Reaping the full benefits of the strategies, tactics, drills, and skills the renowned coaches tell us are possible, would be a lot easier if we had access to the same resources they typically take for granted. To get an appreciation of the assets some of these coaches have to work with, let's take a look at a couple of well-known collegiate athletic programs. During the 2011 fiscal year alone, The Ohio State University Athletic Department reported spending a total of more than $131 million — over $34 million on football alone. The same year, their rivals at the University of Michigan laid out a "paltry" $23.5 million on the single sport of football and just under $96 million overall (United States Department of Education 2011). But don't think for a minute that it's only big-time college and professional teams that are different from ours in terms of the money they pour into facilities and equipment.

Battle of the Bucks

Nestled in a small, southern Georgia town of 45,000, Valdosta High School invests close to a half-million dollars each year in its football program as it strives to retain its self-proclaimed title of "Winnersville, USA." Resources such as these enable this high school team to play its games in a stadium that was recently renovated to the tune of $7.5 million — including the obligatory armchair seating for season ticketholders, and a "football museum." Head Coach Rick Darlington, who was hired in 2003 after a national search, brought three former assistants with him (he says he could have brought "*as many as I wanted*") to his new position where he is given an $87,000 contract, a $36,000 Dodge Ram pickup, and his own Thursday evening television show. Perhaps most astonishing is that all this spending took place at a high school where teacher salaries ranked 120th (and administrator salaries ranked 145th) among the 180 Georgia school systems in the state (Wieberg 2004).

Although Valdosta may be the exception, it is by no means the only high school program that differs substantially from yours. Here's a few more that were reported in a recent *USA Today* article by Steve Wieberg:

- West Monroe High School (Louisiana): Recently spent $400,000 on a new synthetic playing surface and is spending an additional $340,000 on turf for its two practice fields. A local bond issue financed a new football fieldhouse and the athletic director boasts that his football team has 17 different uniform combinations.
- Minnetonka High School (Minnesota): The booster club of 150 members raised $280,000 of a $2.2 million project to put synthetic turf in the stadium and install an inflatable dome to protect the field in the winter.
- Hoover High School (Alabama): The Buccaneer Touchdown Club contributes over $300,000 per year so the football team has access to an air-conditioned training trailer to take on its road games. On those trips, the team travels on chartered, rather than school buses. Ten other booster clubs for other sports brought the total contribution to more than $854,000 (Winberg 2004).

As if to prove that that there's a lot of truth in the old saying, "Everything's bigger in Texas," Allen High School, situated in a northern suburb of Dallas, is now home to the most expensive high school football stadium in the country. In the fall of 2012 finishing touches were put on the $60 million stadium that includes a 38-foot-wide HD video scoreboard, two private luxury boxes, and a state-of-the-art press box (SportsIllustrated.com 2012).

Does any of this sound like your athletic program? Most coaches have nowhere near that kind of money to devote to facilities and equipment. As a result, when we hear these well-known coaches trying to convince us that their experiences will transfer to our program, we need to consider whether our program is funded at a level that is conducive to similar success.

Technical Knowledge May Not Be as Important as You Think

Here's an interesting quote that would probably sum up many coaches' view of the current state of our profession...

There was a time — not long past — when a coach who knew his [sic] game ... was thought to be sufficiently well equipped to enter the profession. It is becoming clear every day, however, that the most successful coaches are psychologists of no small ability. They may never have studied psychology as a science and they would hardly be at home in a psychological laboratory; but they have acquainted themselves with some of the pertinent facts about human behavior and their success in their profession rests in no small measure upon this knowledge [Griffith 1926, 8].

The preceding quote was written over 85 years ago by the "Father" of sport psychology, Coleman R. Griffith. Although sport has changed a great deal since that time, his observation that coaching success requires far more than "knowing the game" is as true today as the day it was written.

Imagine, for example, you are attending a coaching clinic. Two sessions are being offered at the same time. The session in the room to your left is advertised as ... "The Details of the Offensive Scheme We Used to Win the National Championship *Four Years in a Row!*" In the adjacent room, to your right, they are promoting the following session ... "Effectively Communicating with Your Athletes: The *Real* Key to Athletic Success!"

Now be honest. Which of these two sessions are you more inclined to attend? What is it about that particular session that you find more appealing? Are you choosing to attend that session because you think it will be more entertaining? Are you choosing to attend that session because you think you will be able to implement what you learn with your athletes? Are you choosing to attend that session because you really need to gain a better understanding of this information in order to be a better coach? Now go back to the first page of this chapter and examine Figure 1.1. Can you see that your decision regarding which coaching session to attend may be similar, in some respect, to the unproductive, three-step process you often see in your athletes?

Believe it or not, top-notch coaches are often quick to point out that whatever success they've experienced is not as much a result of their vast game-related knowledge — the Xs and Os — as their understanding of human behavior. Unfortunately, you might not recall hearing too many coaches saying that. Many of us don't hear what we don't expect, or want, to hear. In case you missed these messages, the remainder of the chapter will be devoted to a small sample of some of the most successful coaches in all of sport trying to convince us that it is not really mastering the Xs and Os that made them — or will make us — successful coaches.

We might just as well start at the top. I know of a basketball coach whose teams accomplished some of the most remarkable feats in the history of sports. For example, over the years he and his teams...

- Won over 80 percent of their games
- Went through the entire season undefeated on four occasions
- Won 10 NCAA National Championships (7 in a row)
- Won 88 consecutive games
- Won 38 consecutive NCAA Tournament games

The teams he coached were so successful, in fact, that he was named "College Basketball Coach of the Year" seven times and ultimately was selected "Coach of the Century" by ESPN and *The Sporting News*. You've probably already guessed that these coaching accomplishments could only belong to arguably the best coach of all time, the legendary John Wooden. But what's really interesting is what Coach Wooden has to say about the relative contribution technical knowledge (Xs and Os) and "people skills" have on our success. In his own words, Coach Wooden tells us:

> There is very little difference in technical knowledge about the game of basketball among most experienced coaches. However, there is a vast difference between leaders in their ability to teach and to motivate those under their supervision. Knowledge alone is not enough to get desired results. You must have the more elusive ability to teach and to motivate. This defines a leader; if you can't teach and you can't motivate, you can't lead [Wooden 1997, 122].

Do you want to reconsider the session you chose to attend at our hypothetical coaching clinic? Perhaps you need a little more convincing from the Coach. Okay, here's what he has to say about his own coaching strengths and weaknesses:

> There is no area of basketball in which I am a genius. None. Tactically and strategically I'm just average, and this is not offering false modesty. We won national championships while I was coaching at UCLA because I was above average in analyzing players, getting them to fill roles as part of a team, paying attention to fundamentals and details, and working well with others, both those under my supervision and those whose supervision I was under [Wooden 1997, 113].

People skills — the ability to communicate and work effectively with others to achieve a desired outcome — are what Coach Wooden believes made him successful. Not his mastery of the Xs and Os.

With this in mind, let's revisit the previously described coaching clinic. Prior to the sessions, let's imagine you had the great fortune to be standing in the hallway chatting with Coach Wooden. As the sessions are about to begin, the two of you start to make your way toward the doors. Which of the two sessions do you think Coach Wooden — the greatest coach of all time — would most likely feel the need to attend? Are you absolutely certain you shouldn't be in that session with him?

Another coach with equally impressive credentials was Tennessee Volunteer Women's Basketball Coach Pat Summitt. Coach Summitt, at the time of her retirement in 2012, was the winningest coach in college basketball history with 1,098 victories in her 38 years as a Head Coach. She guided her teams to victories in 84 percent of their games, while winning 32 Southeastern Conference Tournament and Season Championships, and eight NCAA National Championships. The success Coach Summitt and her teams had resulted in her being named NCAA "College Coach of the Year" on seven occasions as well as "Naismith Coach of the Century in April of 2000." In an interview for the History Channel's documentary *The Dream Teams* Coach Summitt addressed the relative importance of "people skills" versus Xs and Os in her coaching success. Notice how Coach Summitt reinforces Coach Wooden's view that knowledge of Xs and Os only contributes a small portion to the overall success of an athletic program:

> I've often said, as a coach, the least of my concerns tends to be the Xs and Os. It's more about the organization. It's more about personalities. It's more about the mental aspect and the psychological aspect of working with the personalities on the team... If I had it to do over again, clearly, psychology would have been at least a minor — if not a major — for me [A&E Television Networks 1999].

Pat Summitt's counterpart in the men's game is Coach Mike Krzyzewski who has guided his teams to more NCAA Division I men's basketball victories than anyone in history. At the conclusion of the 2012 season, Coach K's teams had registered 927 wins, four NCAA National Championships, 11 NCAA Final Four appearances, and 25 Atlantic Coast Conference regular season and Tournament Championships. Also like Pat Summitt, Coach Krzyzewski is quick to point out the relative importance of developing people skills over the mere mastery of Xs and Os. In his own words, "We aren't coaching Xs and Os, we are coaching people. So, the more we learn about people the better ... I just think coaching is about relationships. It goes way beyond Xs and Os" (ChampionshipCoachesNetwork 2011).

And it's not just the best college basketball coaches of all time who understand that success, as Coleman Griffith wrote over 85 years ago, is more closely linked to understanding "pertinent facts about human behavior" than "knowing the game." Two-time Super Bowl Head Coach Dick Vermeil, when talking about his relationship with his quarterback Trent

Green candidly indicated, "I want to treat him like he is my son ... and how I would treat my son. I care about him — I know he cares about me — and it goes way beyond Xs and Os — way beyond" (ESPN 2003).

Even irascible old Bill Parcells, who led three teams to the Super Bowl is seen by his former players as relying more heavily on his "people skills" than his "tactical skills" to achieve coaching success. In the words of his former quarterback, Phil Simms, "[Parcells'] greatest trait — he had a special way of dealing with people and that's what made him get to the Super Bowl three times — is that dealing with people. It wasn't the Xs and Os. There were no secrets there" (ESPN 2003).

It should be easy to see that it takes far more than merely "mastering the Xs and Os" to make you a successful coach. It's often said that only 15 percent of our success comes from our technical knowledge whereas 85 percent of our success is attributable to our attitude and people skills (Ziglar 2000). If we trust the views of proven winners like John Wooden, Pat Summitt, Mike Krzyzewski, and Dick Vermeil we can see that this is as true in coaching as in anywhere else. We often waste valuable time trying to learn a few more tricks that we think will make us successful. Whenever we are tempted to learn more Xs and Os, it would be wise to remind ourselves of one final quote from Coach Wooden — "If you spend too much time learning the tricks of the trade, you may never learn the trade" (Wooden 1997, 93). Accordingly, the remainder of this book is devoted to ways we can become better coaches — not by merely learning more and more techniques and strategies — but by changing our attitudes and improving the way we interact with people in our immediate sport environment: athletes, parents, other coaches, game officials, and administrators. The quote by Bill Walsh with which we began this chapter puts it best, "People matter most — more than equipment ... or Xs and Os. People are at the heart of achieving organizational greatness" (Walsh 2009, 202).

Myth No. 2

"Playing on My Team Means Playing by My Rules"

It goes back to my oldest theory in coaching; that a player-coached team is better than a coach-coached team.

—Coach Tom Izzo[1]

Do we build and fund schools so teachers have a place to teach? Of course not. We all know that the best schools are dedicated to continually meeting the academic, social, and emotional needs of their students. Similarly, I'd be willing to bet that if you did some research into the development of your athletic organization — regardless of the level of competition — you would find that there is no mention of creating an athletic organization so people, like you and me, have a place to coach. Instead, you'll probably find that your athletic program was established solely to serve the needs of your *athletes*. It's *their* team — not yours. As coaches, we merely serve as trustees to make certain our athletes get the best experience possible from their involvement in the program (you might take some solace in the fact that it's not their parents' team either — but more on that point in the Myth No. 13 chapter).

Now, keeping in mind it's really your athletes' team, let's examine who makes most of the team decisions. In Table 2.1, I've listed a number of decisions that need to be made throughout the season that have considerable impact on your team (and each individual athlete). Please put a check mark indicating who, in your organization, is primarily responsible for each decision listed on the left. When you've finished, simply count the checkmarks you've made in each column. How many of these important team decisions are made primarily by your athletes? If you, your athletic organization, and your team are typical, your athletes are not routinely involved — or even consulted — in regard to most of these decisions.

19

Table 2.1: Athlete Involvement in Team Decisions.

On your team who decides ...	Athletes	Coaches	Administrators	Parents	Others
athlete eligibility requirements?					
the size (or number) of teams?					
the coach (or team) for whom an athlete will play?					
which athletes make the team and which will be "cut"?					
how long the season will be?					
how many competitions take place during the season?					
locations of the competitions?					
the uniforms the team will wear (colors, style, etc.)?					
the equipment athletes will use during competitions?					
how the team will travel to and from competitions?					
the specific rules for competition?					
on the hiring of game officials to enforce the rules?					
positions or events in which athletes participate?					
the amount of playing time given to each athlete?					
how many practices will be held per competition?					
where and when the practices will be held?					
the length of practices?					
the amount of practice time spent on each drill or skill?					
team goals (practice, game, season, off-season)?					
team strategies to attain the team goals?					
athlete and team rewards and punishments?					

Number of Checkmarks in Each Column =

So now we find ourselves in the rather awkward position of reconciling the following facts: (a) our team "belongs" to our athletes, (b) our team decisions should be based on the athletic, social and emotional needs of our athletes, but (c) rarely, if ever, are our athletes actually involved in making the decisions that affect them. I'd like you to think about how you would explain this apparent inconsistency. Put the book down for a moment and ponder the following question as it relates to your team: "Why don't I involve my athletes in more of our team's decisions?" Whenever I've asked this question of coaches and coaches-in-training they've generally respond in one of three ways:

(1) "It would be far too time consuming to arrive at a consensus among my athletes for each and every decision that needs to be made" (i.e., it's a matter of *efficiency*).

(2) "Coaches, administrators, and parents are in a better position to know what is best for the athletes" (i.e., it's a matter of *expertise*).

(3) "It's our job — asking for input from our athletes would make us appear indecisive thereby damaging our credibility and undermining our authority" (i.e., it's a matter of *ego*).

Certainly there are elements of truth in each of these statements. Issues such as efficiency, expertise, and ego are important considerations when determining responsibility for decision-making. Additionally, as coaches, administrators, and parents, we are legally and ethically bound to provide our athletes with a safe, secure learning environment and therefore must have input in many of our team's decisions. Our need to participate in these decisions is not, however, a sufficient reason to exclude our athletes from this process. In fact, in their widely acclaimed *Bill of Rights for Young Athletes* Rainer Martens, Founder of the American Sport Education Program (ASEP) and Vern Seefeldt, Director Emeritus of the Institute for the Study of Youth Sports at Michigan State University, affirm that in youth sports there exists the inherent... "Right of children to share in the leadership and decision-making of their sport participation" (Martens and Seefeldt 1979, 23). Their call for us to share decision-making with our athletes is echoed in Standard 18 of the *National Standards for Sport Coaches* which specifically states that it is the responsibility of every coach to "provide athletes with responsibility and leadership opportunities as they mature" (NASPE 2006, 14). To see if you might be able to increase the role your athletes play in making team decisions, let's examine each of the reasons coaches, like us, give for not involving their athletes in their team's decision-making process.

Reason #1: It would be far too time consuming to arrive at a consensus among my athletes for each and every decision that needs to be made — it's a matter of efficiency.

Even very young and inexperienced athletes can be included in the decision-making process by allowing them to make *structured choices*. Most parents use this structured choice strategy very effectively to make sure a decision is appropriate while still allowing their children to feel part of the decision process (and to the extent it reduces the likelihood of them throwing a temper tantrum). I, however, recently had the misfortune of standing behind a parent (and his three-year old son) at McDonald's who hadn't yet discovered the benefits of structured choices. When they reached the counter, Dad simply asked the boy "What would you like to eat?" Now this may have been a perfectly appropriate question to ask his wife, but his young son became completely overwhelmed. We stood there for what seemed like an eternity while the little guy agonized over every conceivable "McPossibility." Finally, (much to my relief) Dad's patience began to wear thin. He decided to order for his son. This decisive action was, of course, immediately met with ear splitting shrieks of *"No, no, no! ... Not that! ... I don't want that!"* By simply narrowing the boy's options down to an acceptable and manageable few ("Would you like a cheeseburger or chicken nuggets?") and presenting him with this structured choice, Dad would have given his son the opportunity to take "ownership" of his decision (and avoided the deliberation and tantrum).

Coaches can use this approach to include their athletes in decisions that directly impact their lives. Suppose you are planning your practice. If you are like most coaches, you probably feel there are several areas in which your athletes would benefit from further practice. Instead of you deciding and dictating what they will do in practice today, why not allow the team the option of working on any of the skills you think are important (as well as the specific drills used to enhance these skills)? Your athletes will feel as if they have more ownership in their team and work harder if they know it was their choice. You'll also be teaching them an important lesson — life is all about making choices and taking responsibility. Notice that in addition to providing your athletes with the valuable experience of taking responsibility for the inner workings of their own team, using this structured choice strategy is one way to reduce the inefficiency we often believe is associated with bringing the athletes into the decision-making process. As athletes mature they develop the ability to make more complex decisions and are able to incorporate a wider array of options without becoming overloaded.

I recently witnessed, firsthand, how a softball coach made the best decision of all by deferring to the members of his team. The team was participating in a weekend tournament which required them to play one game Friday afternoon, four games on Saturday, and perhaps, depending on the outcome of these games, an additional two games on Sunday. After a close loss on Friday the coach and I discussed the advantage of involving the team in the decision-making process. When the team played poorly in the opening game on Saturday, the coach's initial reaction was to hold an impromptu practice session before the next game. Thinking back to our conversation, however, he asked his players what *they* thought would most likely help their performance. To his surprise, they indicated that what they really wanted to do most of all was simply sit in the shade and rest. It was a brilliant decision! The team had three games remaining that day and the temperature and the humidity were both in the lower 90s. The team was exactly right — given the schedule and the weather, sitting in the shade and resting was far more likely to help their performance than one more 45-minute practice session.

Reason #2: Coaches, administrators, and parents are in a better position to know what is best for the athletes — it's a matter of expertise.

Although this argument appears logical enough, it probably wouldn't take you too long to think of dozens of examples where the decisions made by coaches, administrators, and parents have obviously *not* been in the best interest of the team or an individual athlete. In fact, it is the basic premise of this book that coaching decisions are as frequently based on myth, folklore, dogma, habit, laziness, and faulty assumptions as they are on what is truly in the best interest of the athletes. Let's discuss a couple of the ways adults (coaches, administrators, and parents) routinely negatively impact children's athletic experiences. If nothing else, these examples should give us pause whenever we are tempted to assume that we always know what's best for young athletes.

Let's begin by examining how adults and children differ in the way they handle a situation that frequently arises in youth sports — inequity of talent level between the teams. Because it's not unusual for one team to begin to completely dominate the other, it's interesting to examine how adults and children attempt to resolve this problem. Think back to your days on the playground, sandlot, or blacktop. Remember how you and your friends tried to make sure teams were evenly matched — even when neighborhood kids of all ages and abilities wanted to play? First of all, you probably took turns selecting individuals to be members of each team in an effort to at least begin the game with teams that were as evenly matched as possible. Although this process can inflict tremendous emotional pain on those chosen near the end, it still isn't as unfair to the spirit of competition as what many adults attempt to do — stack their team with as many good players as possible. When you stop to think about it, the process of recruiting isn't intended to provide for fair competition. Quite the opposite, recruiting is actually the antithesis of competition. It's merely an attempt to collect as many good players as possible so your team will be able to dominate the others. In fact, it's not unheard of for teams to recruit and "stockpile" athletes they have no intention of playing just so those players won't be eligible to compete against them. While this might increase the team's chance of winning, does it sound like something that is generally in the "best interest" of the individual athletes?

Now, for whatever reason, let's suppose one team simply can't compete with the other. The game is on the verge of becoming a rout — it's quickly turning into a complete and total embarrassment for the losing team. How do children and adults differ in the way they deal with this problem? The primary thing on the minds of most children is making sure the game not only continues but remains rewarding for everyone involved. To them, the *integrity of the game* is what is at stake. They have come together to play with their friends and hone their sport skills. They seem to intuitively understand that if they don't take everyone's feelings into consideration — especially those on the losing team — the players will quickly lose interest, causing the game itself to come to an untimely end. Worse yet, members of the losing team might not be willing to return and play the game in the future. If that's the case, this is the one time the game will quite literally be "lost." To avoid this, kids will modify the rules of the game to adjust for the ability differences. Surely you remember the form these modifications take:

- One team only gets two "outs" while the other gets four
- Big kids have to hit/throw/shoot/dribble/kick with their non-dominant hand or foot
- Big kids can only swing the stick/bat/racquet with one hand
- Little kids get to "relay" or "tag-team" while older kids have to do it themselves
- One team has to tackle, the other only touch the player to be declared "down"
- Little kids get a "head start"
- One team gets to have more players than the other
- "Trade" players or choose up sides again right in the middle of the game

Notice that although these game adaptations are ostensibly made "to keep the game going," the kids are also learning very important lessons regarding conflict resolution, compromise, creative problem solving, and compassion. Now let's imagine we're at that same lopsided game only this time the competition has not been "organized" by the kids themselves but by the adults in their lives (remember, these are the so-called "experts" who supposedly "know what's best" for the kids). I don't have to tell you that if you walk onto the field suggesting some modification of the rules so everyone gets to have fun and continue playing, you might be (quite literally as we'll see in the Myth No. 13 chapter) risking life and limb. Adults will have none of this foolishness. To them, rules are rules and whether the children are having fun or get to continue the game is secondary. It's the *integrity of the outcome of the game* adults seek to protect at all costs. The best you can probably hope for from an adult in this situation is a declaration of a "mercy killing" whereby the game is simply called off. The whipping is halted, the dominant team is awarded the victory, and the game (that started out as fun) mercifully comes to an end. There is no opportunity for either team to continue playing. There is no opportunity for either team to continue developing their sport skills. The kids just go home — the winners gloating and the losers humiliated. Some might say that by acting in this way, adults are teaching the kids to respect rules set forth by others (generally those in positions of authority) and to cope with life's failures, disappointments, and frustrations. Now I don't know about you, but I think that life presented me with plenty of occasions to cope with failures, disappointments, and frustrations. I certainly didn't need adults who "knew what was best for me" to purposely structure my playing experiences to make sure I suffered a sufficient amount of failure and frustration. If they were really so concerned about my personal development, why didn't the adults in my life provide me with every opportunity to learn the equally (if not more) important lessons of conflict resolution, compromise, creative problem solving, and compassion? Let's be honest, does the strict control adults exert on their children's games really sound like something that is being done by people who truly understand what is in the "best interest" of all the young athletes involved? The tendency for adults to meddle in children's activities is humorously, but all-too-honestly, depicted in Figure 2.1.

Our adult obsession with administrative efficiency can also negatively impact youth sports. What would you say if I told you there is an enormous amount of scientific evidence indicating that the way we generally create

Figure 2.1: Adult Over-Involvement in Children's Activities. (PEANUTS ©1973 Peanuts Worldwide LLC. Dist. By UNIVERSAL UCLICK. Reprinted with permission. All rights reserved.)

age classifications in youth sport makes it virtually impossible for nearly half of our kids — regardless of their ability or effort — to be athletically successful? You may find it even more surprising to know that top-level administrators of youth sport programs have been aware of this inequity for years but are reluctant to change their existing administrative procedures. I'll give you the hard evidence — but first a word of caution. It's understandable if some of you experience feelings of resentment and anger when you realize that you (or your children) have been systematically disadvantaged by the way youth sports are administered. The unfortunate fact is that many of you had your opportunity for athletic success — regardless of sport — snatched away from you before you even played in your first game.

Here's how it works. We generally assume that talent and effort are the two cornerstones of athletic success. We further assume that talent and effort are evenly distributed among children born at various times of the year. There's no reason to believe, for example, that children born in the months of March or July are any more or less talented, motivated, or persistent than those born in January, August, or November. That being the case, why do you suppose it is that professional (NHL) and Olympic ice hockey players (Boucher and Halliwell 1991) are far more likely to be born in March than October? (No, it's not because February is colder and more conducive to producing ice.) Similarly, why are the highest percentages of elite "Under 18" soccer players likewise born in the first three months of the calendar year (Musch 2002)? Why are similar patterns of success also found in Major League Baseball (Thompson, Barnsley, and Stebelsky 1991) and soccer in France, England, Germany, Sweden, the Netherlands, Brazil, Japan, and Australia (Brewer, et al. 1992; Brewer, Balsom, and Davis 1995; Dudink 1994; Musch and Hay 1999; Verhulst 1992)? In fact, to get a greater sense of this general effect, researchers examined 38 scientific studies published between 1984 and 2007 and found this type of birth date bias across 14 different sports in 16 countries (Cobley, et al. 2009) and that despite the impact of sport globalization, this favoritism toward those born early in the year remains in effect today (Nolan and Howell 2010). What happened to all those kids born later in the year? If ability and effort are evenly distributed throughout the year, why don't they succeed at their sport at roughly the same rate as athletes born earlier in the year?

There's really a very simple administrative explanation. Eligibility to participate on a given team is usually based on the athlete's year of birth. For example, players born in January of 2002 will play on the same team, or in the same league, as those born nearly a full year later — in December of 2002. The athlete born in January is, all things being equal, essentially a full year older physically, mentally, and emotionally than the child born in December (Musch and Grondin 2001). We therefore shouldn't be surprised to find that the older kids generally perform better than the younger kids. Now, if this were merely a one-time occurrence, it would be of little concern. The important thing to remember, however, is that these age groupings will remain intact *indefinitely*. The exact same kids — those born shortly before the cut-off date — will always be disadvantaged and the exact same kids — those born shortly after the cut-off date — will always be advantaged. It will be the case this year, next year, the following year, and forever. How much fun do you think it is to always be the "runt of the litter"? How discouraging is it to "sit the bench" year after year while your technically "same-aged" — but actually considerably "older" — friends always get to play? Is it really surprising to find that children who are systematically disadvantaged by an organization's rigid age classifications drop out of sport at a higher rate and/or ultimately fail to achieve athletic success at the same level as their peers who have been granted perpetual preferential treatment? It shouldn't be — we've known for years that kids drop out of sports when they don't feel they have the ability to compete with others on the team (Roberts 1980; Robinson and Carron 1982). If this idea of what scientists call "relative age effect" sounds familiar, it might be because it was recently identified by Malcolm Gladwell in his best-selling book, *Outliers: The Story of Success* as a hidden advantage that allows only a small percentage of athletes to succeed while most fall by the wayside (Gladwell, 2008).

Perhaps the most disturbing aspect of this "relative age effect" is that many administrators are well aware of the fact they are disadvantaging a certain segment of their athletes. They have been informed that other systems of determining team membership would have less negative impact on kids born shortly before the cut-off (e.g., Boucher and Halliwell 1991; Boucher and Mutimer 1994; Musch and Grondin 2001). But they are reluctant to inconvenience themselves and parents by changing their existing classification system.

Here's a personal story to illustrate the fact that there are sport administrators who are well aware of the built-in bias favoring athletes born in the first part of the calendar year, but have little interest in changing the current system. Back in 1985 my colleagues and I at Michigan State University's Institute for the Study of Youth Sports were working with the Amateur Hockey Association of the United States (AHAUS: which later changed its name to USA Hockey) at its selection and development camps at the U.S. Olympic Training Centers at Lake Placid and Colorado Springs. As the National Governing Body for all amateur ice hockey in the United

States, AHAUS/USA Hockey is responsible for administering youth ice hockey programs throughout the country as well as selecting national teams to represent the United States in international competitions (including the Olympics until professional players were allowed to compete in 1998). After reading a scientific paper published in Canada indicating that Canadian hockey players born early in the year were far more likely to achieve hockey success (Barnsley, Thompson, and Barnsley 1985), we examined the birth records of 271 U.S. hockey players who had recently been selected to participate in National Selection Camps or on National Teams. As you can see

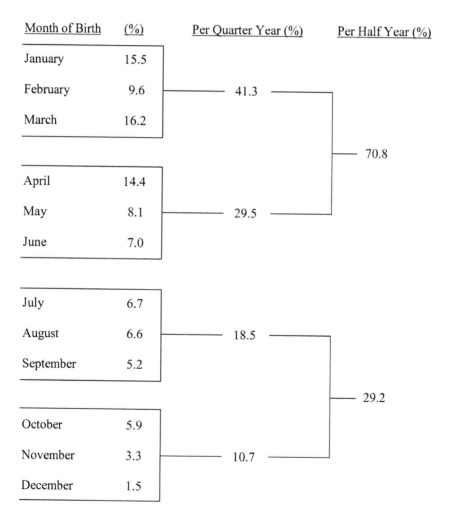

Figure 2.2: Percentages of Elite Hockey Players Born Per Month[2]

in Figure 2.2, our results were identical to those found in Canada — the vast majority of the top U.S. hockey players were born early in the calendar year.

Specifically, over 70 percent of our elite hockey players were born in the first half of the year and well over half (55.7 percent) were born in just the first four months of the calendar year. Perhaps most striking of all was the fact that simply being born in January rather than December made a player more than 10 times more likely to be selected to participate on a national-level ice hockey team.

With these indisputable findings in hand, we appealed to USA Hockey to consider changing its rigid age classifications. We argued that the current system not only causes undue feelings of failure and lowered self-esteem among those who are systematically disadvantaged year after year, it also limits the pool from which the United States selects its international teams. In effect, we select our teams from only those born during the first half of the year, while those born later — even those with great natural ability and dedication — have long-ago elected to drop out of hockey rather than endure continual futility and embarrassment. To give you an indication as to the level of interest administrators had in correcting this ongoing injustice, it is only necessary to note that here we are — more than twenty years later — and the USA Hockey age classification system remains essentially unchanged (see Table 2.2). In fact, the impact may be worst today since each USA Hockey "Age Division" now spans two years. So, instead of a single year separating the oldest and youngest players in each division, there is essentially a two year developmental difference among players. Who knows how many thousands of young hockey players over time have "failed" — not due to their lack of talent or desire, but simply because the deck was stacked against them from the first day they stepped on the ice?

Table 2.2: USA Hockey Age Classifications for the 2012–13 Season.[3]

Youth Teams

Date of Birth	Age Category	Age Division
1994	18 Years	Midget 18 & Under
1995	17 Years	
1996	16 Years	Midget 16 & Under
1997	15 Years	
1998	14 Years	Bantam 14 or Under
1999	13 Years	
2000	12 Years	Pee Wee 14 or Under
2001	11 Years	
2002	10 Years	Squirt 10 or Under
2003	9 Years	
2004	8 Years	Mite 8 or Under

So here's what it boils down to. Until sport administrators change their rigid age classification system, the single best piece of advice we can offer to any parent who wants their child to secure a college scholarship or become a sport superstar is not to concern themselves with specialized training or exotic nutritional supplements. Instead, the way they can provide the greatest advantage possible is to "make arrangements" to conceive their child sometime between mid–April and early June (so they will be born between January and March). Once again, we should keep this example in mind whenever we are tempted to think that we, as adults, should be responsible for most of the administrative and team decisions solely because we know what's in the best interest young athletes.

Reason #3: It's our job — asking for input from our athletes would make us appear indecisive thereby damaging our credibility and undermining our authority — it's a matter of ego.

Giving your athletes an opportunity to make team-related decisions for themselves won't make you appear indecisive, nor will it damage your credibility as long as you go about it the right way. The main thing to remember is that you are not turning over the decision-making to the athletes because you are indecisive and "wishy-washy." Rather, you are intentionally bringing them into the process. Coach Wooden — who many consider the most credible coaching authority of all time — frequently used this approach himself. As he put it, "In the huddle I let them decide what man will shoot. I know what their decision will be. Only if their decision disagrees with mine would I over-rule. Almost always they make the right decision on their own" [Reger 2002, 30].

Let your athletes know the reason you have consciously decided to allow them so much input — because it's their team and you want them to accomplish the things they feel are most important. Also let them know you value their opinions. Depending on their age and experience level, athletes can often have more insight than the coach. Just think about it. The athletes are out there in the thick of the battle and are seeing things develop firsthand — from the performer's perspective. Coaches, on the other hand, often admit to having "the worst seats in the house" when it comes to seeing what's really happening on the field. It's therefore easy to see why the wisest coaches will always begin any discussion with their athletes by asking the players for their insights and opinions.

Let's revisit the example we presented earlier. You prepare yourself in advance and go to practice with three or four specific "areas in need of improvement" in mind. Upon your arrival, the first thing you do is ask the team members for their impressions. In which areas do they think they need the most improvement? Seriously consider their opinions. Then share your observations with the entire team. Let them know what you think the team needs to work on. Make sure they understand that all of these things are important, and will have to be dealt with at some time, but the decision as to what they want to work on first is entirely up to them. Once they've chosen the skills they think are most important, you can then ask if they have any ideas regarding specific drills that will help them improve these skills. If they've left out some important drills, let them know but then give them a choice as to which they would like to use in today's practice. Because you've obviously come to practice well-prepared, with detailed observations, suggestions as to improvements that are needed, and a list of specific drills that will help them improve, your athletes are not likely to see you as indecisive. On the contrary, your athletes are more likely to see you as a coach who has given a great deal of thought about the important elements of a good practice. Keep in mind that one of the most important aspects of a good practice is the high level of ownership, enthusiasm, and motivation you can foster in your athletes by simply allowing them to actively contribute to their team.

Factors Influencing the Effectiveness of "Team" Decisions

As coaches, it's important for us to understand that although involving our athletes in the inner workings of their team will generally produce positive outcomes, your athletes — and the environment in which they perform — have distinctive characteristics that have been shown to moderate these outcomes. We've already mentioned, for example, the fact that younger, less experienced athletes need to be presented with considerable structure to keep them from being overwhelmed. However, as they get older, they will generally be capable of sorting through far more complex and sophisticated choices. But there's more to it than age or maturity.

Gender difference is another factor that coaches must consider when devising their decision-making strategy. For whatever reasons, relative to their male counterparts, girls and women tend to prefer coaches who involve them in the decision-making process (Horne 2002). This difference was humorously depicted in a *Sports Illustrated* column entitled "Out of Touch with My Feminine Side" by senior writer Rick Reilly who, after working with boys for 11 years, described coaching his daughter's seventh-grade basketball team. The new coach concluded the following:

Another difference between boys and girls: Girls have many questions. Our team meetings were sometimes longer than our practices. Apparently girls use team meetings as a chance to process feelings, whereas boys use team meetings as a chance to give each other wedgies. During our first meeting we had long, emotional deliberations over what our huddle cheer would be and whether we should wear matching bracelets [Reilly 2002, 102].

In addition to the personal athlete factors of age, experience, and gender, there are several situational or environmental conditions that also impact the success of shared decision-making. Two of these are pretty straightforward and easy to understand — *group size*, and *time availability*. Obviously, as the size of your team increases, the more you will experience difficulty trying to let everyone voice their opinion. There are, however, some simple ways to alleviate the problems associated with large group decisions. One way is to break the group down into smaller, more responsive units. Football teams, for example, often have a hundred or more players on the roster. Groups of this size have difficulty making sure everyone feels a part of the larger team. So what do football teams do? They first split up into "offensive" and "defensive" units. Further, these still rather large groups are broken down into "positions" (linebackers, defensive line, defensive secondary, running backs, receivers, offensive line, kickers, etc.). It's not uncommon to find only five to ten people comprising each of these position groups. It's at this small-group level the athletes can be given considerable decision-making responsibility.

Again, common sense tells us that the more *time* you have to deliberate over a decision, the easier it is to get everyone involved. If, for example, we are trying to determine what our team uniforms should look like and the purchase order doesn't need to go in for a couple of weeks, we can obviously take time to seriously consider everyone's opinion. On the other hand, deciding on the next play our team is going to run within the confines of a 30-second play clock is quite a different matter. Although it may be impossible to elicit everyone's opinion on every play, there is no reason they can't be consulted when they come off the field or at halftime.

The *type of athlete interaction* required will also have a direct bearing on the degree to which you can allow your team to engage in group decision-making. When faced with several possible choices — and when the actions of several athletes must be totally integrated to accomplish a task — it is often useful to have one person make a final decision as to what is to be done. For example, in football, it is essential that everyone on the team executes the same play. If half the team decides to run the ball to the left and the other half decides to go to the right, we can't expect the play to work. However, in individual sports such as golf, gymnastics, swimming, track and field, etc., there is little reason for one person to "make the call." Input from everyone involved is not only possible but preferred in these situations.

Yet another factor that must be considered when determining the extent to which your athletes should be consulted regarding team decisions is their *phase of learning.* Simply put, when *planning* in advance of a performance, a democratic process can often be undertaken. Once the planning phase is complete, however, the emphasis shifts to the *execution* of the skill. At this point, a single opinion must be given preference. An autocratic style of leadership may be desirable at this stage.

Finally, an important factor that coaches must consider is the *leadership tradition* within the organization. Let's assume for the moment that, under previous coaches, the team you've just inherited has been given a great deal of freedom to voice its concerns and opinions. How will they view you if you come in and institute an authoritarian "top-down" decision-making style? Because they are accustomed to having input in the running of their team, they'll probably see you as an unresponsive dictator or tyrant. The reverse is also true. Let's now assume the team has an authoritarian tradition—previous leaders have always taken on the role of primary decision-maker. If you arrive and immediately turn important decisions over to the team, you'll probably be seen as dithering and indecisive.

Now go back to Table 2.1 and examine the decisions that need to be made. How many of these decisions absolutely *must* be determined solely by coaches, administrators, or parents—with no input whatsoever from the athletes? My guess is very few. We (ourselves and our athletes) would all benefit greatly by keeping the following ideas in mind as we coach:

- Although coaches must always be perceived as credible, they should rarely seek credit.
- Although coaches must always remember that they are an authority figure, they should rarely be authoritarian.
- Although coaches must always provide a sense of direction, they don't always need to give directions.

It seems appropriate to end our discussion by thoughtfully reconsidering the Coach Izzo quote we started with, "It goes back to my oldest theory in coaching; that a player-coached team is better than a coach-coached team" (Prisco 2009). Regardless of our level of competition, we would all do well to consider making this one of our "oldest theory" too.

MYTH No. 3

"A Coach's Main Job Is to Motivate Athletes"

When you are enthusiastic, you are a catalyst to those around you. Your unabashed love and emotion for what you are doing is contagious.

— Coach Mike Krzyzewski[1]

When coaches find out I have a Ph.D. in sport psychology, one of the first questions they ask is, "What can I do to motivate my athletes?" They are often taken aback by my typical response — "You usually don't need to motivate your athletes — they generally come to you already highly motivated." If you've coached for any period of time at all, I can probably guess that at this point you're thinking to yourself, "Ph.D. or not, this guy either knows absolutely nothing about athletes or he's just plain nuts!"

Let's use simple common sense and logic to examine how motivated most of our athletes really are. You'll have to agree that today's youngsters have thousands of opportunities — thousands of ways to spend their spare time. The options available to them are virtually limitless. Some ways they may choose to spend their time are productive — others are destructive. Some are legal — others are illegal. Some are moral — others are immoral. They can, for example, decide to join another athletic team or participate in a different sport; they can sing in the choir, act in school plays, join the debate team, join the chess club, watch T.V., join a scout troop, learn to play a musical instrument, play video games, sell drugs, join a band, work a part-time job, go on dates, listen to music, hang out with friends, join a gang, read a book, volunteer for a charity, surf the Internet, or engage in literally hundreds of other activities. Most of these activities are mutually exclusive — if they choose to engage in one, they are, by definition, choosing not to engage in all the others. Now here's the important point we, as coaches, sometimes overlook: When our athletes show up on the very first day of practice they are, by their very actions, telling us one thing: "Even though I have thousands of other ways of spending my time, I have consciously decided to forgo all the other opportunities I have. More than anything else, I want to be right here, right now, with you—on this team."

Now, is this the message you'd expect to hear from an "unmotivated" athlete? The mere fact they have chosen to participate demonstrates their high motivation level. Because they come to us highly motivated, our main job is not so much to motivate them but rather, to keep from destroying the motivation they brought with them on that first day of practice. Unfortunately, there are too many cases where athletes arrive with great expectations and high hopes for the season only to have their natural motivation squelched by a coach who does not understand how to take full advantage of a young athlete's pre-existing desire to have fun, be with friends, and develop new sport skills (Ewing and Seefeldt 2002).

I'll be the first to admit there will always be the exceptions—athletes with parents who are forcing them to participate against their will. But let's be totally honest—this is not nearly as common as we often try to make others—and ourselves—believe. Just think about how difficult it is to get even the youngest child to do something he or she is absolutely dead set against. If you are a parent, I'm sure you know exactly what I'm talking about. In addition, if you've ever worked with athletes beyond the age of 13 or 14, you know as well as anyone that it becomes almost impossible to make adolescents or young adults do anything against their will. Even on those rare occasions when a youngster doesn't come to us already highly motivated, there are still many ways we, as coaches, can structure the situation so he or she will soon realize playing on our team is a truly rewarding and worthwhile experience.

What Exactly Is Motivation?

Before we go any further, it would probably be a good idea to come to an agreement as to what this thing we call "motivation" really is. As you know, most of the time we simply assume athletes are motivated if we see them doing things like trying hard, obeying our instructions, concentrating on the task at hand, performing well, persisting at a difficult task, engaging in extra practice, etc. (Roberts 2001). If you look carefully at this list of behaviors, however, you will notice that these things aren't really examples of motivation at all—they are merely examples of behaviors that come about because of motivation. Although these may be the things our athletes do when they are motivated, that still doesn't tell us what this thing we call motivation actually is. What causes our athletes to behave this way? If you're beginning to get a bit frustrated by the fact you might not really know what motivation is, don't feel bad. Even scientists who have spent their entire careers studying athlete motivation have a hard time agreeing on a single definition of motivation (Roberts 2001). At least for now, one thing the scientists agree on is that motivation is the desire people have to show (themselves and others) how competent or proficient they are at something. It is this degree to which our athletes desire to demonstrate their competence that causes them to try hard — or not; obey our instructions — or not; concentrate on the task at hand — or not ... simply stated, to be motivated — or not.

There is one other thing most scientists agree on. Your athletes come to you with individualized predispositions for how they determine their competence levels. Basically, all athletes will try to assess their competence at a given task in one of two ways: (1) by comparing their performance to others (e.g., "Am I better at this task than another person?") or (2) by comparing their performance to their own previous performances or goals (e.g., "Am I better at this task than I used to be?"). The sport scientists who study motivation describe athletes who tend to draw conclusions about their competence on the basis of how they see themselves stacking up against others (for example, "Did I win?" or "Am I better than Billy?") as being "competition-motivated" (motivated by beating others). On the other hand, athletes who prefer to evaluate their competence by looking inward (for example, "Am I turning in better times than I did last year?" or "Did I throw that last pitch where I wanted?") are said to be "mastery-motivated" (motivated by mastering a task). Notice that an athlete who is competition-motivated determines whether he or she is competent by the result or outcome of the performance whereas an athlete who is mastery-motivated determines his or her competence by the quality of the performance itself (this is an issue we will discuss in greater detail in the Myth No. 5 and Myth No. 6 chapters when we consider the topic of goal setting).

Now imagine you had a magic wand that would help your athletes enjoy their sport more, put forth greater effort, attend practice more often, feel more competent and confident about their skills, continue to persevere longer in the face of obstacles or setbacks, and believe that effort is the true key to their success. Would you ever be tempted to use your magic wand? Well, research has shown that if you spend time helping your athletes develop more mastery-motivation (and less competitive-motivation) that's pretty much what will happen (Lloyd and Fox 1992; Ommundsen and Roberts

1999; Seifriz, Duda, and Chi 1992; Treasure 1997). In a minute we'll be more specific as to how you can alter your coaching in ways that will help your athletes develop more of this mastery-motivation orientation. But, before we get too far ahead of ourselves, it is time to talk about the one thing — above all else — that will likely have the greatest impact on your athletes' motivation levels ... *you!*

Motivate Yourself First

Instead of fabricating a series of rousing stories and corny slogans in an attempt to trick your athletes into being more motivated, your time will be much better spent doing something you'll find a lot more enjoyable and rewarding — making sure *you* are getting everything you need out of coaching. At first glance this may sound rather selfish and self-centered, but remember that if you don't take care of your needs, you're probably not going to be around long enough to take care of the needs of anyone else — including those of your athletes. I often tell coaches to seriously consider what every airline flight attendant on every commercial flight tells us to do "in the unlikely event that the cabin loses air pressure"—*put your oxygen mask on before trying to assist others.* The harsh reality is that if you don't take care of yourself first, both you *and* those you are trying to help are more likely to pass out and die. The same principle applies in coaching (or teaching, ministering, counseling, doctoring, parenting, supervising, etc.). If you don't take care of yourself, you won't be in any position to take care of others.

So, it's plain to see that our primary responsibility, as coaches, is to make sure we motivate ourselves. This is also the best place to start because, quite frankly, you know more about yourself than you'll ever know about anyone else. For example, you know, better than anyone else, the things you like, the things you don't like, the things you think are important, the things you don't think are important, and so on. In effect, you know just about everything there is to know about you. Can you say that about anyone else? Will you ever really know your athletes as well as you know yourself? Of course you won't. That being the case, let's consider the following question: If you know everything there is to know about yourself and you still can't quite figure out how to get yourself excited and interested in what you're doing, how effective do you think you are going to be at motivating a group of people you hardly know at all — your athletes?

Another advantage of "motivating yourself first" comes from the fact that motivation is contagious. It's often been said that the best coaches "lead by example" and this is never more apparent than when we are trying to motivate our athletes. Just think about the coaches, teachers, or bosses in your life who you think were the greatest motivators. It's a pretty safe bet you got the impression these people were highly motivated themselves. On the other hand, think about people you've been around in the past who simply appeared to be "going through the motions." These people rarely gave you the impression that they cared about what they — or you — were doing. How motivated did you feel when working with them? For better or worse, athletes take their cues from the coach. As coaches, we generally understand that we serve as role models for our athletes in terms of sportsmanship, healthy lifestyles, cooperation, compassion, etc. What we sometimes forget, however, is that our athletes are often looking to us to provide them with motivational cues as well — not through the use of smarmy clichés and pretty posters but through our own personal example. To bring this point home, try this simple experiment. The next time one of your coaching friends begins to whine about having more than his or her fair share of "unmotivated athletes," see if you can imagine why that might be the case. More often than not, you'll see exactly how the coach's "unmotivated athletes" got that way.

Simply put, you can exert control over your own motivation levels in a way you will never be able to control the motivation of others. That's not to say it will be easy. Society sends us so many messages telling us we shouldn't be happy or excited about our lives that we hardly notice them. Advertisers, for example, make a very good living convincing us that our lives are not nearly what they should be ... or would be ... if we just bought their product. Here's yet another example that is so pervasive most of us don't give it a second thought. I'm sure you've heard the expression "TGIF." What does this acronym stand for? Of course, it stands for "Thank God It's Friday." Have you ever asked yourself why you should be so happy that you don't have to work for the next couple of days? Are we really all just "working for the weekend?" To be successful at anything, including coaching, we need to do everything we can to foster within ourselves a more productive TGIM (Thank God It's Monday) attitude (Kohn 1993). When I say that, people usually can't help but giggle. Unfortunately, to most people, the whole notion of looking forward to your job sounds so ... well ... ridiculous. You should have a little smile on your face every time you think of working with your athletes. If you don't, you're doing something wrong. I sometimes try to grab the attention of my students by telling them that "coaching is a lot like sex ... if you and those you're with are not having fun, you must be doing it wrong." When you can hardly wait to get to practice or a workout session with the team, that's when you'll know you're on the right path to developing a TGIM attitude. And once you've developed your own TGIM attitude, it won't be long until you start seeing it show up in your athletes too.

Control Only Those Things Under Your Control

Perhaps the most important coaching (or life) lesson any of us can learn is neatly summed up in the first three lines of a popularized version of Reinhold Niebuhr's *"Serenity Prayer"*

> *God grant me the serenity to accept the things I cannot change...*
> *Courage to change the things I can...*
> *And the wisdom to know the difference* [Sifton 2003].

Becoming a "control freak" is an occupational hazard for coaches. Some coaches even view it as such a positive and useful professional trait they take great pride in referring to themselves that way. As is implied in the "Serenity Prayer," however, trying to exert control over a particular situation is not, in itself, inherently good or bad. What is important, is to consider whether or not you are attempting to control things that are truly under your control. Unfortunately, many coaches have come to *believe* they control far more of their environment than they actually do. When you stop to think of it, coaches rarely control their athletes' behavior — on or off the field. Coaches rarely control the outcome of competitions. Coaches rarely control the calls made by officials. Coaches rarely control how other people (fans, players, parents, media, administrators, officials, etc.) react to things they've said or done. Coaches rarely control player injuries or illnesses. And, most relevant to our current discussion, coaches rarely control their athletes' motivation level. To be sure, there are several ways you might be able to exert influence on the motivation levels of your athletes (we just discussed how your own motivation level might have an impact the motivation level of those around you) but operating under the delusion that you have true "control" over someone else's motivations will, more often than not, result in little more than failure and frustration.

To better appreciate exactly which aspects of our athletes' motivation we can — and can't — control, we need to understand what actually "determines" a person's motivation level in the first place. As seen in the Figure 3.1, the motivation our athletes exhibit is the result of an interaction between the things they bring with them to the sport situation (their unique per-

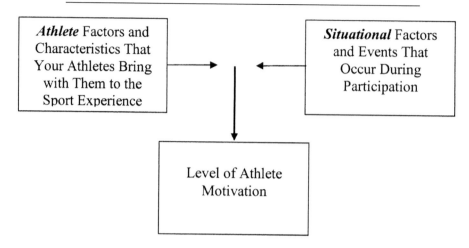

Figure 3.1: What Motivates Our Athletes? (adapted, with permission, from R.S. Weinberg and D. Gould, 2007, *Foundations of sport and exercise psychology,* 4th ed. Champaign, IL: Human Kinetics, 54).

sonalities, prior experiences, expectations, needs, interests, etc.) and their perception of the experiences they have once they are in the sport situation (e.g., the manner they are treated by the coach or other members of the team, the anxiety or pressure they feel during a performance, the success or failure they experience, the degree to which their expectations are met, etc.).

Most coaches have no difficulty accepting the idea that both the factors that athletes bring with them to the sport and the way the sport is structured will contribute to motivation levels. For example, you probably recognize that a player's unique personality traits such as his or her laziness, enthusiasm, leadership, dedication, or stubbornness will, to some extent, impact the behaviors we interpret as indicators of motivation. Similarly, you are also well aware of the fact that the way a player perceives the situation he or she is in will affect his or her motivation level.

Now here's the million-dollar question: If you can improve your athletes' motivation levels by altering either, (a) the personal factors they bring with them to the situation, or (b) the sport environment in which the athletes find themselves, which should you spend most of your time trying to change? The answer is, of course, you should spend your time changing the *situation* so that it will enhance your athletes' motivation. Now, let's see if you can answer a second, equally important question: Do you know why changing the situation is going to be a more efficient way to increase motivation than trying to change the athlete? Okay, here's a hint: Go back and reread the first three lines of the *Serenity Prayer.* Of course, it's because you, as a coach, control so much of what goes on in the situation (in case you need to remind yourself just how much control you typically have over the situation, go back to the Myth No. 2 chapter and reexamine Table 2.1). On the other hand, think about how difficult it will be for you to change someone's personality. Are you a trained psychiatrist? Do you have five or six years to devote to intensive one-on-one psychoanalysis sessions with an athlete? If not, you're likely to be seriously disappointed with your results.

A second important reason to focus on changing the situation rather than changing our athletes is that if we come to the conclusion that it is our athletes who need changing, we have automatically — and rather conveniently — blamed them for the fact they are not motivated. In essence, we have convinced ourselves that it must be our athletes — certainly not our beloved coaching style — that have created the "motivational problem" (Treasure 2001).

Let's start thinking of how we can take some practical steps to structure our practices and games so they will enhance (or at least maintain) our athletes' motivation levels. One way to approach this is to consider setting a new coaching "TARGET."

TARGETing Your Coaching to Increase Athlete Motivation

It's now time to revisit the discussion we were having about how athletes who estimate their competency on the basis of the quality of their performance — and not on how their performance compares to others — tend to enjoy their sport more, put forth greater effort, attend practice more, feel more competent, continue to work longer on tasks, and believe that the effort they put forth is the key to success. But there's a problem. In the real world of sports, society generally places a much higher value on the *outcomes* of performance than the performance itself. Just think about it. When you were a little kid and you came home from playing Little League baseball or youth soccer, what was the very first question your parents asked as you walked through the front door? I'll bet most of you were asked whether you won or lost — not whether you had fun. As you were growing up, how many trophies were you ever given for "getting better?" Does anyone ever get their contract extended or their picture on the cover of *Sports Illustrated* for trying harder? Be honest, doesn't it really bug you when someone gives you that old cliché about "It's not whether you win or lose, but how you play the game?" (Rice 1941). In an environment that is entirely built on competition, how can we foster mastery motivation in our athletes?

One way we can modify our coaching in a way that will enhance our athletes' natural motivation level is to better "TARGET" our coaching energies. The acronym TARGET stands for the need to pay close attention to the way we structure our coaching in regard to the way we:

- Design Tasks
- Determine Authority
- Promote Recognition
- Construct Groups
- Conduct Evaluations
- Control Timing [Epstein1988; 1989]

Designing Tasks. The way we organize practices, drills, exercises, and workout activities will determine how our athletes gather information about their competencies and the competencies of others. If, for example, we configure these activities so several athletes are performing the same tasks, in the same place, at the same time, it encourages the athletes to evaluate themselves by comparing their performance to that of others (competitive-motivation). On the other hand, by emphasizing individualized workouts and skill development regimes (with proper feedback) on specific areas where they need improvement, our athletes will be inclined to evaluate their competence on the basis of their individual progress (mastery-motivation). Because it is this mastery-motivation that has been shown to be associated with increased enjoyment, effort, confidence and perseverance, we can motivate our athletes by increasing the variety and uniqueness of their tasks while drawing their attention to their personal improvement rather than how they stack up against their teammates.

Determining Authority. In the Myth No. 2 chapter we discussed the advantages of involving our athletes in the team decision-making process. There's really no need to belabor the point further other than to say that research has consistently shown people (particularly children) tend to evaluate themselves as having more ability when they are given control over their own skill development (Ryan and Deci 2000; Vallerand 2001).

Promoting Recognition. It is interesting to note that the rewards we give our athletes are often considered more important than the accomplishments they represent. Obviously, if we are attempting to foster mastery-motivation (and downplay competitive-motivation) we need to make sure we provide rewards and recognition on the basis of effort and performance — not just the outcomes of performance. For example, we need to emphasize public awards for "hardest worker," "most improved player," and "most inspirational player" at least as much — if not more — than the more traditionally valued "most valuable player," "all-star selection," or "top scorer." In addition, don't overlook the importance of giving private (one-on-one) recognition. As a coach, our words of encouragement and praise for progress made can be more important than almost any other type of recognition a player can receive (Treasure 2001).

Constructing Groups. As coaches, we naturally treat players differently — and that's not always a bad thing. Coach Wooden, for example frequently said he never attempted to treat all of his players the same. "I didn't treat all players alike ... [but] almost every player I coached knew that he would be treated fairly, that he would be given exactly what he had earned and deserved. They worked harder as a result" (Wooden 1997, 115). Ah, there's the key — even though you often need to treat your players *differently*, can you always say you treat them *fairly*? Unfortunately, there have been several studies that demonstrate teachers and coaches often treat their players — or groups of players — not only differently but in a way that unfairly keeps them from developing their skills. Perhaps the most interesting finding is that if we *think* an athlete has talent (even if he or she has never demonstrated it) we will tend to favor that athlete with elevated expectations and more technical instruction. Of course the reverse is also true — if we don't believe an athlete has a great deal of natural ability we don't expect much from them and we don't provide them with the instruction or opportunities to improve. This differential treatment ultimately results in what we expected in the first place. Originally called a "self-fulfilling prophecy" (Merton 1948) it is frequently referred to today as the "Pygmalion Effect" or the "Rosenthal Effect" (Rosenthal and Jacobson 1968). By systematically favoring the athletes we *think* are more talented, they ultimately become more talented. Of course we then take great pride in our apparent knack for assessing athletic potential.

Think about how often you've seen something like this happen. In fact, imagine you're a basketball coach and you have your team practicing running the fast break. On one of the trips down the court a player you believe has a lot of talent throws an absolutely horrible pass and the ball goes out of bounds. What would be your immediate reaction? If you're like most coaches, you probably offer a few "choice" words to show the entire team you expect a better performance from this player. Then you might give the player some technical instruction regarding what needs to be done differently and tell him or her "run it again — and this time, do it right!" Now let's keep the situation exactly the same with one small exception. Instead of (what you believe to be) a good player throwing the ball away, one of your players you don't think has a lot of talent makes the same bad pass. Do you react the same way? Many coaches don't. In the second situation they will be more inclined to simply ignore the mistake and say "next!" Two things are important here. First, this differential reaction is based on what the coach *thinks* regarding the talent level of the two players (which may or may not be accurate). Second, the player whom the coach thinks is better receives more instruction and more repetitions at the task. If this is repeated over and over again throughout the season, it should be no surprise to find that the first player becomes, in fact, much more skilled than the second. But that would be true even if they were equal in ability at the beginning of the season — simply because one got more instruction and practice time than the other. A question all coaches should ask themselves is whether their "first string" players are better than the "second stringers" because they truly have more natural ability or is it only because they have been in the group that received better instruction and more reps. Finding yourself to be a member of the continually disadvantaged, devalued, and dismissed group is hardly a motivating experience.

Conducting Evaluations. An important part of every coach's job involves evaluating athletes. These evaluations don't have to be a painful experience. In fact, they should be designed to be informative and motivational. Unfortunately, many coaches think pitting one athlete against another is the best way to "motivate" both players at the same time. However, a much more effective way to use the evaluation process to enhance mastery motivation is to base evaluation on our athletes' effort and personal mastery of important performance goals — and not how the performance compares to that of their peers.

Controlling Timing. We've all heard the old adage "timing is everything." Nowhere is this more evident than when it comes to working with your athletes in a way that will maintain motivation. As coaches, we all know that spending too much — or too little — time on a drill or activity will diminish motivation. Too much time leads to boredom and lack of attention but too little time leads to a lack of adequate skill development.

This book was designed to help coaches identify the aspects of coaching we have under our control (and those we don't). The one thing that is always under our control is our attitude. This brings us back to the quote from Coach Krzyzewski we used at the beginning of this chapter "When you are enthusiastic, you are a catalyst to those around you. Your unabashed love and emotion for what you are doing is contagious. (Krzyzewski 2006, 57). In other words, Motivate Yourself First!

"Mental Toughness: Some Players Have It — Some Don't"

It's about that killer instinct, the great teams have that and we need to look for it. We need to teach our team that killer instinct.
— Coach C. Vivian Stringer[1]

Two things are readily apparent in the preceding quote from Coach Stringer. The first is her deliberate use of the verb *teach*. With this single word she makes it clear that what we generally refer to as "Mental Toughness" is something coaches not only can, but should, set out to develop within their athletes. Second, she implies that teams — and athletes — need to acquire these skills if they have any hope of achieving true competitive greatness. In the remainder of this chapter we will discuss ways coaches can instill a higher level of "mental toughness" in their athletes — all their athletes — while redefining appropriate expressions of "competitiveness."

Signs of a "Great Competitor"

All too often we hear coaches and athletes use the excuse that they are "competitors" to justify their inappropriate behaviors. The next time you hear an athlete or coach begin a sentence with the words "I'm just a very competitive person..." I'd like you to pay close attention to what they say next. As often as not, they (or their apologists) will go on to point out that their extraordinary competitiveness somehow absolves them from some type of ill-mannered, immature, or boorish behavior. What they're really trying to get us to believe is their high level of competitiveness somehow entitles them to:

- Curse, swear, or threaten officials, players, coaches, fans, or anyone in the vicinity whenever they feel like it.

45

- Belittle, insult, or embarrass anyone who has made a mistake.
- Throw temper tantrums, pout, stomp their feet, scream at the top of their lungs, smash water coolers, get into fights, or throw things (like chairs) when things aren't going their way.
- Show off and make a spectacle of themselves by being as rude and as crude as they want to be.
- Break or bend rules, etiquette, and sportsmanship in their relentless drive to win.

These self-proclaimed "competitors" not only see their bad behavior as acceptable, they sometimes even managed to convince themselves that it serves as irrefutable evidence of their highly competitive spirit.

When we hear players and coaches attempt to dismiss their childish behaviors on the basis of their competitiveness, we need to remind ourselves that although nobody likes to lose or perform poorly, these actions aren't really the signs of a competitor but rather a person lacking in self-discipline, maturity, and commitment to the team. True competitors — for the very reason they don't like to lose or perform poorly — are only interested in, and therefore only focus their energy on, three things: *Improving* themselves, *improving* their teammates, and *improving* their sport. To the true competitor, everything else is self-centered showboating. Putting forth a constant effort to improve performance — in yourself and others — is the single true indicator of mental toughness and competitive greatness.

What Is Mental Toughness?

Although it may be difficult to generate a complete list of specific skills that an athlete must possess in order to demonstrate "mental toughness," most of us seem to "know it when we see it." An indication of this is contained in the somewhat trite but true adage that we've all heard a hundred times — and many of us have actually used — "When the going gets tough, the tough get going." Now look carefully at that old cliché. Notice that at the same time, it seems to tell us everything — and nothing — about mental toughness. On the one hand, it gives us a general indication of how important mental toughness is, and that when things get progressively more challenging, those who "have it" tend to use it more often. On the other hand, it never really defines what this essential "it" really is. Do your athletes (or you) really have any idea what you're asking them to do when you holler out vague words of encouragement such as "show me some heart!" or "pay attention!" or "get tough out there!" or "suck it up!" or "get in the game!"? How much do you think these pieces of sage advice actually improve your athletes' performance? How realistic is it to expect your athletes to have, or do, something neither you, nor they, can even define? As you can see, our first order of business is to come to a clear understanding of what mental toughness is.

To help us identify exactly what mental toughness entails, let's reexamine the cliché "When the going gets tough, the tough get going." What mental, or psychological skills do you think would help your athletes perform at a higher level when "the going gets tough" or when their "best is needed"? Look at the list of mental skills presented in the left hand column of Table 4.1 and circle how you think each would affect your athletes' performance when "the going gets tough."

Table 4.1: Assessing the Skills Your Athletes Need to Become "Mentally Tough."

If my athletes could...	*Their "mental toughness" and athletic performance would...*		
Relax when faced with a "high-pressure" situation	Improve	Remain the Same	Get Worse
Block out distractions and focus concentration on important cues	Improve	Remain the Same	Get Worse
Feel confident they can do what is required in a particular situation	Improve	Remain the Same	Get Worse
Mentally prepare for competition by rehearsing or practicing situations ahead of time	Improve	Remain the Same	Get Worse
Work hard so nothing within their control gets in the way of accomplishing their pre-set goals	Improve	Remain the Same	Get Worse
Positively encourage themselves and others at all times — especially when things are toughest	Improve	Remain the Same	Get Worse

Notice that by doing this simple task, the "mental toughness" skills you expect from your athletes are no longer abstract — you have clearly identified at least six important things a "mentally tough" athlete should be able to do: (1) relax under pressure, (2) focus their attention properly, (3) feel confident that they can perform what is asked of them, (4) mentally prepare for competition, (5) strive to accomplish pre-set goals that are under their control, and (6) use positive and encouraging ways of talking to themselves and others. You may want to list other skills under this heading of "mental toughness" but the important thing you've just proven to yourself is that when you boil it down to the basics, the ways that you want your athletes to demonstrate their mental toughness — or their competitive greatness — involve skills that can be identified and taught.

Mental Toughness Is a Skill

Have you ever stopped to think about the difference between "skills" and "abilities?" In everyday conversation, we often use the two terms interchangeably. The confusion is not all that surprising when you consider that abilities and skills interact with one another to produce an overall athletic performance, but on closer examination, there is an important distinction to be made. *Abilities* are relatively enduring — often innate — personal traits such as strength, stamina, flexibility, balance, coordination, etc. (Fleishman 1975; Stallings 1982). Although with practice and training we can develop and extend these natural abilities to some extent, we generally don't think of them as things we learn how to do. On the other hand, *skills* must be learned.

To illustrate the difference between abilities and skills, let's examine an overhand serve in tennis. In order to develop a really good serve, a tennis player must practice this specific movement hundreds — even thousands — of times. It is a skill that doesn't "come naturally," it must be learned through practice and repetition. But the building blocks for this skill are the player's basic natural abilities such as hand-eye coordination, balance, and strength. Because everyone has different levels of each of these abilities, we are not surprised that when we're teaching a group of people to serve a tennis ball for the first time, they will differ greatly in the quality of their performance. Although some might be considerably better than others, none of these novice players will be very good because serving a tennis ball is a skill that can only be developed through many hours of deliberate practice (Ericsson, Nandagopal, and Roring 2009). I've heard some describe the distinction between abilities and skills this way, "Abilities [natural talent] load the gun ... but skills [learned and practiced behavior] pull the trigger." Although the absolute upper limit of our athletes' potential may be genetically determined and relatively unchangeable, the degree to which they approach these natural-born limitations is determined by the skills we help them learn and develop.

This brings us back to our discussion of mental toughness. The mistake many coaches make is to assume that mental skills — such as those we considered in Table 4.1— are abilities rather than skills. If we consider them abilities, we view them as unchangeable — our athletes either have them or they don't. Logically, there is no reason for us to devote valuable practice time to helping our athletes improve in these areas if they can't be dramatically changed anyway. Notice that it's also pretty convenient for us to arrive at this conclusion because most of us don't know how to help our players develop these mental skills anyway. That leads us into a discussion as to why we, as coaches, tend to spend most of our time helping our athletes work on their physical skills and simply ignore the mental skills required for performance.

Think about the last time one of your athletes turned in what you thought was a very poor performance due to a lack of mental toughness. To help you reconstruct this performance, write the important details of this event in Table 4.2 below. Indicate the name of the athlete, the specific situation he or she was facing, what was done, what should have been done, and why you think it happened...

Let's get right to the important stuff. Did your athlete perform poorly in this situation primarily due to insufficient abilities or skills? To the extent that the poor performance was due to a lack of abilities (either physical or mental), there is very little you can do that will improve the athlete's future

---

Athlete's name: _____

What was the specific situation this athlete faced?

What *did* this athlete do?

What *should* this athlete have done?

Why do you think this athlete performed poorly in this situation (check all that apply)?

☐ Insufficient *physical abilities*

☐ Insufficient *mental abilities*

☐ Insufficient *physical skills*

☐ Insufficient *mental skills*

Table 4.2: Assessing Your Athletes' Performance Errors.

performance (remember, abilities are — for the most part — permanent). If, on the other hand, you feel the poor performance occurred because the athlete did not possess adequate physical or mental *skills,* you will need to structure practice time in such a way that will give the athlete (and his or her team-mates) the opportunity to learn these skills that will make them successful. Notice that regardless of whether the deficient skills are physical or psycho-logical, the remedy is the same — additional practice time specifically designed to develop the skills required for successful performance. If we stop to think about it, there is really nothing to be gained by blaming our athletes' poor performances on their lack of ability — there's very little we — or they — can do to change that. The important thing we need to identify is the degree to which the poor performance resulted from a lack of physical *skills,* psycho-logical *skills,* or a combination of physical and psychological *skills*— and then schedule practice sessions that will help them improve.

Athletic Performances: Physical, Psychological, or Both?

Unfortunately, this is the point where many coaches make another seri-ous mistake. Over the years, coaches have learned to behave as if most — perhaps all — of the factors that determine athletic success are physical, and our athletes can therefore master the keys to success by simply working on their physical skills. Interestingly enough, although most of us *behave* as if athletic performances are determined solely by the physical skills our athletes possess, we don't actually *believe* it! Just look at the topic we are currently discussing — mental toughness. If you even think there is such a thing as mental toughness, and that it can improve performance, you are admitting that there is a lot more to an athletic performance than simply learning physical skills. To make this point even more obvious, look at all the terms listed in Table 4.3. Have you ever heard coaches use any of these expressions? Please circle any of these personal characteristics you believe have a positive impact on athletic success. As you can see, you really *do* believe that there is a great deal more to athletic performance than mastering physical skills.

Table 4.3: Psychological Characteristics of Successful Athletes.

Aggressiveness	Attention	Attitude
Coachability	Cohesiveness	Commitment
Competitiveness	Concentration	Confidence
Courage	Dedication	Dependability
Desire	Determination	Discipline

Drive	Effort	Enthusiasm
Focus	Guts	Hustle
Integrity	Intensity	Leadership
Loyalty	Mental Preparation	Motivation
Passion	Perseverance	Poise
Pride	Sacrifice	Self-Control
Spirit	Toughness	Work ethic

You may find it reassuring to know that you're not the only one who thinks psychological skills play an important role in athletic performance. Many of the most successful coaches and athletes actually agree in principle — if not arithmetically — with Yogi Berra's well-known assertion that "Baseball is 90 percent mental, the other half is physical." Let's examine, for example, what a Hall of Fame basketball coach and a future Hall of Fame NFL quarterback have to say about the relative role physical and mental skills have on athletic success.

In the summer of 2003, Green Bay Packer General Manager Mike Sherman asked legendary basketball coach Bob Knight to deliver a 30-minute speech to the Green Bay Packers. Knight — who finished his career five years later as the winningest coach in men's college basketball — talked about the things he believes are most important to winning. Surprising many of the players in attendance, (and perhaps some of you) Knight began by telling the Packers that: "Talent is not anywhere near the top of the list of things necessary to win, because everybody has talent." If that wasn't shocking enough, he went on to share with them what he has discovered by working with high-caliber athletes over the past half-century, "It's my belief, in all the years I've been around sports, I believe very strongly that the mental is to the physical as 4 is to 1" (Havel 2003). In other words, Bob Knight believes that 80 percent of winning or losing is a result of mental — not physical — preparation and execution. In case you think that the rough, tough professional football players in the audience disagreed with Knight's observation, you should know that Brett Favre, a three-time NFL Most Valuable Player, indicated his total agreement with Knight's assessment. "It's really true" was his only comment when asked to react to Knight's assertion that the physical aspects of sport contribute only about 20 percent of a winning effort.

To see how common this view is, every time I conduct a college coaching clinic I begin by asking all the coaches in the room what percentage of a "successful" performance in their sport is determined by the physical skills their athletes possess and how much is determined by their mental, or psychological skills. You might be surprised that across all sports — from golf to football and swimming to soccer — the coaches typically indicate that psychological factors such as confidence, focus, motivation, goal setting, and anxiety control are probably responsible — depending on the sport — for something in the range of 60 percent to 90 percent of success or failure. It's pretty clear that most coaches understand the important role psychology plays in athletic performance. What's not nearly as clear is what they do about it.

How Much Time Do Your Athletes Spend Practicing Their Mental Skills?

If, like most coaches, we agree with Bob Knight and Brett Favre that roughly 80 percent of success in sport is mental and 20 percent is physical, we then have to ask ourselves the tough follow-up question: "What percentage of practice time do I devote to that part of the game most likely to help my athletes succeed?" If you're like most coaches, you are reluctant to set aside much — if any — of your valuable practice time to help your athletes develop the very skills you — and most coaches — know are the true secrets to success. If that's the case, you have structured your practices so that virtually 100 percent of your time is spent working on the skills (physical) that will contribute to roughly 20 percent of your athletes' success. Meanwhile, you have consciously decided to spend little or no time whatsoever helping your athletes work on the skills (mental) that are likely to constitute about 80 percent of your team's success. When you think of it that way, is it really any mystery why you teams haven't experienced the level of success you were hoping for?

And it's going to become even more important that you teach your athletes both physical *and* mental skills in the future. There's a whole new breed of coaches out there who are being educated — in college courses and at coaching clinics — on the value of spending more time working on the mental side of the game. Let's briefly examine the kind of coaches you will be facing in the future.

Mentally Preparing for a National Championship

In 2005, the Michigan Wolverine softball team won their first NCAA Division I National Championship. What you may not know is that three years earlier, Wolverine Head Coach Carol Hutchins purposely instilled in her team the mental toughness they would need for this champion-level performance by making her players read and discuss the book "*Heads-Up Baseball: Playing the Game One Pitch at a Time*" by sport psychologists Ken Ravizza and Tom Hanson (Ravizza and Hanson 1994). The entire team began setting aside practice time to learn not only the physical skills of hitting, pitching, fielding, and throwing but the mental skills related to confidence, relaxation, goal setting, and — most of all — playing the game one pitch at a time. According to Hutchins, these mental skills sessions taught her players "the importance of forgetting mistakes" and "staying in the now" (Weber, 2002).

That season, the Wolverines won the Big Ten regular-season title, the Big Ten tournament, and the NCAA regional championship. But the real payoff would come three years later when the team — despite having to play their first 33 games of the season on the road — drew on their mental toughness training to become the first softball team east of the Mississippi to win the NCAA Division I title.

Coach Hutchins knew what more and more coaches are learning everyday — that to play to their full potential, her players were going to have to develop more than their physical skills. More importantly, she was also willing to set aside valuable practice time to teach them the "other 80 percent" of an athletic performance — mental toughness.

You may find the story of Coach Hutchins and her National Champion softball team interesting — but it's more than that. It should also serve as a clear warning. In the years to come, your athletes and your teams will be competing against athletes who have been systematically trained, like hers, to improve their skills in the part of the game that is likely to determine 80 percent of winning and losing. Think about what that means if you've decided — and it is your decision — to neglect training your athletes to develop their mental skills. Imagine, for example, you're a Big Ten softball coach. Even if you happen to be blessed with athletes who are as naturally gifted or who have perfected the same physical skills as those playing for Michigan, they still won't be able to compete on a regular basis because you haven't set aside time to teach them the skills necessary for them to acquire mental toughness.

Why Coaches Don't Teach Mental Toughness

We all know that coaches are notorious for going to great lengths — in extreme cases, unethical or illegal lengths — to gain even the slightest advantage over their competition. So how can we explain the fact that most coaches make no attempt whatsoever to give their athletes the mental toughness skills that would almost certainly enhance their performance? As we already discussed, many coaches simply make the mistake of thinking mental toughness as an unchangeable ability — "you have it or you don't." But there may be a number of other reasons coaches resist implementing mentally training their athletes. In their book *Foundations of Sport and Exercise Psychology*, Weinberg and Gould (2011) set forth a number of reasons athletes and coaches might be reluctant to engage in mental skills training.

Lack of knowledge. We generally learn how to coach by example. Unfortunately, when most of us were formulating our views as to what coaches "do and don't do" we were rarely exposed to coaches who recognized the value of setting aside time for mental training. As a result, we tended to develop, like those who taught us, a personal bias that causes us to ignore — or even disparage — any form of mental skills training. Our coaches' failure to use mental training not only left us with the impression it wasn't necessary, we even feel uncomfortable thinking about incorporating it into our practices.

Lack of time. If you talk to any coach for more than a couple of minutes you'll probably hear them complain about the fact they never have enough practice time. Because they feel that their practice time is so limited, most coaches are not about to "waste" any of it on mental skills training (especially if they don't know how to do it anyway). Although practice time certainly is finite and priorities need to be set, there are a couple of questions coaches need to ask themselves before they conclude mental skills training would be a waste of their practice time. First, as we've stated throughout this chapter, how can we possibly consider working on skills that will determine 80 percent of our success, to be a waste of time? Second, because coaches at a given level of competition usually have roughly the same amount of practice time, why do we need so much more time than everyone else? In several chapters throughout this book we'll detail how you can improve the efficiency of your practices by helping your athletes set and accomplish important personal goals during practice (Myth No. 5), thoughtfully planning and organizing practices (Myth No. 8) and reducing the amount of practice time wasted by punishing athletes for performance errors and misbehaviors (the Myth No. 9 chapter).

Because few coaches have an adequate understanding of mental skills training, it's not surprising that they have developed many erroneous beliefs and expectations that keep them from teaching these skills to their athletes. For example, it's not unusual for coaches to mistakenly think that psychological skills training will benefit only "problem" athletes with serious personal issues or elite athletes at the highest levels of competition. As we've seen, however, learning how to relax under pressure, focus on essential performance-related information, feel more confident, mentally prepare for competition, and set attainable goals are skills all athletes need to develop. But these important mental skills — just like the physical skills we teach — require continuous practice. Unfortunately, many coaches who are willing to give mental training "a try" get discouraged when they don't see immediate improvement after one or two mental skills training sessions. The sad truth is that there are few "quick fixes" in sports. When we expect immediate results — from short bursts of either physical or mental practice — we're usually going to be very disappointed.

It's not enough to simply set aside time to teach our athletes mental toughness. We have to continually demonstrate — by example — what mental toughness is. It's not throwing temper tantrums when things go badly. It's not using or abusing others to satisfy our "win at all costs" view of sports. It's being prepared, remaining calm and composed under pressure, staying focused, and building confidence — in ourselves and others. In short, it all comes down to what Coach John Wooden labeled "Self-Control" in his well-known "Pyramid of Success." The coach was keenly aware that self-control wasn't something only his athletes needed to develop, "I wanted those under my leadership to see me always on an even keel — intense, of course, but even. How could I ask others to control themselves if I couldn't do it? And emotional control is a primary component of consistency, which, in turn, is a primary component of success" (Wooden 2005, 108). When coaches exhibit mental toughness — "controlled intensity" as Coach Wooden might call it — they pass this essential skill on to their athletes.

MYTH NO. 5

"Winning Is the Ultimate Goal in Sport"

If in my own mind and heart I had defined success purely as winning, I might have seen myself as a failure... Had I done so, I might have completely stopped believing in myself and the possibility of realizing my dream.

— Manager Joe Torre[1]

No doubt you've heard the old expression "Money is the root of all evil." This, like most of the coaching myths and misunderstandings that make up the chapters of this book, is simply another example of a distortion of the truth that we mindlessly pass on from one person to the next. The precise biblical passage is "For the *love* of money is the root of all evil: which while some coveted after, they have erred from the faith, and pierced themselves through with many sorrows" (I Timothy 6:10, King James Version; emphasis added).

Interestingly, the same can be said of winning. It's certainly not a "sin" to enjoy winning—we all do. Participating in sports wouldn't make any sense if we weren't "in it to win it," but the single-minded and relentless pursuit of winning—"coveting" as the Bible would call it—can cause us to "error, and pierce ourselves with many sorrows." There are two primary reasons that those of us who set goals based on winning are more likely to end up losing—both as a coach and as a person.

First, focusing so much of our attention on wins and losses often deceives us into thinking that winning is the ultimate purpose of sport. It is not. Do any of us truly believe that participating in sport only becomes a worthwhile experience when we win? Can we even argue that playing sports is somehow made "more valuable" by winning? Probably not. While sports can teach us many valuable lessons, few—if any—require winning.

Second, most of the things that actually contribute to whether we win or lose are—and this might be a surprise—beyond our control. Although we can generally determine our own actions, we have little or no control over others — and it's often what others do that directly affects whether we win or lose. So it's pretty easy to see that, to the extent that we pursue goals beyond our control, we are inadvertently setting ourselves up for sport experiences full of disappointment, disillusionment, and frustration — "piercing ourselves with many sorrows" indeed.

It's Natural for Coaches and Athletes to Set Goals

It's unimaginable to even think that there might be successful coaches out there who don't routinely set goals for themselves — and their athletes. Setting individual and team goals is about the most natural thing coaches and athletes can do. In fact, it's so natural I challenge you to resist this temptation and force yourself to go through an entire season — or even a single competition — without setting a goal for yourself or your team. It's impossible.

But if goal setting comes so naturally to coaches and athletes, why do they need instruction on how to do it? The answer is really quite simple. Because goal setting *appears* to be so natural, our coaches, teachers, or parents probably never felt it was necessary to sit us down and let us in on an important little secret — all goals are not equal. So we continue to mistakenly believe that merely setting a goal — any goal — is all that matters. The truth is, however, some of the goals we set for ourselves will probably help our performance, some will have little or no effect, and still others, believe it or not, are actually likely to cause more harm than good (Kingston and Hardy 1997). Isn't it a shame no one told us that? But let's not be too hard on our coaches, teachers, or parents. Most of them didn't know this secret either because their coaches, teachers and parents didn't tell them ... and theirs didn't tell them ... and theirs didn't tell them ... well, you get the idea. In general, coaches and athletes don't understand — because no one has ever taught them — many of the aspirations they have are actually making it *less* likely they will accomplish their goals. What it boils down to is that although setting goals is a very natural thing for coaches and athletes, *effective* goal setting is something that must be learned — and therefore needs to be taught.

Setting (and Helping Others Set) Effective Goals

Obviously, if some goals are more effective than others, there must be several types of goals. The first two types, long-term goals and short-term goals, play an important role in improving performance, but the big payoff comes when we learn to distinguish between three other kinds of goals — outcome, performance, and preparation.

Long-term goals. The old philosopher Yogi Berra was onto something when he once said, "You have to be very careful if you don't know where you're going, 'cause you might not get there" (Berra 1998, 102). And that's really the purpose of long-term goals — to let us know where it is we want to go. As their name implies, long-term goals may take weeks, months — even years — to achieve. If you want examples of long-term goals, just stop by any playground, blacktop, or sandlot and ask the kids to tell you about their athletic goals. Many of the youngsters will say they want to become a professional athlete, obtain a college scholarship, or to be the starting quarterback on their high school team. Although these long-term aspirations are important because they provide a general sense of direction, they have two distinct limitations. First, by themselves, long-term goals are often little more than dreams or fantasies. Even though millions of kids would love to someday be a pro athlete, simply wishing for it won't make it happen. Second, by their very definition, we won't really know whether or not we've accomplished these goals for a long, long time. Maintaining our motivation and staying focused while working on long-term goals can be very difficult because there is so much we need to accomplish over such an extended period of time. That's where short-term goals come in.

Short-term goals. As important as our long-term goals are, we render them worthless when we fail to support them with a series of short-term goals. The purpose of short-term goals is simple — they keep us focused and motivated on the task at hand by constantly reminding us of the next step we must take if we are to accomplish our long-term goal. Sometimes it helps to think of short-term goals as our "personal roadmap" to success. Once we know where we want to go (our long-term goal) we can use our map (short-term goals) to make sure we're always on the right track. If we find we're headed in the right direction, we are motivated by the fact we're making progress and getting a little closer to our ultimate goal. If, on the other hand, we find we're veering a bit off course, we can make the adjustments that will get us back on the right road to reach our destination. In either case, these daily checkpoints help us move ever closer to our long-term goal. Simply put, short-term goals help us answer the important question, "What do I have to accomplish *today*— in this game, during this practice, or at this training session — to remain on track to meet my long-term goals?" Although it's easy to see that using a combination of long- and short-term goals will increase the chances that we will attain our athletic goals, our fondness for setting outcome-based goals is another matter entirely.

Why Winning Isn't Everything... Or Even a Useful Goal

Coaches, athletes, and fans naturally focus on outcomes. We tend to measure our athletic successes and failures on the basis of wins, losses, playoff appearances, bowl games, tournament seedings, medals, championships, rankings, all-star selections, Hall-of-Fame inductions, home runs, rushing yards, scoring averages — even salaries. In fact, it's safe to say that the very thing many people like so much about sport is the finality of the competition. Although we sometimes disagree as to how and why a win or loss occurred, the identity of the winners and losers is rarely open to debate.

Look closely at Table 5.1 and the list of goals we commonly set for ourselves. Now rate the degree to which you believe each is an "appropriate" goal for coaches or athletes to set for themselves or their team.

	I think this is a...			
	"Great" Goal	"Good" Goal	"Poor" Goal	The reason I think that is...
General Athletic Goals:				
Win today's game	O	O	O	
Win the league championship	O	O	O	
Make it to the playoffs	O	O	O	
Lead the league in scoring	O	O	O	
Be selected "All-Conference"	O	O	O	
Be named team "MVP"	O	O	O	
Become a "starter"	O	O	O	
Be elected team "captain"	O	O	O	
Sport-Specific Goals:				
Strike out the next batter	O	O	O	
Pitch a shutout	O	O	O	
Hit a home run	O	O	O	
Rush for 100 yards	O	O	O	
Catch 10 passes	O	O	O	
Score a touchdown today	O	O	O	
Score 25 points in the game	O	O	O	
Score a goal in today's game	O	O	O	
Place in the top 3 in my event	O	O	O	
Beat my main personal rival	O	O	O	

Table 5.1: Rating the Appropriateness of the Goals We Set.

At first glance, these look like perfectly fine goals don't they? But here's the real shocker. Even though most of us grew up setting—and being encouraged to set—exactly these kinds of goals, *none* of them will really do much to improve our performance! Now that you know there's something very wrong with setting these kinds of goals, look at them more carefully and see if you can identify why such seemingly fine goals are unlikely to be anything but a total and complete waste of time.

For starters, notice that all of these goals focus on the nice things we will experience as a *result* of a good performance. If you carefully examine each of the goals listed above, you will see that they tell us absolutely nothing about what we must do to execute the performance that will bring about these desirable results. We're simply left to hope our performance will somehow be good enough to allow us to experience these nice outcomes—not surprisingly, it rarely is.

A second problem with these result-oriented or "outcome-based" goals is that they are generally outside of our control (Burton 1989; 1992; 1993). Another glance at the list will show us that although we might *contribute* in some way to accomplishing each of these goals, our teammates, opponents, coaches, officials—even dumb luck—will exert a tremendous influence over whether or not we achieve these goals. Unfortunately, setting goals that are at the mercy of others can be frustrating because we often tend to view anything short of meeting our goals as a sign of personal failure.

To illustrate the futility of setting goals we can't control, let me pose a question. What would you think if a fellow coach told you his goal for today was to "have it rain"? Your first reaction would probably be that this seems like a pretty silly goal for someone to set for himself—and you'd be right. But what's really important here is to understand what it is that allows all of us to immediately recognize this as such a "silly" goal. The fact is, the only problem with this goal is that the person making it doesn't have any control over whether it happens or not. He may *need* it to rain. He may *want* it to rain. He may *hope* it will rain. But there is nothing he can do to actually *make* it rain. When we don't have total control over our goals—whether they are directed toward making it rain or winning a national championship—they become little more than a waste of valuable time and energy.

If you're still not completely convinced that outcome goals, like those listed in Table 5.1, are rendered useless because we can't control them, let's look at a couple of examples. There's probably no better place to begin than right at the top of the list with the one goal every athlete and coach has set at one time or another—"My goal is to win today's game." Keep in mind that you may *need* to win, you may *want* to win, and you may *hope* to win but the important question here is the extent to which you can *control* whether you win or not—and the answer is that you can't.

Our inability to control outcomes in team sports. In team sports your performance is blended together with that of everyone else on the team. You may perform at your absolute best, but that doesn't necessarily mean your team will win. Let's use an example from baseball. You could hit a home run every time you're at bat in a game and cleanly field every ball hit in your direction but that certainly doesn't mean your team will win. On the other hand, it's also very possible for you to strike out every time you bat and boot every ball hit your way and—provided you are surrounded by quality teammates or good fortune—your team may win despite your poor personal performance. Although you can certainly contribute to a victory, it's impossible for you to actually *control* whether your team wins or not.

Consider the case of Alex Rodriguez. Since he broke into the big leagues "A-Rod" has been considered by many to be one of the best all-around baseball players on the planet. In fact, during his first 10 season in the major league he hit more home runs, scored more runs, drove in more runs, collected more extra-base hits and racked up more total bases than anyone in baseball. But during that time, his teams (Seattle, Texas, and New York) accomplished little (during his three year stint in Texas—when he probably performed at his best—his team's overall win-loss record was a whopping 28 games under .500).

Our inability to control the outcomes in individual sports. It may be tempting to argue that because there is little or no reliance on the performance of teammates, the outcomes of individual sports—such as golf, bowling, swimming, gymnastics, figure skating, and track and field—are more within our control. Not really. One of the clearest—and craziest—examples of how the outcome of an individual sport can be determined by something other than the performance of an athlete happened during the 2002 Winter Olympics in Salt Lake City, Utah. Canadian pairs figure skaters David Pelletier and Jamie Salé undoubtedly turned in a performance that should have easily won them the gold medal. But something beyond their control came into play. Judge Marie-Reine Le Gougne of France intentionally gave them a score that dropped them into second place behind Russian skaters Elena Berezhnaya and Anton Sikharulidze. Overall, the judges' scores were so out of line with the athletic performances that an investigation was immediately undertaken. It was soon discovered Pelletier and Sale were given their undeserved low scores because the French had struck a deal with the Russians that would later give the ice dancing gold medal to France in return. As a result of these extraordinary circumstances, the decision was later made to award *both* the Russian and Canadian skaters with gold medals in the event (ESPN.com 2002).

Although winning or losing may not be affected as much by teammates, most individual sports require the athlete to simply turn in a performance and then stand back to see if someone else can beat it. If they can, there is really nothing the athlete can do but stand there and suffer the defeat — regardless of how well they may have performed. Because there is typically no "defense" in individual sports, there's little we can do to stop an opponent from beating even our best performance. Take the example of a high-jumper who turns in a personal best — clearing the bar several inches higher than she's ever jumped in her life. Does this fantastic individual performance mean she'll win — or even place — in her event? Of course not. That will depend, in large part, on how well the other jumpers performed in that event. What's worse, if her goal was to win the competition, she may even view her tremendous personal achievement as a failure simply because she didn't accomplish her outcome goal. As you can see from these examples, even in an individual sport you can only control the quality of your performance — not the positive or negative outcomes your performance brings.

What Winning Means to the Winningest Coaches

It's interesting to note that some of the winningest coaches in all of sport devote a tremendous amount of time trying to convince their athletes to *stop* thinking about winning. Coach John Wooden, for example, coached his UCLA basketball teams to a remarkable 10 national championships, 88 consecutive victories, 38 consecutive NCAA Tournament wins, and 4 undefeated seasons. You might think that a coach who won that many games must have stressed the importance of "winning" to his team at every opportunity. In reality, nothing could be further from the truth. In fact, Coach Wooden has frequently stated that a large portion of his success was probably due to the fact that neither he, nor his athletes, ever believed winning was their primary goal. As the Coach is famous for saying,

> I never mentioned winning or victory to my players. I never referred to "beating" an opponent. Instead I constantly urged them to strive for the self-satisfaction that always comes from knowing you did the best you could to become the best of which you are capable. That's what I wanted: The total effort. That was the measurement I used, never the final score [Wooden 1997, 88].

And John Wooden isn't the only coach who dominated his sport by deemphasizing winning. Bob Ladouceur, the Head Football Coach at De La Salle High School in Concord, California, guided his teams to such a gaudy level of success that it's easy to think that the high school football record books must be full of misprints. Between 1992 and 2003, for example, Ladouceur's Spartans racked up 151 consecutive wins — that's 12 straight years without a loss against some of the toughest competition in the country. To put "Coach Lad's" accomplishments into perspective, during his first 27 years at the helm, his teams amassed an overall record of 287–14–1 while posting more perfect seasons (17) than losses (14). Entering the 2012 season, Coach Ladouceur's career win-loss record stood at a remarkable 384–25–3. Again, you might think this level of success demands a constant focus on the importance of winning. You'd be wrong. In his book *When the Game Stands Tall* sports reporter Neil Hayes arrived at the following conclusion after spending the entire 2002 season with the De La Salle football program:

> There is no specific training technique or motivational play that explains why Ladouceur's teams have not lost a game in more than a decade, but many threads intertwine with a philosophy as unique as the head coach himself: He has won more consecutive football games than any other coach in history by not emphasizing winning. Winning is a byproduct of a larger vision [Hayes 2003, 2].

Wooden and Ladouceur aren't the only successful coaches who have downplayed winning in order to win. Duke basketball coach Mike Krzyzewski has racked up more men's Division I college basketball victories than anyone in the history of the game. By the end of the 2011–2012 season he had guided his Blue Devils to four NCAA National Championships, 11 NCAA Final Four appearances, 12 Atlantic Coast Conference (ACC) regular season titles, and 13 ACC Tournament championships. "Coach K" later led yet another team — the men's USA Olympic basketball team — to two gold medals in Beijing (2008) and London (2012). That's an awful lot of winning at the highest level of competition — especially when you consider he never sets specific goals to win games or championships. As he puts it:

> Actually, I never have a goal that involves number of wins — never... When we win a game, everything isn't right. And when we lose a game, everything isn't wrong. As a matter of fact, sometimes a loss can be a win... If we're constantly looking at win-loss record to determine whether we are doing well, we're not looking at the right barometer [Krzyzewski 2000, 28; 60].

So far we've discussed how the top coaches in college basketball and youth football purposely shy away from setting result-oriented goals in order to help them win. But what about the rough, tough, "winner-take-all" game of professional football? Surely in this cutthroat league where millions of dollars and the careers of every player and coach are on the line in each game there has to be a tremendous pressure to set "winning" as the primary goal, right? Not really — at least not for some of the most successful men to ever coach in the National Football League (NFL).

Chuck Noll guided his Pittsburgh Steelers to more Super Bowl victories (4) than any coach in the history of the NFL. With success like that, we might be tempted to think that Noll was preoccupied with winning. But he understood — like Wooden, Ladouceur, and Krzyzewski — that winning is simply a byproduct of performance. Nothing sums up Noll's distinction between winning and performance better than a quote that has had a lasting impact on one of his former assistants — himself a Super Bowl winning Head Coach — Tony Dungy of the Indianapolis Colts. According to Dungy, Noll understood that it was better to set a goal to strive for a good performance than a victory. In the words of Noll, "I would rather play well and lose than play poorly and win" (Dungy 2007, 139). How many of us would be of the same opinion?

Chuck Noll's de-emphasis on winning as a formal goal helped him collect what no other Head Coach has — four Super Bowl Championship rings. But right behind him with three of his own is Bill Walsh, former Head Coach of the San Francisco 49ers. In 1979 Walsh took over a 49er team that in his words,

> [W]as a demoralized, chaotic, and near-mutinous organizational culture of failure that was epitomized by a team that produced a 2–14 record the year prior to my arrival (and was even worse than that record suggests). One writer declared that the San Francisco 49ers were the worst franchise in all of professional sports. Not just football — all professional sports [Walsh 2009, 13].

Within two short years Walsh transformed the miserable mob of misfits he inherited into champions. Between 1981 and 1988 his 49ers were the dominant team in the NFL, winning the Super Bowl in 1981, 1984, and 1988. His team's success earned Walsh recognition as the NFL "Coach of the Year" in 1981 and 1984 and ultimately, a well-deserved spot in the Pro Football Hall of Fame. The 49ers achievements speak for themselves but even more relevant to our current discussion is *how* this miraculous turnaround was accomplished. We needn't look further than the title of Walsh's book, *The Score Takes Care of Itself: My Philosophy of Leadership* for a clue as to how he and his teams racked up more titles than any other NFL team in the decade (and set the stage for two additional Super Bowl Championships under his successor, George Seifert in 1989 and 1994). Particularly informative is an early section of the book he provocatively labels, *The Prime Directive Was Not Victory* in which he discusses his true goal-setting philosophy:

In pursuing this ideal, I focused our personnel on the details of my Standard of Performance — trying to achieve it — rather than how we measured up against a given team.... I directed our focus less to the prize of victory than to the process of improving — obsessing, perhaps, about the quality of our execution and the content of our thinking; that is, our actions and attitude. I knew if I did that, winning would take care of itself [Walsh 2009, 20–21].

Notice that it is an unyielding goal of improving *performance*— not the *results* of performance — that has guided each of these outstanding coaches — Wooden, Ladouceur, Krzyzewski, Noll, Dungy, and Walsh — throughout their exceptional careers. Despite these models, some coaches, even at elite levels of competition, still don't understand the apparent paradox that by placing a premium on winning they will often increase the likelihood of losing all the more. Here is one unfortunate example.

After several years of being the "doormat" of the NFL, the Detroit Lions hired Tampa Bay Assistant Rod Marinelli as their new Head Coach. In his first game, Marinelli's Lions played remarkably well but experienced a hard-fought, last-second loss to the previous year's NFC Champions, the Seattle Seahawks. During his first post-game press conference, the rookie coach told his team something he thought would motivate them — but it ended up destroying any chance they would win again.

"It's not good enough," Marinelli said of his players' tremendous effort. "I'm not interested in playing hard and well; I'm interested in winning. There's no option, there's no solution other than winning. That's it; I won't accept anything less.... I'm not going to throw them a rose and say 'good job'" [Scout.com 2006].

Oh really? Lions' fans who were forced to endure the remainder of that miserable 2006 season would have probably been thrilled if Marinelli's team had continued playing "hard and well" throughout the season. Had they consistently played "hard and well" the team would have certainly won more than three games that year. At the end of that dismal season I wrote a column in *The Grand Rapids Press* suggesting that the Lion's horrendous performance wasn't really that difficult to explain (Albrecht 2007). After all, on the very first day, the "head man" publicly announced to the entire team that their outstanding effort and performance was of no value. The new coach got so caught up with winning, he completely forgot that consistently playing "hard and well" — the two things he publicly stated he had no interest in — is exactly where all winning takes root. To those who understand the power of setting performance-based (as opposed to outcome-based) goals, it was no surprise that Coach Marinelli ended up being fired two years later after amassing an embarrassing career win-loss record of 10 wins and 38 losses. In fact, his last team, the 2008 Lions, turned in the worst performance in the entire history of the NFL — going winless in all 16 of their regular season games. Notice the stark contrast between Marinelli's relentless pursuit of the outcome of a performance and the approach toward improving the performance itself espoused by NFL Hall of Fame coaches Chuck Noll and Bill Walsh. Like Marinelli, the more we focus our attention on winning and neglect the underlying performances that make it possible, the more we'll end up losing.

As interesting and instructive as it may be to examine how some of the most successful coaches in all of sport use goal-setting to enhance their athletes' performance, it is important to keep in mind that the central theme of this book is that we must resist the temptation to merely copy the techniques of other, even highly successful, coaches. Our coaching-related decisions must be based on what we *know*, not what we *think* we know. So let's turn our attention to what the many scientific investigations into goal setting can tell us about how we — and our athletes — can benefit most when setting goals.

Improving Performance by Setting Performance-Based Goals

If the traditional outcome-based goals our coaches, parents, and society as a whole led us to believe were appropriate do little to help our performance, what kinds of goals should we be setting? The answer is deceptively obvious. We need to focus our attention on goals designed to improve the quality of our performance instead of on the rewards, results, and payoffs the performance might — or might not — bring our way.

It's pretty easy to see why performance-related goals are generally more effective than outcome goals. First and foremost, performance goals are more likely to be under our control.

Let's reconsider for a moment, the cases of the baseball player and the high jumper we mentioned earlier. As we saw, "winning" was not something these athletes could control. But they could — and should — be constantly striving to turn in their best possible performance. The true secret of effective goal setting is learning to replace natural — but uncontrollable — outcome goals with performance-improving goals. Let's practice this important skill with another baseball example, the Natural "Outcome" Goal: "My goal is to strike out the next hitter."

Based on our previous discussion of outcome goals, it's easy to see why this goal — as good as it may seem — will do little to help our pitching performance. It doesn't specify what we actually need to do in order to increase our chances of striking out the next hitter, and — believe it or not — striking out the next hitter isn't really totally under our control anyway. Whether or not we achieve this particular goal will, to some extent, be determined by the calls made by the umpire, the hitting skills of the batter, and even dumb luck. Now let's look at how we can rephrase that outcome-based goal in a way that will most likely improve our performance, with the Revised "Performance" Goal: "My goal is to throw my next pitch with the velocity, location, and movement I want."

Notice how focusing on our performance (how we will throw the ball) rather than the *outcome* of our performance (whether or not the batter strikes out) produces a more effective goal. We now know exactly what we have to do when we throw the next pitch — nothing more, nothing less. It also forces us to recognize that the pitch, but not the result, is completely under our control. It's still possible that the batter will hit our "perfectly thrown" ball out of the park. But that can only happen for one of two reasons: (1) the batter is really talented enough to hit what we considered to be our best pitch, or (2) the batter just got lucky and swung the bat where the ball happened to be. In either case, what could we have done to prevent the home run? The answer is nothing. We can't perform better than our best. This is exactly what Coach Wooden means when he says, *"Did I win? Did I lose? Those are the wrong questions. The correct question is: Did I make my best effort? That's what matters. The rest of it just gets in the way"* (Wooden 1997, 56).

High-quality performances (like throwing a baseball with the "velocity, location, and movement" needed to be successful) don't happen by accident. Sure, they require a certain amount of natural talent but, by in large, they result from hours and hours of hard work and close attention to detail. Setting performance-based goals, however, doesn't mean setting the vague goal to "do my best." In fact, research has shown that simply trying to "do your best" usually does little to improve performance (Klein, et al. 1999). Instead, we need to set specific goals that will eventually allow us to perform at a high level. This is where our short-term, performance goals combine with our "preparation" goals. The question that should direct our goal setting each and every day is, "What must I do today to develop the skills necessary to perform at my best?"

The Process of Preparing for a Performance

There are many things we have to do to prepare ourselves to give our best effort. And setting goals to improve in each of these areas is the only way we can ever hope to "be the best we can be." But many coaches and athletes limit themselves by failing to set goals beyond competitions (and even those are generally unproductive "outcome" goals). If we are to truly perform at our best, we need to set a series of preparation or "foundational" goals in *every* aspect related to our performance. Setting a daily goal for practice, fitness training, nutrition, hydration, rest, rehabilitation, and academics will help our athletes come closer to reaching their ultimate performance.

Setting practice goals. How often do your athletes set specific, stated goals for what they want to accomplish during a particular practice session? Unfortunately, for most athletes practice is a matter of spending a couple of hours doing whatever the coaches tell them to do. If you find this hard to believe, go out and prove it to yourself sometime by observing a practice run by another coach. It's a good bet it will look something like this:

> A coach shows up and blows a whistle and tells the athletes to do something ... they all run to where the coach wants them to be and begin doing the things the coach wants them to do. A few minutes later, the coach blows the whistle again and tells them to do something else ... and they all run to the new location and once again begin doing as they're told. Later still, the whistle blows and the athletes carry out the coach's new instructions. Finally, the whistle blows for the last time and the athletes are told to "hit the showers" ... as always, they do exactly as they're told.

Practice is over and what did the athletes actually try to accomplish during this two-hour session? Nothing—beyond following the coach's directions and doing as they're told. Because they had no specific goals for practice the athletes weren't really trying to achieve anything—and "nothing" is probably about all they did accomplish in this practice. By simply taking a couple of minutes at the beginning of every practice to allow each athlete to write down a specific and measureable goal he or she wants to accomplish during today's session, we can focus their attention on something that will help them get just a little better every day. Then, at the end of practice, have everyone reassess and evaluate whether or not they accomplished what they thought was important.

Setting training and fitness goals. Back in the early 1970s, I was at dinner with several NFL players and one of them asked another how he was staying in shape during the off-season. The second jokingly replied, "Walking from my apartment to the elevator." In fact, this second professional athlete was doing quite a bit to retain his general fitness level during the off-season but it was pretty unstructured—a little weightlifting in his basement recreation room and a daily game of basketball with some of his teammates. Those days—if they ever truly existed at all—are long gone. To perform their best, today's athletes have to commit themselves to ongoing training regiments — in and out of season. Part of this commitment means striving to attain daily training goals that will allow them to compete at their top level of physical condition.

Setting nutrition and hydration goals. Most athletic performances require enormous expenditures of energy. As coaches we need to help our athletes set daily dietary goals to help them fuel their bodies so they have the energy they need to perform at their best. For most athletes, a diet low in fat and high in carbohydrates will provide more energy and decrease the storage of body fat (Martens 2012). The problem is our athletes live in a "junk-food" culture that makes it difficult for them to stick to an ideal "athletes' diet" without a tremendous amount of self-discipline. That's where setting daily dietary goals can help. By getting our athletes to set goals restricting their high fat calories (e.g., "My goal is to never eat more than one burger and one order of French fries in a given week") and increasing carbohydrates (e.g., "I will eat at least four servings of fresh fruits and vegetables today") we can help them get the energy necessary for performance — without resorting to unproven or potentially dangerous nutritional supplements (Baume, Hellemans, and Saugy 2007). Because dehydration hurts performance in many ways (Martens 2012) our athletes will also benefit from daily goals regarding the amount of liquid they take in each day (e.g., "I will drink at least 16 ounces of water or sport drink two hours prior to practice every day").

Setting sleep, rest, and recovery goals. Coaches are notorious for adhering to the "more is better" theory. Between mandatory film sessions, chalk talks, practices, weight training, and academics, we attempt to squeeze every drop of energy out of our athletes — confident in the knowledge that every minute of work is moving them one step closer to success. But in athletics, sometimes "less is more." Excessive training and inadequate recovery time can lead to physical breakdown and psychological burnout (Martens 2012). After strenuous exercise the body needs time to rejuvenate and repair itself. Adequate rest and recovery time is as important to performance as hard work and training. Because so many of our young athletes are "burning the candle at both ends," helping them set goals for rest and recovery (e.g., "I will get at least 9 hours of sleep every night during the season") will do wonders in terms of enhancing their performance. Amazingly, recent studies conducted at the prestigious Stanford Sleep Disorders Clinic and Research Laboratory have found that increasing the number of hours of sleep an athlete gets — even beyond the normal eight hours — has a dramatic effect on their performance (Mah, et al. 2011).

Setting rehabilitation goals. When athletes are injured, they need to develop an effective plan that will help them safely return to action as soon as possible. Rehabilitation, by its very nature, is a physically and psychologically painful process. The physical pain is excruciating as the athlete manipulates horribly damaged bones, tendons, and ligaments back into some semblance of their pre-injured selves. Psychologically, the pain can be even worse. Fear, anxiety, and loss of identity are only a few of the psychological reactions that can interfere with a full recovery (Pargman 2007; Petitpas and Danish 1995). Unlike goals set in other areas that are basically designed to motivate athletes to increase their levels of activity, goals associated with rehabilitation must be developed to strike a delicate balance between too little and too much activity. Because athletes are often highly motivated to return to action, they can fall prey to the misconception that "if a little rehab is good, a lot of rehab is better." Daily goal setting can be used to motivate and push our athletes forward through the difficult rehabilitation process while holding them back from excessive rehabbing that will probably only result in re-injury and psychological setbacks.

Setting academic goals. Because athletes participating at the interscholastic and intercollegiate levels are — first and foremost — students, rules require them to perform at a minimum academic level before they can even be eligible for sport competition. Simply put, if they don't perform in the classroom, they won't be allowed to perform on the athletic field. When you consider that an athlete's performance requires academic success, it's easy to see that academic goals (e.g., "I will attend all my classes every day and sit in the front of the room" or "I will turn in every homework assignment on time and in complete accordance with all requirements") are directly related to athletic performance.

Of course the additional benefit of focusing on improving performance in all of these areas — practice, nutrition, hydration, fitness, conditioning, rest, recovery, rehabilitation, and academics — is that the more our athletes accomplish here, the more *likely* it is they will achieve some of the natural by-products of their performance — like "winning."

Setting "SMARTER" Goals

We sometimes need to remind ourselves that the real value of sport participation is not in the winning, but in the pursuit of personal excellence. It's easy for coaches to help their athletes set productive goals if we just remember that we always want our athletes to set S-M-A-R-T-E-R goals than their opponents (Doran 1981). Goals that will improve our athletes' performance the most will be those that are:

Specific: Vague goals such as "I'll do my best," "I want to give 110 percent," or "I'm going to be more aggressive," don't indicate what athletes actually need to do — or how to do it. Specific goals are also easier to measure and to evaluate.

Measurable: Goals that are easily measured help our athletes see if they're making progress. Because it is difficult to accurately measure someone's level of "trying" we shouldn't set goals to *try* to do something. There is a famous line in the movie *Star Wars: Episode V—The Empire Strikes Back* where the renowned Jedi master, Yoda, admonishes Luke Skywalker for saying he is willing to *try* to accomplish his goal, "*No! Try Not! Do or do not! There is no try!*" Setting specific and measurable goals allows coaches and athletes to notice even small gains. And there are few things more motivating than signs of improvement.

Agreed-upon: It's important that everyone involved — athletes, coaches, and parents — agree on the value of every goal. Sometimes coaches or parents want to dictate what an athlete's goal should be. It's important to remember that goal-setting isn't something that is "done *to* you," but instead, it's something you "do *for* yourself." The problem is most athletes won't put forth a total effort to attain a goal they don't personally see as important. This is the exact point Coach Krzyzewski is making when he says, "I worked with the 1991 team to set a couple of goals that had nothing to do with winning ball games. I say 'worked with the team' because every team, in part, dictates what goals are set. After all, they are the ones who are going to have to achieve the goals" (Krzyzewski 2000, 60).

Realistic: Maybe the trickiest thing about setting useful goals is that they must be both challenging and realistic. If our athletes' goals aren't challenging enough, they won't make any progress. On the other hand, unrealistic goals usually result in frustration and disappointment.

Timely: Goals must be accomplished in a given time period. For example, we can help our athletes set goals they can meet "during my next time at bat," "during practice today," or "every day this week." By setting a timeframe in which they want to meet their goal, they'll know when it's time to go back and evaluate their performance.

Evaluated: Simply put, our athletes need to examine whether they've accomplished their goals or not. Without evaluation, there's no way they can really know if they're making progress. If, during evaluation, they find they've met their goal, it's time to help them set another; if not, we need to help them understand why they fell short (usually the goal was either not under their control or it was unrealistic).

Recorded: All specific, measurable, agreed-upon, realistic and timely (SMART) goals need to be written down. Recording their goals reminds our athletes (and their coaches) what they wanted to accomplish and how much progress is really being made.

Keep Winning in Perspective

There is a famous line in the 1953 Fritz Lang movie *The Big Heat* when Gloria Grahame's character states the obvious, "I've been rich and I've been poor. Believe me, rich is better." So it is with winning. As coaches, we are all going to experience both winning and losing. And it's pretty safe to say that most of us will find that "winning is better." But that doesn't mean winning should be our only — or even our primary — concern. Neither we — nor any of our athletes — can control whether we win or lose. We can only put forth the absolute best effort of which we're capable — in both our preparation and performance. We need to learn to be satisfied with the results of our best efforts. Go back to the beginning of the chapter and reconsider how Joe Torre came to understand that a relentless focus on winning can actually be such a distraction from what really matters — performance — that it makes winning less likely, "If in my own mind and heart I had defined success purely as winning, I might have seen myself as a failure... Had I done so, I might have completely stopped believing in myself and the possibility of realizing my dream." And who are we to argue with one of the most successful managers in Major League Baseball?

Myth No. 6

"There's No 'I' in Team"

The best way to improve your team is to improve yourself.
— Coach John Wooden[1]

Of the hundreds of clichés that permeate sports, the most used — and abused — is undoubtedly "There's no 'I' in team." The mindless repetition of this saying is so common that it has become the punch line of jokes. A great example was a beer commercial (Anheuser-Busch, Inc. 2003) popular a few years ago that humorously depicted a self-centered football player — Leon — during a post-game interview...

REPORTER: *Leon, your reactions following today's devastating loss...*
LEON: *Football's a team sport, man, so I got to put the loss squarely on the shoulders of my supporting cast. Look man, I've been carrying these guys the whole season but I can't do it all. I need some help.*
REPORTER: *So your four fumbles weren't a factor in your mind?*
LEON: *Not if one of those other guys would have jumped on the ball. Again, Leon can't do everything.*
REPORTER: *There's no "I" in team...*
LEON: *Yeah, well there ain't no "we" either.*

Although this well-worn coaching favorite is usually meant to caution against self-centered behavior like Leon's, there's one slight problem — it's simply not true. Think about it. In your entire life have you ever seen a *team* throw a block, hit a home run, make a great catch, intercept a pass, score a goal, steal a base, run a race, block a shot, pin an opponent, serve an ace, dribble a ball, nail a landing, or haul in a rebound? I doubt it. These specific skills, and virtually every other accomplishment in sport, have to be executed by an *individual*— an "I." As Coach Wooden's quote at the beginning of this chapter suggests, team achievements can only be realized through the combined performances of individuals. Rather than robotically repeating the old coaching platitude "there's no 'I' in team," we'd be further ahead to remind ourselves — and our athletes — that teams are actually noth-

73

ing but a collection of I's — all contributing in their own special way to a common team objective.

When you stop to think of it, individual athletes can't do much about how others on their team perform. Oh sure, they can provide a struggling teammate with a few general words of encouragement or an occasional technical suggestion but when it comes right down to it, an individual can only do his or her own job — not those that are assigned to teammates.

Maybe this would be easier to see if we compare the role an athlete plays on a team to that of a musician in an orchestra. The violinist, for example, can't help the clarinetist play his part correctly. The clarinetist, in turn, can't assist the drummer, and the drummer has all she can handle without thinking too much about what the trombonist is doing. In fact, some might go so far as to suggest that an "orchestra" actually doesn't exist at all — it's merely a collection of very talented people performing their separate tasks individually. And isn't it the same with our so-called athletic "teams?" After all, an offensive lineman in football can only protect the quarterback by blocking properly. It's the quarterback's job to read the defense and throw a catchable pass to an eligible receiver. If the quarterback doesn't perform these tasks there's nothing the lineman, the receiver — or anyone else on the team — can do. Similarly, what can a baseball pitcher do if his shortstop doesn't field a ground ball properly or the centerfielder strikes out every time he bats? What can a point guard do if her center fails to properly box out after a crucial shot or turns the ball over to the other team every time she touches it? What can a swimmer do if another member of his relay team doesn't swim very fast? Nothing.

You Are the "Maestro"

Just because most of what we think of as team performances are nothing more that a bunch of individual performances all put together, that doesn't mean we — as coaches — aren't interested in overall team execution. In fact, it's one of our primary concerns. If we go back to our previous example of the orchestra it might help us identify the way coaches blend the execution of individual performances into overall team achievement. As we said, one musician in the orchestra can't help another play his or her instrument any more that one of our athletes can help a teammate execute an essential physical skill. But it is the job of the orchestra's conductor — the "*Maestro*"—to first select a musical arrangement that best fits the band's capabilities and then adjust the tempo, volume, and tonal inflection of each individual musician's performance to transform dozens of otherwise disconnected solo efforts into a single coherent — even beautiful — group performance.

And so it is with coaches. We are the "Maestros" of our team. By selecting strategies and tactics that are proper for our athletes' skill level and constantly fine-tuning every individual performance so it blends perfectly with every other player's performance, we can sometimes create the appearance of perfect "team" execution out of what might otherwise be little more than selfish chaos.

When — and Why — Individuals Let Their Teams Down

We sometimes think that successful athletic teams are somehow "greater than the sum of their parts." Unfortunately, the exact opposite is far more likely to be the case. Social psychologists have been studying groups (like our teams) for decades and one indisputable finding that comes up again and again is that even the best teams usually perform at a level *below* what we would expect by simply adding up each player's individual potential (Karau and Williams 1993). Although we may think that members of a team tend to play harder due to a sense of obligation and commitment to the team, the fact is that being part of a team usually reduces the effort put forth by individual athletes. And several possible reasons have been given for this counter-intuitive finding that scientists call "social loafing" (Latané, Williams, and Harkins 1979). What's essential for coaches to understand is that when our athletes subconsciously shirk their responsibilities to the team, it's usually because we haven't convinced them of how important their contributions — as individuals — are to the overall success of the team.

In order to help us better understand how we might get our players to contribute more of their athletic potential to the team, researchers from Clemson University and the University of Toledo examined the results of 78 scientific studies of social loafing and concluded that when our athletes don't perform as well as they should, it is often because of the way they view their individual contributions to the team (Karau and Williams 1993). For example, if our players don't truly believe their performance is necessary for the team's success — either because they feel their teammates are capable of carrying the entire load (e.g., "our team is so good, we'll do fine regardless of how I play") or their contribution is redundant (e.g., "my teammates and I perform basically the same role on the team so I am not providing anything unique to the team performance") — there is little incentive for them to perform at their highest level. Simply put, they don't see the unique individual value of their contribution to the team's performance. Still another reason our players sometimes unconsciously shirk their team responsibility is that they don't believe they will be held individually accountable for their performance (e.g., "our coaches keep telling us that it's only the overall team results that matter so win-or-lose, my performance won't be closely examined and evaluated").

Here's the good news: As coaches we can rather easily persuade our players to perform closer to their physical potential by simply letting them know exactly how their individual contributions are an essential part of the team's overall success and that there is a system in place to constantly evaluate the degree to which every member of the team is doing his or her part to contribute to the team. And now for the bad news. Although we are in a perfect position to combat the "social disease" of social loafing (Latané Williams, and Harkins 1979), most of us unintentionally do more to hurt our team's performance than help it.

Why Team Goals Don't Help (But Sometime Hurt) Performance

Most coaches have convinced themselves of the importance of setting team goals. They're so convinced, in fact, that anyone who has the audacity to challenge the conventional wisdom that says "setting team goals will improve a team's performance" is seen as a heretic to the profession. Coaches routinely spend valuable time trying to encourage their team to "win the league championship," "win today's game," "out-rebound our opponent," "commit fewer turnovers than in our last game," or "make at least 50 percent of our shots in today's game," etc. Unfortunately, as worthwhile as these goals appear to be, they tend to hurt, rather than help, most team performances — by focusing on uncontrollable events, downplaying the importance of individual contributions, and generally fostering an environment that promotes social loafing.

There's little doubt that accomplishing team goals such as those mentioned above will improve the likelihood of team success. But, as we mentioned at the beginning of this chapter, *teams* can't accomplish these tasks. Teams don't have arms or legs, or hands, or eyes, or brains. Only a *person* can run, jump, catch, throw, swim, shoot, rebound, dribble, or hit. When you think about it, it's no exaggeration to say that when we emphasize team-related goals to our athletes, nobody (literally "no body") on the team is ever designated — or responsible — for the execution of the required skills. As noted sport psychologist and coaching authority Rainer Martens puts it, "*Team goals should not be confused with personal goals. In fact, team goals are hardly needed if one of the personal goals of each team member is to make the best contribution possible, given his or her current skill level*" (Martens 2004, 132).

Instead of simply assuming that by focusing our players' attention on some abstract team goal they will somehow improve their performance, we need to remind ourselves that to be of any use, every aspect of a team goal must be executed at the individual level. In order to reduce the affect of social loafing, we must be perfectly clear as to what each and every athlete has to do to contribute to the group goal. Obviously, like all the "SMARTER" goals we discussed in the Myth No. 5 chapter, these individual goals should always be Specific, Measurable, Agreed-upon, Realistic, Timely, Evaluated, and Recorded. Only when these individual performances are executed at their fullest can the "Maestro" in us blend them into a high-level team achievement.

How Setting Team Goals Can Contribute to "Upsets"

Few aspects of coaching are more frustrating than watching your team play down to the level of their competition and ultimately lose an important game or match to a considerably weaker opponent. Although many things can contribute to an underdog pulling an upset, probably the last thing in the world we would think of blaming the loss on is the losing team — and their coach — placing *too much of an emphasis on winning*. But more often than not, that's exactly what's happened. At first glance it may seem utterly ridiculous that focusing our players' attention on winning increases the chances they'll lose — especially to teams they should have no trouble beating — but knowing what we do about team goals and social loafing, it's pretty easy to see how this can happen.

Coaches constantly preach against "being overconfident" or "looking past an easy opponent" or "taking an inferior team lightly" but despite these dire warnings, it's impossible for a team — or even a coach — to truly consider every opponent on their schedule an equal challenge. Some of the teams we'll face are simply better than others and — all our lip-service to the contrary — we (and our players) know it. You can prove this to yourself by simply ranking each team you'll face in the upcoming season on a 1–10 scale (1 = among the worst team you'll face this year and 10 = among the best).

Notice that just being able to complete this exercise demonstrates that we, like all the players on our team, are fully aware of the competitive challenge — or lack of it — posed by each opponent on our schedule.

To illustrate how our perceptions regarding the relative strengths and weaknesses of our opponents — and an all-consuming goal to beat them — can result in our team's inconsistent and erratic play, let's rank five fictitious teams on our schedule — the Colts, Tigers, Cubs, Broncos, and Jets. Our first opponent is a mediocre team called the Colts. We'll give them a middling strength ranking of 6. Our second game, however, is against a team we consider to be the best in our league — the Tigers. Certainly, the Tigers deserve a ranking of 10. Game three is against what appears to be a rather poor Cubs team. We'll give them a 2. A very good Broncos team follows (we'll give them a ranking of 8) and we wrap up our hypothetical season with a game against a so-so team called the Jets. We'll give them an average team strength ranking of 5.

Notice that if our team enters each of these games with "winning" as its primary goal (as opposed to optimal performance) it is possible to perform at various levels — depending on the opponent — and still accomplish its goal. For example, when we play the highly-ranked Tigers, our team probably understands it needs to "bring its A-game" if it is to have any legitimate shot at reaching its goal. On the other hand, every member of our team is equally aware that attaining the exact same goal (winning) against the lowly Cubs will likely not require anywhere near the same quality performance.

Figure 6.1 shows that if our team's primary goal is to simply beat the opponent, there is a natural tendency to play up — or down — to the level of the competition. This erratic performance from one game to the next also sets the stage for tremendous upsets. Look at the game we have scheduled against the Cubs. By all rights, the Cubs shouldn't have much of a chance to beat us — that would at least be the case if every member of our team set the goal to individually perform at the highest level possible. However, by focusing not on their individual performance, but on a desirable team outcome (winning) our team knows they can still accomplish their goal without putting forth a total effort.

If our original assessment that the Cubs deserved a strength rating of 2 was correct, any performance by our team above that should set us up for a victory. But what if our perception of the Cubs' talent was even slightly off? What would happen, for example, if we should have rated them a 3 instead of a 2? They still aren't a very good team but if we entered the game assuming that any performance above a 2 would put us in good position

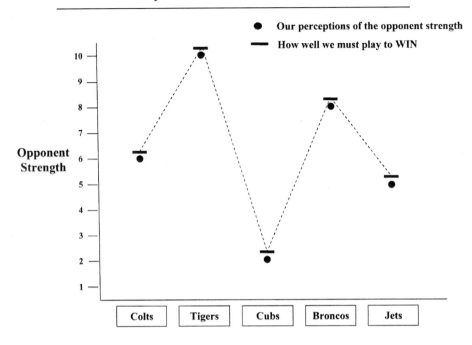

Figure 6.1: How Setting a Team Goal "To Win" Affects Team Performance.

for a win, we are likely to be upset. In addition, consider that the Cubs probably view our team as being superior — sort of the way we view the Tigers. If their goal is — like ours — to beat their opponent, they understand that attaining this goal will require an all-out effort on their part. As a result, they work extra hard in order to meet their goal. At the same time, we work far below our capability in order to meet ours. It's an upset just waiting to happen.

Although the emphasis we place on winning often causes a reduction in performance against relatively weak opponents, rarely do we recognize it is our setting of team outcome goals rather than individual performance goals that are actually responsible for the loss. Listen closely to what Michigan State University basketball coach Tom Izzo said after his Spartans who were then ranked seventh in the country (with a 7–1 record in the Big Ten), played probably it's worst game of the 2007–8 season and lost 85–76 to lowly Penn State (then 2–6 in the Big Ten): "It's my job to make sure our team respects another team. I do not think we respected that team like we should have. That's what it looked like to me.... We did not respect them" (LansingStateJournal.com 2008). It's pretty apparent from this quote that Coach Izzo knows his team underachieved because it underestimated Penn

State. Less clear is whether he understands that the overemphasis he and his players placed on winning that game — rather than performing at their highest level — probably led step-by-step from the underestimation, to the underachievement, and ultimately to the upset.

The Law of the (Athletic) Jungle

The subtle interdependence between team and individual performance is perhaps best illustrated in the Rudyard Kipling poem *Law of the Jungle*. The opening stanza of the poem so powerfully expresses the indisputable connection between team and individual success that its recitation has become a solemn ritual of high school, college, and professional teams across the country. The poem, for example, is a long-standing tradition at the University of Nevada where the Wolfpack student section leads the crowd in a chant of its recitation before every home football and basketball game (CBS Interactive 2012). Similarly, under head coach Lloyd Carr, the defensive starters on the Michigan Wolverines football team developed a ritual that included gathering together the night before each game, dimming the lights and reciting the poem to one another (Greene 1999). Finally, Coach Phil Jackson — also known as the "Zen Master" who lead the Chicago Bulls and the Los Angeles Lakers to 11 NBA championships stated in his book *Sacred Hoops* that he frequently read Kipling's *The Law of the Jungle* to his players prior to playoff games (Jackson 1995).

The last two lines of this powerful poem accurately sums up the "one-for-all; all-for-one" reliance every team has on individual performance and every individual's contribution to the team:

> For the strength of the Pack is the Wolf,
> And the strength of the Wolf is the Pack [Kipling 1895, 29].

It's easy to see from Kipling's poem that there certainly is an "I in team." In fact, individual success is absolutely essential for team success. Or, as Coach Wooden phrased it for us at the beginning of this chapter, "The best way to improve your team is to improve yourself" (Wooden 2004, 111).

MYTH NO. 7

"Injuries Interfere with Athlete and Team Development"

I believe God gave us crises for some reason — and it certainly isn't for us to say that everything about them is bad. A crisis can be a momentous time for a team to grow — if a leader handles it properly... But success in handling a crisis situation depends to a very large extent on what has developed (or not developed) prior to the crisis ever taking place.

— Coach Mike Krzyzewski[1]

As coaches, we devote an enormous amount of time and energy to making sure our athletes are as safe as possible. We spend hours getting them into the best physical condition; we match them up against others of approximately the same size and ability; we teach them the safest methods of play; we never ask them to perform skills beyond their capability; we give them adequate rest and rehabilitation time; we preach the importance of good nutrition and warn of potential risks associated with drug use; we regularly inspect their equipment and playing surfaces and we train ourselves to handle a variety of emergency situations. And that's the way it's supposed to be. Nothing we do as a coach is as important as protecting the physical and emotional safety of our athletes.

Despite our efforts, however, injuries remain an unfortunate reality in sports. Thankfully, most sport-related injuries are relatively minor. Some are not. Coaches, parents, and athletes themselves must be prepared to handle both serious and minor injuries in a way that will help athletes take full advantage of what injuries can truly be — blessings in disguise. In the quote at the beginning of this chapter Coach Krzyzewski reminds us that, "A crisis can be a momentous time for a team to grow if a leader handles it properly" (Krzyzewski 2000, 151). And every coach knows that injuries are one type of crisis that every athlete and every team will face at some time.

There are few things in this world that coaches hate more than injuries.

It's in our blood. Usually that's a good thing because it motivates us to do everything we can to keep our athletes safe. But, once they occur, this natural hatred sometimes keeps us from acknowledging how beneficial injuries can be — to the individual athlete and the team. It essentially becomes a negative "self-fulfilling prophecy." By refusing to even consider the possibility that injuries can have positive consequences, we almost certainly guarantee they won't.

The "Benefits" of Injury

Many coaches find the entire discussion of "benefits of injury" completely and utterly ridiculous. After all, we "know" from our personal experience just how devastating injuries can be to an athlete and a team — or do we? What we need to teach ourselves — and our athletes — is that these setbacks are generally temporary and, once we open ourselves up to the various ways injuries can actually improve our performance, that's exactly what happens (Wrisberg and Fisher 2004).

Whenever our athletes get hurt, their bodies are sending messages that something's gone terribly wrong. And it's our job to help them "listen" to what their bodies are trying to tell them (Al Huang and Lynch 1992). For example, when our athletes suffer from overuse injuries (sometimes called "repetitive micro-trauma" injuries) such as stress fractures, tennis elbow, swimmer's shoulder, Little League elbow, runner's knee, jumper's knee, or shin splints, the injury may be telling us there's a problem with inadequate warm-up, excessive activity, incorrect technique, or improper equipment (American Orthopaedic Society for Sports Medicine, 2008). Acute traumatic injuries such as concussions, broken bones, shoulder separations, ligament tears, or sprains, on the other hand, should motivate us to reexamine our existing safeguards. We may find that our current rules, equipment, or playing conditions need to be altered to better protect our athletes. In either case, these injuries can do us the great favor of providing important information that can be used to prevent future injuries — but only if we are willing to listen to the message they're sending.

Coaches generally take a very narrow and short-sighted view of injuries. We focus solely on the possibility that even a relatively minor injury might somehow cause our athletes to "lose their competitive edge." Despite the fact that we've all seen it dozens of times with our own eyes, it's difficult for us to accept the fact that injuries can ultimately *improve* an athlete's individual performance by providing recuperation time, performance insights, and opportunities to develop new skills.

Injuries can force performance-enhancing rest and recovery. Many athletes and coaches are so competitive (some may even say "driven") that they find it almost impossible to voluntarily pull back and give their bodies time to rest. We frequently operate under the false assumption that when it comes to training, "more is better." To illustrate this point, think about how difficult it would be to address your team during the final couple weeks of their season — when the pressure to perform is more intense than ever — by saying, "You know, it's been a long season and our bodies are really in need of a rest. Let's take a break from all our training for the next couple of days." Even though a rest may be exactly what would help our team's performance the most, few of us would even consider reducing the training schedule just as the competition reaches its peak. Ironically, when our athletes' bodies start sending signals that they're wearing down — with inexplicable decreases in performance — we often feel compelled to push them all the harder to compensate for the drop in performance. Many coaches and athletes simply refuse to reduce their training until an injury finally gives them no choice. That's why it's not uncommon that after taking an injury-induced rest, many athletes bounce back refreshed, rejuvenated, and performing at a higher level than ever (Udry 1999).

Injuries can reveal performance insights. In the words of that old sage Yogi Berra, "You can observe a lot by watching" (Berra 2008). Similarly, as odd as it sounds, sometimes the best thing athletes can do to improve their performance is to stop performing and start watching. By lowering the stress and anxiety levels that often accompany performance, athletes are better able to focus their attention on the essential elements of their performance (Easterbrook 1959). The logic is the same as when we sometimes remove a poorly performing quarterback or point guard from the game — not to punish them — but to let them relax and take in the subtleties of the game without feeling the constant pressure to perform. Once they are relaxed, the game seems to slow down and previously hidden aspects of the performance present themselves. Similarly, injuries can give our athletes the rare opportunity to improve individual performance by simply "watching and learning."

Injuries can improve under-developed skills. As we discussed in the Myth No. 1 chapter, all of us — including athletes — have a natural tendency to practice our strengths and avoid working on our weaknesses. When an injury takes away the very thing an athlete has relied on for success, however, he or she will have no choice but to compensate by developing other, previously neglected, skills. Because athletes are forced to focus on these less-developed aspects of their game, they often come away with a wider range of skills after recovering from the injury. This was indeed the case with three of the best players in college basketball during the past decade: Brandon Rush, J.J. Redick, and Morris Peterson.

One coach who has no problem recognizing the benefits of injury is Bill Self, head basketball coach of the 2008 National Champion Kansas Jayhawks. In the spring of 2007, one of his team's (and the country's) best players, Brandon Rush, suffered a badly torn anterior cruciate ligament (ACL). Rather than mope around about how devastating this injury could be to his star player—and his team—Coach Self immediately recognized the injury for what it really was—a perfect opportunity for Rush to take his game to the next level. Self let his counterintuitive views regarding the potential benefits of the injury be known early on, "I think it's a great opportunity for him [Rush] to become a better ball player. He can concentrate on skills and not rely on athleticism as much. He can improve his ball-handling, shooting, and ability to read screens. Then, when the hop comes back, he'll be a more complete player" (Schlabach 2007). Coach Self's positive approach to what most of us would view as a disaster was internalized by Rush himself—with some support from his mother, Glenda. "This might be a blessing in disguise—that's what my mama said" Rush announced after returning to the line-up in the fall of 2007. "My mom always knows what she's talking about, especially about basketball" (Tucker 2008). And it turns out that Brandon's mom was right again this time. Not only did Self, Rush, and the rest of the Jayhawks team come up with a 75–68 overtime win over Memphis to earn the 2008 NCAA National Championship but Rush also went on to be the first-round pick of the Portland Trail Blazers in the 2008 NBA draft. It's also important to note that Brandon Rush isn't the only NBA player to experience the way an injury can improve individual performance.

By the time he graduated from Duke University in 2006, J.J. Redick was considered by many to be the best college basketball player in the country, winning all three national "Player of the Year" awards (i.e., the Rupp, Wooden, and Naismith trophies). Basketball fans agreed that Redick's greatest asset was his phenomenal shooting accuracy that enabled him to finish his college career holding the Atlantic Coast Conference record for most 3-point shots made, most consecutive free-throws made, and the second-best career free-throw percentage in the history of college basketball (91.2 percent). What most fans didn't know, however, was that a series of injuries played a major role in Redick becoming one of the greatest shooters of all time. When he was in junior high, Redick broke his right (shooting) wrist twice and his left wrist once. Instead of hurting his performance, the casts on both wrists forced him to focus on his shooting mechanics and perfect what would later become his trademark fluid release (Teel 2004). We can only guess what would have become of J.J. Redick without the "benefit" of the broken wrists.

After leading his Michigan State Spartans to the 2000 NCAA Men's Basketball National Championship, Morris Peterson was a first-round draft pick of the Toronto Raptors in the 2000 NBA draft. But "Mo Pete's" basketball future didn't always seem so bright. After a good, but less than stellar, high school career, Peterson broke a bone in his hand. Although he could have continued playing, his coach, Tom Izzo, convinced him to sit out the season as a "medical redshirt"—a decision that paid immeasurable dividends by giving Morris an extra year to mature physically, emotionally, and academically. But despite the extra year, he was still far from a complete player. In fact, during his sophomore year Peterson's defense was so bad Izzo once joked with reporters that "Morris is wandering around campus, trying to find someone he can guard" (Ebling 2002). And things only got worse from there—at least that's what many thought when Peterson broke his right wrist. But that "break" also turned out to be one of the best he'd ever get. Instead of having the luxury of continuing to rely on his impressive offensive talents, things had to change. Peterson is quick to point out how the injury helped him become a more complete basketball player, "When I broke my hand, I had to develop my game in different areas. I dove for loose balls, played defense and even whacked a few guys. It gave me a chance to be an all-around player" (Ebling 2002). That "all-around" ability—and his tremendous defensive improvement—resulted in Peterson being named the Big Ten Conference "Player of the Year" in 2000, and a first- or second-team selection to virtually every post-season All-American team.

Injuries can reveal undiagnosed problems. One of the most frustrating experiences for any coach is to have a player who doesn't seem to be performing up to his or her potential. Such was the case with Kelvin Torbert, a highly touted recruit on the Michigan State University basketball team. In high school, Torbert received nearly every award imaginable. He was a first-team selection on every All-American team and was voted "Mr. Basketball" in the state of Michigan. He was even named the "Gatorade National Player of the Year" as a high school senior. But his adjustment to college basketball was slower than many expected. Even after bone chips were removed from his ankle during his sophomore year, he didn't seem to have the explosive leaping ability that made him such a prep school sensation. Things got so bad for Torbert that in February of 2003 *Sports Illustrated* college basketball guru, Seth Davis, nominated him for a spot on his "All-

Disappointment" team (Davis 2003). Fortunately, nine months later something wonderful happened to Kelvin Torbert — he got hurt. He sprained the same ankle he had surgery on a year earlier. Although the injury wasn't all that serious, it required a new set of x-rays. When the medical staff examined the pictures, they saw old bone chips — missed during the original operation — still floating around in the ankle joint (Grinczel 2002). Once the remaining bone chips were removed Torbert began to develop into the player everyone thought he could be — helping his team reach the NCAA "Final Four" in 2005 with back-to-back wins over Kentucky and Duke before losing to eventual national champion North Carolina.

Injuries can provide opportunities for personal growth. Improvements in physical performances after injuries — such as those experienced by Brandon Rush, J.J. Redick, Morris Peterson, Kelvin Torbert, and thousands like them — have encouraged sport scientists to examine the ways injuries might positively influence the way athletes think about themselves (Gould, et al. 1997; Podlog and Eklund 2006; Rose and Jevne 1993; Udry, et al. 1997). These studies have consistently demonstrated that there are several ways injuries can strengthen an athlete's mental approach to his or her sport. First, athletes gain an increased sense of confidence from overcoming these performance obstacles. By demonstrating to themselves that they "have what it takes" to triumph over adversity, athletes are more likely to approach future setbacks with a stronger belief in themselves and a sense they can — and will — conquer any challenges that stand in their way. In addition, many athletes have found that being forced to give up their sport due to injury — even for a short time — gave them a renewed appreciation of their love for the game and the importance of sport in their lives (Podlog and Eklund 2006). When athletes stop taking their participation for granted, they begin to enjoy their sport more and perform at a higher level.

From the previous examples it's plain to see the injuries can often lead to improvements in individual performance — but what about the team? Doesn't it hurt the team's overall performance when a key player is injured and unable to compete? Maybe — but then again maybe not.

Injuries can reveal hidden talents of teammates. One of the most obvious ways an entire team can benefit from an injury is when it provides other members of the team with an opportunity to showcase talents that might have otherwise gone unnoticed. Take, for example, the remarkable case of future NFL Hall of Fame quarterback Tom Brady. After leading his New England Patriots to five Super Bowl appearances (winning three of the five) and after being selected Super Bowl MVP twice and NFL "Player of the Year," many have conveniently forgotten that Brady probably wouldn't have

been a starting quarterback in the NFL at all if his teammate, and starting quarterback for the Patriots, Drew Bledsoe, hadn't been seriously injured. Brady joined the Pats as a lowly 199th overall pick in the 6th round of the 2000 NFL draft and, as a result, wasn't expected to contribute much to the team — that is, of course, if he even made the team at all. But, in his first year, he worked his way from the team's fourth string quarterback to Bledsoe's backup. In September of 2001 Bledsoe received a vicious hit from New York Jets linebacker Mo Lewis that severed a blood vessel and caused his chest to fill with blood. Although he would fully recover, Bledsoe was out, Brady was in. Brady took charge of the team and led the Patriots to their first Super Bowl victory, and the rest is history. If the Patriot's starter hadn't been injured would Brady have ever become a Hall of Fame quarterback? Would he have ever even started a game for the Patriots, or any other NFL team? More importantly, would New England have made it to the Super Bowl if Bledsoe had remained their quarterback during the 2001 season? ... or the 2003 season? ... or the 2004 season? ... or the 2007 season? ... or the 2012 season? Those things we'll never know. What we do know, is that even this terrible injury to the Patriot's starting quarterback did not interfere in the least with the team's overall performance.

Injuries can push other members of the team to improve their performance. As coaches, we would all love to have a superstar on our team — that one person we can count on to put the team on his or her back and carry it to victory. But having a great player on the team can sometimes limit what other members of the team contribute. During our discussion of "social loafing" in the Myth No. 6 chapter, we discovered that sometimes athletes don't perform as well as they should because they subconsciously view their individual contribution to the team as being unnecessary for the team's success (Karau and Williams 1993). It's easy to see that having a real "go-to" superstar on the team who generally "carries the load" can actually increase the likelihood that some members of the team feel they don't have to play their best to realize their team goal — to win (recall that this is one of the biggest problems with focusing on team outcomes rather than individual performance). So what happens to team performance if this superstar is unable to play due to injury? For most of us the answer is obvious — the absence of the great player will hurt the team's performance. But think again. If some of the members of the team have been subconsciously "loafing" because they think their contributions aren't needed, there may now be an increase in their performance to make up for the loss of their valuable teammate. As a result, the replacement player not only gets a chance to develop his or her skills, other players often feel the need to "step up their

game" to make up for the missing teammate. For this reason, it's not uncommon for the reconstituted team to actually perform at a higher level in the absence of the original player. That's exactly what happened at the University of Tennessee in 1996. Chamique Holdsclaw — perhaps the most dominant player in college basketball at the time — partially tore a ligament in her right knee. Everyone was certain that her injury would have a disastrous impact on the team's performance. But when her Lady Vols ended up winning the national championship, Coach Pat Summitt explained their accomplishment this way: "Her [Holdsclaw's] injury was the key to the Championship. When she went down, all the others realized they had to do more. It made us a better team" (Gelin 1996). Let's look at Coach Summitt's astonishing quote once again. When the winningest coach in the history of college basketball says straight out, "Her injury was the key to the Championship ... it made us a better team." There isn't much more that needs to be said. Injuries obviously don't always hurt — and can even help — overall team performance.

Injuries can improve a team's ability to overcome future adversity. Sometimes teams that are forced to deal with a teammate's injury gain an inner strength that would be impossible to learn in any other way. Such was the case for the 2000 NCAA College Basketball Champions — Michigan State University. We've already seen how a wrist injury to one of the stars of that team, Morris Peterson, gave him the opportunity to develop into a more complete player — one capable of helping his team capture a national championship. But that championship team benefitted from an injury to another key player in a different way. After being tabbed by many as the preseason favorite to win the national championship, the Spartan's All-American point guard and inspirational leader, Mateen Cleaves, suffered a stress fracture in his foot that caused him to miss the first 13 games of the season. Not surprisingly, the injury to Cleaves took its toll on the team. With perhaps the toughest pre-conference schedule in the country, the team struggled and fought its way to a mediocre 9–4 record. They had been forced to play against some of the nation's top basketball teams — Arizona, Kansas, Kentucky, North Carolina, and Texas — without their best player and emotional floor leader. Despite the frustration everyone associated with the team felt over their disappointing start, they had learned a valuable lesson — one that would actually help them win the national championship three months later. After Mateen's return, the Spartans reoriented themselves and won both the Big Ten regular season and tournament titles. They were now on a roll and beat each of their first five opponents in the NCAA Tournament by double digits. Then, in the National Championship game against Florida the unthinkable happened. Barely holding on to a "two possession" lead over

the Gators, Cleaves drove to the hoop and "got his feet tangled" (some are still convinced it was a deliberate foul) with Florida's Teddy Dupay. Cleaves fell to the floor in a heap. He had severely twisted his ankle. After writhing in pain for several minutes, Cleaves was finally carried off to the locker room. The Spartans, who were hanging on for dear life against a feisty Florida team were now faced with over 16 minutes of game time without their leader. But that wasn't anything new. They had played without Cleaves against some of the best competition in the country for 13 games at the beginning of the season. They had proven to themselves they could match up with any team — with or without Cleaves. So in this, the biggest game of their lives, as their leader was being carried to the locker room, the young Spartans huddled up and listened as their coach, Tom Izzo, reminded them of what they had already shown themselves to be capable of, "You know what, guys? We have a war on our hands. But you played without Mateen for 13 games. For the next few minutes, revert back to what you did" (Albom 2000). Amazingly, with Cleaves on the bench for the next five minutes his teammates not only maintained — but extended — their margin over the Gators. When Cleaves left the game his team led by six. By the time he limped back onto the floor the Spartans had extended their lead to a nine-point advantage at 58–49. They won the National Championship that evening by a score of 89–76. We can only guess what the score would have been — or if they would have won at all — had the early-season injury to Cleaves not convinced this team they could compete with any opponent — regardless of who was on the floor.

As we've seen, injuries — when dealt with properly — can improve both individual and team performance. But it's not just athletes who stand to benefit from injuries. We often become better coaches as we help our athletes cope with the physical and psychological challenges associated with their injuries. For example, we certainly are better coaches when we modify our training regiments based on the "early warning signals" injuries generally provide. In addition, we will also be better coaches when we learn to stock our "coaching toolkits" with positive examples of athletes and teams who have not only recovered from — but excelled as a result of — their injuries.

Injuries can help us "accentuate the positive." During the dismal, dreary, and deadly days toward the end of World War II, one of the most popular songs on the radio was constantly imploring the entire country to "Ac-Cent-Tchu-Ate, the Positive" (Mercer, 1944). This optimistic musical message reminded everyone — just when they needed it most–that every half empty glass is also, by definition, half full and it's our choice whether we preoccupy ourselves with the portion of the glass that is useless and beyond our control or the part we can still put to good use. When injuries occur, we need to remind ourselves that as the leader of the team it is our job to help athletes who are suffering through an injury-related setback by "accentuating the positive"—searching out, locating, and pointing out the silver linings on even the darkest of clouds. To see the impact a coach can have in changing a potential disaster into something positive we need only reconsider how University of Kansas Coach Bill Self convinced Brandon Rush to focus on the "great opportunities" his knee injury presented or the way Michigan State Coach Tom Izzo reminded his Spartans that they could use the painful lessons they learned during a 13 game early season absence of Mateen Cleaves to propel them to a National Championship.

Injuries can enhance our empathy for injured athletes. Sometimes it's the insights we've gained from fighting our own personal battles with injuries that serve us best when helping our wounded athletes. That's certainly been the case for the most successful coach in the history of college basketball, Pat Summitt. During her senior season at the University of Tennessee-Martin, Summitt suffered a knee injury so severe that an orthopedic surgeon told her that she would never play basketball again (Smith 1998). Despite the devastating prognosis, Coach Summitt dedicated herself to spending countless hours of excruciating rehabilitation which eventually resulted in her being named Co-Captain of the USA's first women's Olympic basketball team. As is the case with many athletes, Summitt learned important personal lessons when she was challenged by her injury, "I learned a lot about myself. I learned how hard you have to work if you really want to be good at anything and if you want to overcome adversity." But the painful lessons would not only benefit Summitt as a player. She now recognizes that going through the denial, disappointment, anger, frustration, and ultimate recovery from a serious athletic injury actually helped her become a better basketball coach. As she puts it, "It helped me as a coach because I coached while I was rehabbing. And I think I connected better with the players—just to know the ones who had injuries or the ones who really were struggling—that I could be there and understand what they might be going through" (A&E Television Networks 1999).

Not only does Coach Summitt use the story of her personal recovery to console her injured Lady Vols, she even uses it to occasionally provide "aid and comfort to the enemy." In March of 2008, Oral Roberts University guard Mariana Camargo tore the ACL in her left knee when she apparently slipped on a sign one of the Tennessee cheerleaders was using to fire up the Volunteer fans (videotape later revealed she was injured just prior to landing on the sign). After the game, Summitt sat down with Camargo. "First, I had to hold back tears." The tough old coach said after their meeting, "It was such a freak thing, the way it happened. I was thinking, "Why?" But Summitt used the opportunity to relate her own knee injury experiences — and the positive outcomes that are possible through hard work and a positive attitude to Camargo, "I've been there." she told the anguished ORU guard. "It's all about the rehab" (Fleser 2008).

Helping Athletes Cope with Their Injuries

It's essential for us, as coaches, to understand that we hold the key to whether our athletes will improve or implode after an injury. As the indisputable leader of the team, the way we behave — before and after an injury — will probably be the single best indicator of how our players will react when faced with an injury of their own.

Good coaches will spend considerable time thinking about how they can best deal with an injury once it happens. Better coaches understand that as important as that may be, it's how they choose to act *before* the injury occurs that will determine whether the battle to effectively cope with an injury is often won or lost.

Recognizing and valuing our athletes for being more than athletes. Although it's perfectly natural for anyone suffering an injury to feel a certain amount of psychological distress, this can be particularly devastating for those who have come to define themselves solely on the basis of their athletic competency. Athletes who have somehow convinced themselves that their only real value — to their teammates, their coaches, their family, their friends, and the society in general — stems from their athleticism, run the risk of imagining that even a relatively minor injury has the potential to render them essentially worthless as a person (Brewer, VanRaalte, and Linder 1993). Even before an injury occurs, we can do a lot to help our athletes develop the healthy (and far more accurate) perspective that their personal worth has little to do with their athletic accomplishments. To bring about this improved self-image we, as coaches, need to take every opportunity to show our athletes that their true value extends far beyond their ability to run, jump, throw, or catch. For example, when athletes are dealing with a personal or family issue that requires them to miss a practice or competition, we need to make sure they understand that our only concern is for them as a person — not how their absence might impact the performance of our team. Once again, Coach John Wooden's words and actions serve to guide our interaction with our players as we try to foster a broader sense of self-worth in all our athletes,

One of the finest things a player could say about me after he left the team was that I cared every bit as much about him as an individual as I cared about him as an athlete. It was important to me because I really did care about them. I often told the players that, next to my own flesh and blood, they were the closest to me. They were my extended family and I got wrapped up in them, their lives [Wooden 1997, 151].

Constantly letting our athletes know that we truly "care every bit as much about them as an individual as we care about them as an athlete" will help them realize that they have worth beyond the playing field. Once they define themselves as more than mere athletes, even the prospect of a career-ending injury becomes almost bearable. But, as important as our support prior to the injury is, what we do after the injury will probably still be the key to helping our athletes effectively cope with the psychological aspects of their injury.

Obviously, no coach worthy of the pea in his or her whistle is going to make an already bad situation even worse by intentionally neglecting the psychological and emotional needs of an injured athlete. However, the operative word here may be "intentionally." This entire book is based on the premise that we all-too-often pattern our coaching behaviors on the actions we've seen from others rather than what's in the best interest of our athletes.

Providing injured athletes with emotional support and encouragement. One indication that we may need to reexamine the way we deal with our injured athletes is evident by the fact that so many athletes report being dissatisfied with the level of support their coaches provide them during the rehabilitation and recovery process. For example, after conducting a series of interviews with previously injured athletes, Shelley (1999) concluded that "At one time or another, all of the subjects felt as though they were isolated, abandoned, ignored, misunderstood, or unsupported by their coaches, teammates, or both" (p. 314). These personal accounts verify the commonly-held impression that coaches often neglect their athletes after an injury occurs. There are several reasons we might not give our injured athletes the support they need. First, we may feel we simply don't know what we should do or say to help. Second, we might think our obligation to the team means our time is better spent working with the remaining athletes. Third, we might erroneously believe that caring for injured athletes is primarily the responsibility of medical specialists such as our athletic training staff or team physician. Finally — and this is something we must always guard against — there may be times when we subconsciously feel that an athlete who cannot contribute directly to the team's success is of little value. Let's be honest, it doesn't take a great deal of training or expertise to keep our athletes from feeling isolated, abandoned, or ignored. It only requires a little time, some compassion, and an absolute commitment to making our athletes feel they are — and always will be — an integral and important part of their team. Just think how encouraging it is for injured athletes to have their coach take time to sit down with them and talk about how they're doing — not because the coach is selfishly trying to assess when the athlete might return to action but because the coach is truly concerned with the fact that, someone Coach Wooden would call "a member of their extended family" is going through a very difficult time. And here's another idea — why not show up unannounced at some of our players' rehab sessions? It's a great place for one of these periodic chats and it gives us a unique opportunity to personally express our appreciation for the sacrifice they are making and the pain they are enduring as they work toward recovery. Finally, we need to do everything possible to make sure our injured athletes remain a valuable part of the team. They should be invited to every team meeting and event and given an important role whenever possible. For example, most injured athletes make great informal "assistant coaches." After all, who's in a better position to offer a bit of insight and teach a replacement "the ropes" than someone who was performing that task just a few days ago?

Using previously injured teammates as positive coping models. Coming to grips with injuries that threaten to disrupt nearly every aspect of their lives is likely to be one of the most confusing and frightening events our athletes will ever encounter. And the thing that will cause them the most anxiety of all is their overwhelming fear of the unknown. Fortunately, the vast majority of our injured players have yet to experience the range of emotions that accompany a severe injury. In fact, if they are like most athletes, they've had to intentionally train themselves to block out every thought that would even allow them to consider the possibility that some day participation in their sport could hurt them so badly that their season — if not their entire athletic career — might be finished. But we can help ease this haunting fear of the unknown by pairing injured athletes up with one of their teammates — or at least someone like them — who has successfully overcome the reoccurring difficulties and doubts that must be confronted when recovering from a serious injury. A previously injured athlete can demonstrate effective ways of coping by describing and showing how they had suffered from similar setbacks and problems but overcame them by determined effort (Bandura 1997; Feltz, Short, and Sullivan 2007; Flint 1999).

Merely tending to our players' physical needs after an injury is often the easy part of our job. A far greater challenge will be helping our athletes effectively cope psychologically and socially with their injuries (Wiese-Bjornst, et al. 1998). Sport psychologists have studied athletes' reactions to injuries for years. They've documented the fear, anger, frustration, depression, and anxiety that athletes experience when injured. But they've recently discovered something very interesting — nearly all injured athletes eventually say they benefited, in some way from their injuries (Udry, et al. 1997; Wrisberg and Fisher 2004). When it comes to athletic injuries, perhaps the nineteenth century German philosopher Friedrich Nietzsche was on the right track when he said, "*What doesn't kill me makes me stronger*" (Nietzsche 1889/1997, 6). After all, it's pretty much the sentiment expressed at the beginning of this chapter by one of the greatest coaches of all time, "A crisis can be a momentous time for a team to grow — if a leader handles it properly... But success in handling a crisis situation depends to a very large extent on what has developed (or not developed) prior to the crisis ever taking place" (Krzyzewski, 2000, 151–2).

"There's Never Enough Practice Time"

It would take me an hour and a half to plan each practice. I was meticulous about it, because practice was the most important time I spent with our players ... I prepared a master plan of practice in August, which included the times and dates that I wanted to put each part of our plan into place. We also had a weekly practice plan of things we wanted to accomplish in each seven-day cycle.

—Coach Dean Smith[1]

Retail legend John Wanamaker is credited with the pithy observation: "I know that half of my advertising is wasted. I just don't know which half" (Rothenberg 1999). Unfortunately, pretty much the same can be said of most of our practice time — half of the time we spend in organized practice is probably wasted, we're just not always certain which half that is. As coaches, many of us have talked ourselves into believing that if we only had a few more hours — even a few more minutes — of precious practice time our athletes' performances would be magically transformed and we would become more successful coaches. There's only one problem with that line of thinking — it's probably not true.

Coaches, at any given level, have roughly the same amount of time to prepare their athletes. As Coach John Wooden once put it, "I understood that each coach had the same amount of time to teach his team to win ... it is important to acknowledge that you and your rivals are essentially the same in this regard. Therefore, the contest comes down to who uses their allotted time to best advantage ... who has the fewest missteps when it comes to building productivity into each moment of time" (Wooden and Jamison 2005, 156). Consequently, every time we claim that "there's never enough practice time" we're actually just admitting that we don't use our allotted time as efficiently as our rivals. It would probably be closer to the truth if we would simply admit once and for all that "although I am given the same amount of practice time as every other coach, I tend to waste so much of it that I often mistakenly think there's never enough."

Not surprising, coaches who take a little extra time putting together a well-conceived practice plan generally feel less pressured by uncontrollable time constraints. While there are many reasons we don't conduct our practices as efficiently as we could (or should) there are two relatively simple changes we can all make that, although giving us no additional time, will help us better use the finite time we have. The first involves better planning and execution of each and every practice session — like that described by Dean Smith in the quote at the beginning of this chapter — and the other focuses on eliminating the dozens of hidden "time drains" that we have allowed to creep into our practices.

Planning and Executing Efficient Practices

We all plan our practices. It's just that very few of us spend time systematically considering, prioritizing, and sequencing the details that will help us accomplished our goals for a particular practice session. The truth is, most of us are more likely to scribble our random thoughts and considerations for an upcoming practice on a piece of old scrap paper while sitting at a traffic light on the way to the practice field.

Of course our lack of planning turns out to be about as efficient as going to the grocery store without a shopping list (Allen 2001). We end up aimlessly wandering through the store loading our cart with rations based entirely on impulse — tempted by whatever catches our eye and sounds tasty at the moment. Inevitably, we get home and realize that although we bought plenty of snacks and treats, we neglected to purchase many of the ingredients we actually need to prepare healthy and wholesome meals throughout the week. Whether we are shopping for groceries or practicing for a big game, our failure to adequately plan and prepare will ultimately result in a lot of wasted of time and energy.

Like Coach Smith, John Wooden also recognized the importance of planning for every practice. It's no coincidence that Coach Wooden's name has become inextricably linked with the often-heard Benjamin Franklin maxim, "By failing to prepare, you are preparing to fail." As much as we love to use this sage advice to challenge the work ethic of our athletes, we conveniently overlook the fact that these words of wisdom hold as much, and perhaps more, relevance for coaches. Like most successful coaches, Wooden and Smith both understood that although their actual on-court practice time with their players was severely limited, the time they had to *prepare* for practices was not. As a result, they typically spent as much time each day *planning* their practices as they would conducting them. In fact, Wooden readily acknowledged that it was probably this obsession with planning each and every detail of practice that was responsible, more than any other single factor, for his remarkable success, "I was never the greatest Xs and Os coach around, but I was among the best when it came to respecting and utilizing time" (Wooden and Jamison 2005, 162).

Determining and sequencing instruction. Obviously, the first step in organizing effective practices is to decide which skills need to be taught, and in what order. Although planning and organizing an entire season's worth of practices can be daunting, it will usually help if we "begin with the end in mind" (Covey 2004). This simply means specifying what we expect our athletes to be capable of doing by the end of the season. By establishing this long-term goal we are now in a position to consider everything we need to incorporate into our practices that will help the team attain this goal. At this point, however, it's important to remember — as we discussed in the Myth No. 5 chapter — the need to focus on the *performances* of our athletes rather than the *outcomes* of their performances. That means our year-long goals should be written in terms of what our athletes can actually do (perform) not who they might be able to beat (the outcome of a performance). For example, one of the goals a basketball team might have is to improve its shooting percentage over the previous season by working on various aspects of its offensive game. Once we've established this long-term goal, the next step is to create a list of technical (specific body movements) and tactical (decision-making) skills that our players will need to master to improve their offensive production.[2] Depending on the age and skill set of your athletes all these skills may need to be taught at some point during the season. However, since only one skill can be taught one at a time — and some build on the proper execution of others — it's important to consider the proper sequencing of instruction. For example, our athletes will have to master the relatively simple aspects of the "control dribble" before we can teach them the more complex "reverse," "cross-over," or "change-of-pace" dribbles.

Writing up a practice plan. Once all the skills to be introduced during the season are determined and properly sequenced, it's time to incorporate them into your practice sessions. Every daily practice plan needs to be written down in advance. An example of the kind of detailed planning we need is clear when we look at how Coach Smith broke the season into logical segments. Notice again that he prepared a master plan at the beginning of the season, which included the times and dates that each part of the plan had to be taught. The date, starting time, length of practice and objectives for the day should be listed at the top of each daily practice plan. Each 5 to 10 minute interval should be accounted for with special attention being given to keeping the activities quick, snappy, and relevant. Key teaching points that you want to reinforce during each activity should also be written down for easy reference.

Giving effective demonstrations. One of the reasons "a picture is worth a thousand words" to a coach is that an effective visual demonstration (a real-time, moving "picture") uses far less practice time than the "thousand words" we would otherwise need to convey the enormous complexity involved in the performances we expect our athletes to execute. But demonstrations only work if we present them properly. Here are the key elements of an effective demonstration that will help our athletes master essential sport skills in a way that will save us valuable practice time:

• Get (and keep) the athletes' attention. Structure the setting so the demonstration doesn't have to compete for the athletes' attention. Make sure you limit distractions and have everyone's undivided attention.

• Set the stage for motivated learning. Make sure the athletes understand the importance of the skill that is being demonstrated (where, when, and why it's relevant) and how it will help them become proficient at their sport.

• Use a "high-status" demonstrator. It's fine for the old coach to demonstrate — provided he or she can perform the skill properly — but don't hesitate to bring in more advanced or experienced athletes to serve as models. Athletes often learn better from models who are more like them (Bandura 1997).

• Demonstrate each skill from various angles. Showing what a movement looks like from several different perspectives help athletes gain insight as to how the skill is properly performed. It's especially important that the athletes get to see the skill performed from the same perspective they will have when they perform it themselves.

• Use a "whole-part-whole" approach. If the skill being demonstrated is complex, break it down into its logical parts. Introduce the whole skill first so the athletes can see what the total end product will ultimately look like. Then break the skill down into its logical sub-skills or parts. Finally, show the whole skill once again to show how the parts fit together into the complete movement.

• Allow for plenty of practice. As each sub-skill is demonstrated, allow the athletes sufficient time to practice that particular movement. Remember to provide ample encouragement and positive, constructive feedback throughout the practice.

Using mental practice. We all know physical practice is an essential part of athletic development. The truth is, however, there are plenty of times when physical practice is impossible or impractical. Injuries, travel, lack of facilities, inclement weather, and rules restricting practice time are only a few of the things that limit the time our athletes can devote to improving their skills. Or do they? It is certainly true that *physical* practice can sometime be hard to come by but there's no reason our athletes can't use this "down time" to hone their skills by engaging in *mental* practice. Although it would be a mistake to think that mentally rehearsing an athletic performance can in any way substitute for physical practice, it would be equally erroneous to assume that it isn't an excellent supplement to traditional physical practice or a way to improve skills when physical training is impossible (Feltz and Landers 1983).

Getting others to help. One of the best ways to improve the efficiency of a practice is to enlist the help of volunteer parents to serve as "assistant coaches." Having another responsible adult to coordinate and supervise practice activities results in a safer playing environment, smaller groups, less standing around, more individualized instruction and feedback, fewer disciplinary problems, more repetitions, and greater skill development. Giving parents a chance to contribute to the team in this productive manner also keeps them too busy to create many of the problems we typically associate with parental over-involvement (see the Myth No. 13 chapter for further details). Even if the thought of having parents working with the team on a regular basis sends chills down your spine, you still don't need to go it alone. Check with the local colleges or universities in your area. They often have students in physical education or coaching programs who are looking for practically-oriented, entry-level coaching experience. Helping us coach not only provides these students with a valuable learning opportunity, but our athletes will benefit from the additional attention, and we will benefit by getting some much-needed help during practice. Finally, don't forget that using your injured athletes to help out is a great way to take advantage of their expertise and keeps them feeling that they are still an essential part of the team (see the Myth No. 7 chapter for a further discussion of the benefits of having injured player helping out in practice). After all, who is in a better position to provide a bit of help in training the replacement than the player who originally held that position? The important thing is to do yourself—and your athletes—a big favor and get some coaching help.

Assigning "homework" to your athletes (and their parents). As important as our practices are, there's hardly a coach in the country who truly believes that the couple hours of formal training we schedule with our athletes during practice is enough to get them performing at their best. Whether we are coaching 6-year-old "pee-wees" or world-class competitors, it's pretty easy to see which of our athletes have been working on their game outside our structured practice sessions. Athletes who excel do so because they have committed themselves to hundreds of extra practice hours shooting jump shots on the playground blacktop, fielding ground balls on the rocky neighborhood infield, throwing spirals through a tire in the back yard, or lifting weights in a smelly gym. One of the best ways we can boost the efficiency of our practice time is to help our athletes understand what they can — and should — accomplish outside of practice by letting them know what aspects of their game needs additional work — outside of practice.

Setting — and helping your athletes set — practice goals. Think about how often players — and coaches — go through an entire practice without even identifying what they hope to accomplish. Unfortunately, most practices look pretty much the same: The coach blows a whistle and says "Do this," and the players run to do "this"; then the coach blows the whistle again and says, "Now do that," and the players hustle to do "that." This repeats itself several times until, in a couple of hours, the coach blows the whistle one last time and says "Hit the showers," and everybody dashes for the locker room. The simple fact of the matter is that if we're not really trying to accomplish something specific during our practices, we probably won't. Just having each athlete jot down something she or he wants to accomplish during practice each day helps keep them taking the little steps that will eventually make them better athletes (see the Myth No. 5 and Myth No. 6 chapters for a complete discussion of effective goal setting).

Expecting — and planning for — the unexpected. This may sound like an oxymoron. After all, if something is unexpected, how can we go about "planning" for it? The fact is that we do this sort of thing all the time — but rarely when it comes to planning our practices. For example, most of us have (or at least should have) put a bit of money away into a "rainy day" account to help us cope with unexpected financial emergencies. Although the exact nature of our emergency will never be known in advance, most of us have learned, the hard way, that we are all susceptible to Murphy's Law — "Whatever can go wrong, will go wrong" and we had better have a well-conceived back-up plan if — no, *WHEN* — Murphy rears its ugly head. Organizing a team of athletes is a very complicated task with a lot of moving parts. There are dozens of places where our original plans can fall apart during every practice. For example, the practice facilities we expected will not be available; athletes will come to practice without the proper equipment; the weather will turn foul midway through practice; you (or one of your coaches or athletes) will be called away from practice to deal with a personal emergency; there will be an equipment or power failure; an athlete will be injured or begin to feel ill. The list of things that can interfere with practice time is endless. The degree to which we anticipate, plan, and effectively respond to these potential disruptions will contribute greatly to how efficiently we use the practice time we are allotted.

Taking a "Games Approach" to practice. Patterning our practices after those conducted by our former coaches will, more often than not, result in our athletes standing around waiting for their turn to take part in a series of mindless, disjointed drills that bear little resemblance to the skills they will be asked to execute in competition. The sport of basketball, although far from the only sport guilty of such wasteful practices, provides us with a clear example of a drill that is used by nearly every team in the country. Players are divided into two equal lines and one undefended player dribbles a couple times and shoots an unchallenged layup while a player from the other line grabs the uncontested rebound and casually flips the ball to the next shooter. This irrelevant and unrealistic drill goes on and on until each player has several opportunities to assume the role of both undefended dribbler/shooter and uncontested rebounder/passer. To make matters worse, all the other members of the team merely stand around watching as they wait their turn. Does anything approaching this ever really happen during a basketball game? Of course not. In a real game, nearly every dribble, shot, rebound, and pass will need to be made with opponents slapping, pushing, shoving, and bumping our players every step of the way. Then why does nearly every basketball coach in the country engage in such a wasteful and irrelevant activity? The main reason is probably that we all grew up with coaches who had us perform this type of drill so it seems perfectly natural to include it as a part of our practices. Similar mindless training and mechanistic drills can be found in every sport but a new way of conducting practice called the "Games Approach" provides us a way of devising creative, motivating, and realistic ways of maximizing our players' time on task. In the Games Approach, coaches analyze the skills used in a real game and tailor practice activities to provide athletes with a series of game-like situations. A complete description of how coaches can use the Games Approach in a variety of sports can be found in a book entitled *Play practice: The Games Approach to Teaching and Coaching Sports* by former Olympic coach and Games Approach pioneer, Alan Launder (2001).

Use innovative means of communication. Another way to make sure that your entire team is functioning as productively as possible is to take advantage of relatively new social media technology to send and receive communication with your athletes and their families. Setting up a team webpage with general team information (schedules, rules, regulations, contact information, etc.) and sending late-breaking news or "reminders" regarding changes in practice times and locations via social media such as Facebook, Twitter, Tumblr, or text messages will help our athletes and assistant coaches know how to prepare for practice. Although this technology may be new, and a bit intimidating to some of us, it is the way our athletes (and their parents) communicate on a regular basis.

Evaluating your practices. Invite a trusted colleague — perhaps a coach of a different sport — to observe a few of your practices. Have this person offer some suggestions as to how you might enhance the productivity of your practices. It's amazing how much inefficiency and poor time management a "fresh set of eyes" can reveal.

Eliminating Hidden "Time Drains" in Our Practices

Coaches often run their practices by simply flipping on their "automatic pilot" switch — doing what seems natural without seriously considering whether or not they are squeezing every precious second out of the limited time they can spend with their athletes. Unfortunately, the way most of us conduct practice is more likely to be based on how our former coaches ran their practices than on any serious attempt at maximizing the instruction, repetitions, and feedback our athletes receive during every practice.

As strange as it may sound, many of the things we've learned from our coaches, and now take for granted as being a normal part of practice, will actually cut into our preparation time. Conducting long, grueling workouts, punishing athletes when they make mistakes, setting aside special time to condition our athletes, and teaching overly advanced skills are typical ways we squander practice time. But the first thing we have to emphasize is the importance of everyone (coaches and players alike) being on time and ready to start teaching and learning the very minute practice begins.

Stress the importance of being on time. If you have a practice scheduled to begin at 3:30 P.M., why would you want to finally get down to business at 3:35? If you do, and your practices typically last for about two hours, you've just frittered away nearly 5 percent of your allotted practice time for the day — and that's before you've even so much as tooted your whistle. If a couple minutes here and a couple minutes there don't sound like anything to worry about, just calculate that daily loss of preparation time over the course of an entire season. You'll discover that the seemingly insignificant five minutes you waste daily by not starting on time results in your athletes losing the equivalent of one entire practice session each and every month! It's also important that we, as the leaders of the team, serve as a good example regarding the importance of time management. As Coach Wooden puts it, "A leader who is careless about time sanctions the same attitude throughout the organization. Time is about more than the clock; it is about creating and fostering an environment in which discipline and hustle rule over carelessness and a casual attitude about time" (Wooden and Jamison 2005, 163).

Stop punishing your athletes. As we will explore in greater detail in the Myth No. 9 chapter, our natural tendency to punish our athletes for performance or disciplinary errors usually causes more problems than it solves. One of the many problems associated with punishment is that it wastes valuable practice time. Every minute we spend punishing athletes — individually or as a group — is yet another minute we can't use for technical instruction, positive corrective feedback, or additional performance repetitions. Unfortunately, all too many coaches resort to punishment because they don't know their sport well enough to provide constructive suggestions for improvement. Since they don't know what else to do, they punish. Performance errors should be corrected by providing better instruction and discipline problems should be dealt with by removing something the offender truly values — like playing time.

Stop conditioning your athletes. I know that sounds really weird but here's a question most coaches have never asked themselves, "Should I continue devoting so much of my practice time to conditioning my athletes?" Although using practice to condition our athletes sounds like a great idea — at first — it's actually just another way we waste enormous amounts of valuable practice time. The conditioning of most athletes can, and should, be worked right into the normal flow of practice. As usual, a quick look at how Coach Wooden's basketball practices were designed to incorporate conditioning into realistic practice activities serves as a great example of how this can be accomplished. As you read how Coach Wooden conditioned his athletes, think about how it contrasts with the typical way basketball coaches waste 10–15 minutes running silly back-and-forth "suicides" or "end-to-end" sprints sometime during every practice.

We didn't achieve conditioning by doing laps or running up and down stairs or doing push-ups. We did it through the efficient and intense execution of individual fundamental drills. A player who wasn't running in a scrimmage would shoot free-throws until he made ten in a row, and then would go back into the scrimmage while someone else came out to shoot free-throws. Everyone wanted to be scrimmaging, so players put tremendous pressure on themselves to make free-throws and worked intensely while they participated in the scrimmage [Wooden 1997, 134].

Just imagine how much performance-based, motivating, and relevant "hidden" conditioning takes place during 15 to 20 minutes of all-out, full-court, man-to-man, fast-break scrimmaging. Another benefit of this type of conditioning is that it isn't viewed by the athletes as some disconnected "necessary evil" that must be tolerated (and avoided if possible) but rather, an integral part of overall performance. When working with more advanced athletes, we have to recognize that the small amount of "conditioning for the sake of conditioning" we can incorporate into our formal practice sessions will be of little value. Athletes at this level of competition have to be taught the importance of taking responsibility for their own conditioning outside of practice.

Don't do what you don't do. The most efficient coaches understand that it really doesn't make a lot of sense to spend valuable practice time working on skills their athletes will rarely, if ever, be called on to perform in competition. Practice time needs to be focused on those skills that are absolutely essential for competition. One of my first experiences with coaches wasting practice time on irrelevant skill development came when I first started playing Little League baseball. At some point in nearly every practice, our coaches would have us work on turning double plays. They would hit each infielder several ground balls and we would practice throwing the ball to either the second baseman or the shortstop covering second base who would pivot and throw on to first. Now most baseball coaches think this is an important skill for infielders to master—and it might be if we weren't talking about Little Leaguers. Despite our hundreds of repetitions, the first double play I recall my team—or any of our opponents for that matter—successfully executing came nearly 10 years after we began practicing this complicated maneuver. We had essentially wasted 10–15 minutes of practice time every day for a decade on a skill that never once paid off in a game. Surely we could have better spent this time working on more basic skills (backing up throws, forcing the lead runner, running the bases properly, etc.) that we would have used in every competition. As this example illustrates, to avoid wasting time, it's absolutely essential that we engage in a "cost-benefit analysis" of everything we do in practice.

Know when to call it quits. Long, drawn-out practices only cause mental and physical fatigue. When fatigue sets in, it often leads to boredom, frustration, disciplinary problems, performance errors, bad habits, and injuries. Calling it quits before our athletes are totally fatigued is another case where "less is more." Getting our players to work hard and in a focused manner for a single hour of practice is far more motivating and productive than forcing them to stand around wasting time for three. Whenever we're tempted to think our athletes need more practice time we should remind ourselves they can have it — as soon as their coach starts conducting more efficient practices.

The Cost of Not Using Your Practice Time Wisely

Just think about the hours and hours of valuable practice time we throw away every season by failing to...

- Spend an adequate amount of time planning and properly sequencing skill instruction
- Give effective technical demonstrations
- Use mental practice as a supplement to traditional physical practice
- Invite parents, college interns, or retired coaches to help us conduct practice
- Assign our athletes "homework" to improve their skills outside of practice
- Set, and help each of our athletes set, achievable short-term practice goals
- Formulate contingency plans to cope with uncontrollable disruptions
- Use realistic drills that maximize repetitions and relate to actual performance
- Start our practices on time
- Understand that time spent punishing athletes is time that can't be used for instruction and repetition
- Condition athletes though realistic activities rather than specific "conditioning" drills (like running)
- Understand that teaching overly complex skills and plays won't improve performance
- Know when to call it quits before mental and physical fatigue sets in

Now, let's reflect once more on the quote from Coach Smith at the beginning of this chapter. Notice that when we start spending as much time planning our practices as conducting them, we'll probably never find ourselves thinking, "There's never enough practice time."

"A Hard-Nosed Coaching Style Fosters Discipline, Respect, and Performance"

I don't yell a lot... When I get mad I usually talk at the same volume I'm talking now. And when I get really mad—I whisper. So if my voice at this level won't get your attention, and you believe you need someone to yell at you to correct you or motivate you, then we'll probably need to find you another team to play for so you can play your best.

— Coach Tony Dungy[1]

Let's begin by stating the obvious. A coach's success is based on altering behavior. It is our job to engage our athletes in ways that will reduce the likelihood they will repeat their mistakes while, at the same time, inspiring them to continue executing the proper elements of their performances. A coach's "stock in trade" therefore resides in his or her ability to change behavior. To put it bluntly, what good are we if our athletes don't act differently after coming in contact with us? And it goes well beyond coaching. Life itself is largely a matter of exerting influence over others in an attempt to change their behavior. We spend each and every day of our lives attempting to alter the existing behavior of our children, our spouses, our friends, our customers, our clients, our politicians, our students, our co-workers — even total strangers.

The way we choose to influence others is, in large part, a function of how we've seen others behave in similar situations — particularly those we admire and respect. It's no surprise, therefore, that when we, as coaches, want our athletes to behave in a certain way, we tend to rely heavily on recollections of the coaching behaviors of those with whom we are most familiar — coaches we had ourselves and those we frequently see on television. It's important to understand that what we generally think of as our own unique "coaching style" is rarely developed by our deliberate, conscious decisions regarding what will help us accomplish our goals. It is far more likely that we coach the way we do because of gut-level, emotional reactions to events we experienced in the past — often when we were young, vulnerable, and impressionable.

Unfortunately, many of us carry around the mental image of a coach as a tough, rough, gruff, authoritarian who is allowed (even encouraged) to treat the people in their care in ways that would simply not be tolerated in most social settings. I think I first noticed that coaches were allowed special exemptions in regard to the way they treat (mistreat may be more to the point) their athletes when I was in the seventh grade. We had a math teacher who also served as the boy's basketball coach. In class, from 2:00 to 3:00 every afternoon, Mr. Hartley was a reasonably polite, considerate, and effective teacher. When his students struggled and needed a little extra help in algebra, he was always more than willing to do whatever he could to help them gain a better grasp of the material. But when basketball practice started — less than a half an hour later — Mr. Harley purposely transformed himself into such an irascible, ill-tempered coach that he was tagged with the moniker "Mr. Heartless" by the boys on his basketball team. Even though some of these same boys benefited from Mr. Harley's positive encouragement during algebra class earlier in the day, this was obviously a different situation. After all, this was "sport" and apparently the same rules of learning don't apply here. Coach Heartless yelled, screamed, ranted, and raved his way through every practice. Any miscue would result in roughly the same sequence of events: (1) a "blue streak" of curses and oaths from Coach Harley — even though his athletes were young children, (2) an attempt to belittle or embarrass the guilty party for being so stupid as to make such a mistake, and (3) a series of laps or wind sprints for the entire team — the exact number of which to be determined by the severity of the offense. One time Coach Heartless got so frustrated with the team's errors he threw a basketball at one of the players that hit him in the head — leaving a large red welt on the side of his face and the youngster complaining of a headache for the remainder of the practice. Despite being a bunch of naive 12-year-olds, my teammates and I quickly recognized the inconsistency in this person's behavior. When teaching algebra he was Dr. Jekyll but a few minutes later, when he was teaching basketball, he turned into Mr. Hyde. We frequently discussed — even fanaticized about — the fact that if he ever treated us like basketball players just an hour earlier, in his math class, the school board would fire him on the spot and perhaps even throw him in jail (where we hoped he might be subjected to some of the same harsh treatments he imposed on us). Although our team no doubt developed some basketball skills as a result of (or maybe in just spite of) playing for this coach, what we learned above all else, and what will stick with every member of that team forever, was that coaching is somehow "different" from teaching. When it comes to coaching it is apparently acceptable, even appropriate, to brutalize youngsters in the name of athletics — as long as you win enough games.

That bring us to the crux of the matter — winning. Coaches aren't about to forgo their negative coaching styles simply because they feel guilty about the inappropriate social lessons they may be passing on to the next generation. Despite platitudes to the contrary, most coaches (and their supporters) are far more interested in winning games than fulfilling their responsibilities as appropriate role models. Therefore, let's set aside, for the moment, the social ills associated with punishment and focus solely on whether punishment and negativity are likely to help us attain the things we, as coaches, desire most — enhanced athletic performance and increased chances of winning (please refer to the Myth No. 5 chapter for a more complete discussion of the relative importance of winning).

Punishment Doesn't Work

Psychologists define punishment as "the infliction of pain or discomfort upon a subject for failure to conform to a predetermined course of action" (Chaplin 1975, 434). In everyday language punishment is really nothing more than giving people something they don't want for something they've either done or failed to do. Because we have seen so many examples of coaches using this technique in an attempt to alter their player's behavior, we sometimes take it for granted that punishments — whether in the form of *verbal abuse* (e.g., yelling, criticizing, embarrassing, ridiculing), *physical abuse* (e.g., hitting, pushing, shoving, grabbing) or *exercise abuse* (e.g., running, sit-ups, push-ups) — are effective in reducing undesirable behaviors. However, contrary to popular belief, there is little evidence that resorting to these kinds of abuses will really help us become better coaches. The truth is, we can't simply "scare" a bad performance out of our athletes. In fact, by resorting to punishment in our attempt to reduce undesirable behavior, we are usually at risk for doing far more harm than good. Unfortunately, our coaching styles are so deeply ingrained that most of us would rather not think about the potential disadvantages of punishment. Ironically, if we actually knew the negative effects punishment can have on our athletes' performance, most of us would never use these techniques again. We would quickly see that punishment does little more than keep us — and our teams — from accomplishing our most important goals.

This is the point at which some like to offer examples of rough, tough, dictatorial coaches as evidence that punishment obviously "works." There is, however, one big problem with this argument. For every Vince Lombardi there's an equally successful Bill Walsh, for every Woody Hayes there's a Pete Carroll, for every Bobby Knight there's a Dean Smith, for every Bob Huggins there's a Brad Stevens, for every Mike Ditka there's a Tony Dungy, for every Red Auerbach there's a Phil Jackson, for every Bill Parcells there's a Dick Vermeil, for every Ozzie Guillen there's a Joe Maddon, and for every Bobby Valentine there's a Joe Torre. The point here isn't to debate whether one particular coach is "better" than another. What is important is recognizing that choosing to adopt a negative coaching style (and it is a deliberate *choice*) will not make us successful. The "positive" coaches on this list not only enjoyed similar — or even better — results, they also instilled as much discipline and engendered as much respect from their athletes as the coaches who adopted a more negative, dictatorial, command-style approach. Obviously, winning — or losing — can result from either a positive or negative coaching style. It really doesn't matter in the least. What does matter are all the other problems that will come our way if we rely on punishments to correct performance errors (Albrecht 2009).

Punishment Will Only Work When You Are Present

In order for punishment to even have a remote chance of working, three conditions must be met: (1) you must be present, (2) you must be able to detect the undesirable behavior, and (3) you must be willing and able to administer a meaningful negative event (something they really don't want) to the perpetrator. This may sound obvious but its implications are far-reaching. Punishment operates at, and therefore reinforces, a very low level of moral reasoning. It decreases the undesirable behavior by simply linking this "bad" behavior to a very unpleasant outcome. The behavior may change — not in an effort to "do the right thing" — but simply to avoid the punishment. A basketball player, for example, may be driven to work harder on defense not because "I want to be a better basketball player" or even because "I want to contribute more to my team," but because "I want to stop the coach from yelling at me and making me run sprints." Some coaches have said they don't really care what the motive for the performance is as long as it's executed properly. That's terribly short-sighted — and generally untrue. How many coaches really think it's perfectly fine if their athletes use improper techniques or make inappropriate tactical decisions when they are practicing at home or playing on another team in the off-season? Most coaches want the skill to be executed properly on a more-or less permanent basis — regardless of whether they happen to be around to see it.

Training cats — and athletes — to "do the right thing." Let me use a personal story to illustrate the point that punishment only works when you are present and have complete control over the situation. A couple years ago my wife and I got two tiny kittens. Young cats love to explore things and they generally think everything belongs to them. We, on the other hand, were keenly aware that most guests who come to our house for dinner would probably be grossed out if they saw our cats sitting on the dining room table. We knew, therefore, that our cats had to eventually be trained to stay off the table. Now we love our kitties and we wouldn't do anything to hurt them; but we knew we had to somehow keep them from getting on the dining room table. One thing that almost all cats have in common is their hatred of getting wet. Although it doesn't really hurt them, there are few things they detest more. This led me to create a makeshift foxhole in the living room (hiding behind the sofa). Every time the cats jumped onto our dining room table I blasted them with a jet stream of water from a huge water rifle I bought specifically for this purpose. As soon as they felt the water, they headed for cover and it wasn't long before both cats learned to never get on the table. The punishment had worked — or did it? Although we never see them on the table, where do you think our cats are when we go to sleep at night? Yep, nearly every morning there are little "kitty tracks" all over the table. It seems our cats didn't actually learn to stay off the table — only to stay off the table when that "crazy guy" is in the next room with his water rifle. Our athletes are certainly as smart as cats and most of them will quickly realize that they can successfully avoid our punishments as long as they do what we want — at least when we're around.

Why punishing athletes for using drugs won't work. It's not only individual coaches who expect unrealistic behavioral change from athletes by punishing them into submission. Sports fans and policy makers often bemoan the fact that despite spending 40 years and billions of dollars subjecting hundreds of thousands of athletes to ever-more invasive levels of drug testing, drug use among athletes is as prevalent as ever. After all our efforts we have seen, in the past few years, accusations that superstars such as Barry Bonds, Mark McGuire, Roger Clemens, Rafael Palmeiro, Sammy Sosa, Marion Jones, Floyd Landis, and Lance Armstrong (in addition to hundreds of lesser-known athletes) are still using banned performance-enhancing substances to improve their performance. One of the reasons drug testing has never — and will never — significantly reduce drug use is that it's based on the principle of punishment. We aren't sending our athletes the message that "using drugs is wrong" — because we don't actually punish our athletes for *using* drugs (we don't have any idea how many thousands of athletes at all levels *use* drugs). Instead, we unwittingly send the message that *"getting caught using drugs is wrong"* — because that's the only thing we can punish them for. Therefore, like cats on the dining room table, athletes have quickly figured out that one way to avoid being punished is to avoid getting caught. They use drugs that are currently undetectable, they use "masking agents" to hide the fact they are using drugs, or otherwise stay one step ahead of the tests. The rules of this game are really very simple — if you don't get caught, you won't get punished.

Punishment Wastes Valuable Practice Time

One frequent complaint of coaches is "there is never enough practice time" (please see the Myth No. 8 chapter for a more complete discussion of the effective use of practice time). Although we rarely think of it this way, coaches waste an enormous amount of time by devoting large segments of their practice doling out punishments for all kinds of disciplinary infractions and performance errors.

I once played on a basketball team that was a pretty decent free throw shooting team. We probably averaged about 65 percent from the free throw line but in one particular game we missed 18 of 22 free throws (81 percent) in a three point home loss to one of our arch-rivals. Our coach was so furious with our performance that he insisted on an impromptu practice immediately after the fans left the gym that night. To illustrate just how prevalent it is for coaches to purposely waste valuable time punishing their athletes, let me ask you a question. How do you think we spent our extra two hours of practice time that evening? What two activities (beyond constantly yelling and cursing at us) do you think the coach felt were the best ways to prepare us to shoot a higher percentage of free throws in upcoming competitions? If you said we spent the bulk of the practice running sprints and shooting free throws, you're absolutely right. Isn't it interesting that you actually knew what we did that night? After all, you weren't there. How we spent that additional practice time was never reported in the media. In fact, you may not have even been born yet! But notice how we consider punishment (in this case, running) and mindless drills a routine and "accepted" part of practice. As it turned out, this whole practice was nothing but a waste of time. Remember, we didn't miss our free throws because we didn't know how to shoot — we generally made about 65 percent of our shots. We also didn't miss the shots because of fatigue. We missed roughly the same number of shots at the beginning of each half as we did at the end. So why did the coach make us run? It was punishment for our poor performance — plain and simple. Everybody on the team knew it and everybody on the team resented it for the rest of the season.

Coaches need to constantly remind themselves that every minute of practice time we use to punish our athletes is just one more minute of practice time that we can't use to do what is truly expected of us — provide our athletes with the quality instruction that will reduce the likelihood of these errors occurring in the future.

Why we "purposefully" punish athletes and waste practice time. I have a theory for which I admittedly have little hard evidence but I'd like you to consider. After observing coaching behavior for many years it is my view that many coaches readily gravitate to punishment simply because they don't really know their sport well enough to correct errors in a more positive manner. For example, when a football player fumbles the ball, everyone — including the coach — knows something's gone wrong. Obviously, that's not the performance we're looking for. A competent coach, who really understands the finer points of the game, might immediately see that the running back's arms weren't in a position to properly secure the football. Having made this observation, the coach can now provide valuable instruction regarding arm placement so another fumble is less likely to occur in the future. But now consider a football coach who is not as well-versed in the subtleties of the game? Perhaps his lack of knowledge results in his missing the cause of the fumble. Like everyone, he knows very well that "something" has gone wrong but he's not exactly sure what it was or what to do about it. Since he doesn't know how to positively instruct his athlete, he's left with two choices: say nothing, ignore the mistake, and risk being accused of not knowing (or caring about) what he's doing — or scream, holler, and punish the player for the fumble. At least with the second option the coach *looks* like he might be doing something productive. Every time we are tempted to resort to a negative style of coaching we would be well-served to ask ourselves one important question: "Does all of my yelling, screaming, and hollering actually make them play better or just make me look and feel better?"

Making better hitters: Running laps or batting practice? One of the worst examples I've ever seen of punishment being a total waste of practice time occurred at a girls (Under-18) softball practice. It so happened that the team was coming off a terrible loss. In the previous day's game they had faced a hard-throwing pitcher who (I later discovered) was being highly recruited by several Division I college coaches. She was absolutely overpowering. In the seven-inning game she struck out 17 of the 21 batters she faced. Needless to say, the coach of the defeated team was terribly upset about the ineffectiveness her team had shown against this pitcher. In order to demonstrate her displeasure with the team's performance the coach decided to "make her point" during practice the next day. After not-so-gently reminding the team of their horrendous batting performance the previous day (as if any of them had actually forgotten) she informed the team that everyone was going to run one full lap around the entire field, from home plate — to the right field foul pole — to the flagpole in dead centerfield — to the left field foul pole — back to home plate, for each and every one of the 17 strikeouts they had been guilty of the day before. Every member of the team spent the entire practice — not taking additional batting practice or getting technical instruction from the coaching staff (again, I'm not sure the coaches knew enough to give valuable instruction anyway) — but simply being punished for their "sins." When I asked what the coach was hoping to accomplish by devoting her total practice to running laps, she came up with the same tired phrases we often hear from those who try their best to justify their negative approach to coaching, "they needed a 'wake-up' call," and "I had to grab their attention and give them a little incentive to start working harder." Perhaps that was her intent but what actually happened was later that night four of her best players quit the team saying they had "joined this softball team to have fun and improve their skills" — neither of which apparently made any sense whatsoever to a coach who would run them for two straight hours instead of teaching them ways to become better hitters.

Punishment Can Increase a Fear of Failure and Reduce Risk Taking

Still another serious limitation of punishment is that, although it is often used to enhance performance, it can have the exact opposite effect. One way excessive punishment inhibits performance is by fostering a "fear of failure" within the athletes and a subsequent reduction in risk taking.

Regardless of the sport, one thing all quality athletic performances have in common is that they require the taking of calculated risks. In order to be successful, athletes (and coaches) have to push themselves beyond their normal "comfort zone" and risk failure. If an errant pass, missed shot, or blown coverage is met with criticism and contempt, it may be interpreted as a reaction toward the effort itself. I once stood inside the locker room of an elite hockey team during the first intermission and heard a coach scold his players for what he thought was poor shot selection. He ended his tirade by screaming, "Anyone who takes a shot that misses the net during the next period will owe me a hundred sprints at the beginning of practice tomorrow!" As soon as I heard this, I knew there was going to be trouble. Not surprisingly, when they returned to the ice, the team was so intent on avoiding the punishment they took only the safest of shots and ended up losing the game by a single goal. After the game the coach was in such a foul mood I didn't have the courage to remind him of the profound advice that is generally attributed to the greatest hockey player of all time — Wayne Gretzky — "You'll miss 100 percent of all the shots you don't take."

There's one sure way to make certain athletes will never make a mistake — punish them until they become so gun shy they don't do anything at all. Coach John Wooden once said "I believed if you were not making some mistakes, you were not doing anything. You need to do something to make things happen. I'd rather have a 50 percent shooting average and score 100 points than a 100 percent shooting average with 50 points" (Wooden 2004, 74). What most coaches don't realize is they are cutting their own throats by punishing their players for making performance errors. If we want our athletes to do nothing, all we have to do is punish them every time they make a mistake. And when they do nothing, we lose.

Punishment Can Create an Unpleasant Environment and Decrease Motivation

Let's face it. Punishment wouldn't be punishment if it was pleasant. The problem with that is that coaches who rely on punishment to correct errors are at risk of creating what Parker Palmer (1998) in his book *The Courage to Teach*, calls "a culture of fear" on their teams. We need to continually remind ourselves that sports are made to be *played*. They are supposed to be enjoyable and it is a coach's job to make it happen. If sport wasn't enjoyable, what would be the point? Coaches who use punishment run the risk of destroying the intrinsic motivation their athletes have for the sport. In the extreme, athletes might find the coach's "culture of fear" so painful that they stop participating in the sport all together. The research is clear on this. Three of the main reasons kids give for dropping out of sports are "I wasn't having fun," "I wasn't getting better," and "I didn't like the coach" (Weiss and Amorose 2008). The softball players who quit after their coach made them run for an entire practice because they struck out too many times are a good example of how a coach's use of punishment and poor teaching skills can cause athletes to quit participating in sports. They basically said, "There are a lot of different things I could be doing. If my coach isn't going to give me proper instruction to help me improve my skills and is just going to make me run and develop a hatred for the game I thought I loved, I have better things to do with my time." Oddly enough, there are coaches who actually think that it's part of their job to systematically eliminate underperforming athletes. These coaches rely on heavy doses of negative or "destructive" coaching to drive athletes away from their team. In what they perceive as an ongoing struggle of Darwinian survival where only the strongest survive, these coaches purposely structure practices and games in such a way as to "weed out" athletes who "don't have what it takes." Is that really coaching? Let's face it, just about anyone can work with the "good" athletes. It takes a true coach — and a true teacher — to help an athlete who is experiencing difficulty. Coaches who merely discard or punish their athletes until they quit would be like doctors who say "don't send us any more sick people — we don't know what to do with them. Send us healthy patients so we can look like good doctors" (Palmer 1998).

Punishment Can Increase Anxiety and Hurt Performance

Most coaches are well aware of the fact that an athlete's performance generally suffers when he or she experiences high levels of anxiety (please see the Myth No. 10 chapter for a complete discussion of the relationship between arousal and performance). Even under the best of conditions athletic performances can be very anxiety provoking experiences.

To get a good sense of how much pressure our athletes face, just imagine how well you would perform a difficult task — let's say calculating a series of complex math problems — if we brought a hundred or so of your friends and neighbors together in a room to watch you manipulate the numbers. Let's then pick out a couple of these friends and have them go "head to head" with you — calculating the same problem sets — just so we can judge which of you is smarter. Now, let's go even further and fill an entire arena or stadium with thousands of strangers so they too, can evaluate the appropriateness of your every mathematical move. If they can't clearly see the subtle details of your performance, we'll project every one of your pencil scratches onto a huge big-screen television. As you try to concentrate on solving the problems, thousands of spectators will be screaming at the top of their lungs — some yelling obscenities and insults about you and your family to distract you into making mistakes, others yammering words of advice and encouragement. In fact, this is such an interesting spectacle of sound and fury that perhaps we'll even send the television signal out so millions of people across the country can see how well you perform this task. Oh, by the way, every time you make a mistake, we'll show it again and again on "instant replay" with self-appointed "math experts" pointing out exactly where you screwed up. Keep in mind, we are also going to show your biggest blunders again and again on the 24 hour news channel and write about them in tomorrow's newspaper. Of course people who never passed a math class in their lives will sit around dissecting every one of your miscalculations on talk radio for the next week or so and then we'll ask you to show up and do the whole thing over again for our amusement. Now, given the inherent pressure in this situation, to what extent do you think it would benefit your performance to have your math teacher standing over you during your entire week of preparation screaming insults and hitting you with a stick every time you made a mistake? Probably not much.

Yet this is exactly what we do when we punish our athletes as they're trying to master the complex skills involved in sport. Essentially, coaches who rely on a negative style to get their point across are often just an additional and unnecessary distraction. Generally speaking, there are more than enough things for our athletes to concern themselves with while performing without the extra burden that comes from wondering if their unpredictable coach (or parent) is going to have an emotional "melt down" every time they make a mistake.

Punishment Can Decrease Athlete Self-Confidence

Everyday observations and scientific research make one thing perfectly clear — self-confidence is one of the best predictors of sport performance (Feltz 2007). There is little question that when it comes to athletic performance, the importance of confidence can be pretty much summed up by a quote often attributed to Henry Ford, "Whether you think you can, or think you can't — you're right." That's why it's puzzling to hear so many coaches belittling the performances of their athletes. Despite hundreds of scientific studies of confidence, there has been no evidence yet to suggest that we can build our athletes' confidence by tearing them down.

Some coaches believe that ridiculing, degrading, or demeaning their players' performance will get under their skin and cause them to work that much harder just to prove the coach wrong. Even on these rare occasions, is this really the toxic relationship we want to cultivate with our players? Do we really want our athletes to perform at a higher level just because they're convinced we're an absolute jerk and they'll do whatever it takes to show everyone how ignorant and foolish we are?

In 1999 ESPN put together a documentary called *The Season* which depicts a high school football team's journey to the Pennsylvania state championship. In that film — which I still show to every one of my classes — members of the coaching staff curse and swear at the kids while constantly mocking and ridiculing their performances. During one game, for example, a player's effort is belittled by the coach, who's only response is, "You stink ... you stink." As the season goes on, the effect of this constant psychological abuse becomes glaringly evident. The back-up quarterback — who had grown up in with a "screaming Dad" and who admits "Personally, I play better when I'm not being screamed at" — is cleaning out his room with a friend when they come across a handgun (part of a video game). His very first impulse is to pick up the gun, point it to his head and say, "Football's getting to me — I can't take Pettine [his head coach] anymore." Although the gun is a toy, the message being sent is chilling. How many of us would want our players to pick a gun — real or not — and point it at their head and say they "can't take the coach anymore"? The coach, Mike Pettine (who is now the Defensive Coordinator with the Buffalo Bills) dismisses the negativity of his coaching style by saying, "When I'm flipping out or being very critical, I never mean it as a personal attack." Well, coach, how you mean it obviously isn't nearly as important as how it's perceived. And by the way, how can telling someone things like, "You stink ... you stink" or "Mike, aren't you tired of f***ing up?" without it being taken as anything other than a personal attack?

As leaders, we need to understand that every comment we make will have a lasting impact, for better or worse, on our players. They hold us up to be the "experts" — the "top dog." When we continually tell our athletes how terrible they are, or how much they "stink," how long will it be until they finally believe us? After all don't we really expect our players to believe the things we tell them?

Punishment Can Produce Unintended and Undesirable Behaviors

Punishment can have different effects on different athletes. Some might simply internalize their feelings and become a bit more sullen or a bit less confident. Others may react to being punished in a more observable way such as outright rebellion against the coaching staff or quitting the team. Punishment can also bring out a number of unwanted behaviors from our athletes.

Punishments as rewards. Oddly enough, there are a few athletes who take pleasure in the extra attention they receive from being singled out for punishment. Giving these attention-seekers some form of punishment may be exactly what they're looking for. Although this type of unintentional rewarding of "bad" behavior is more prevalent in a classroom setting, athletic teams have also been known to have the occasional "team clowns" who seem more interested in drawing attention to themselves than avoiding punishment. Here punishment only increases the chances of the unwanted behavior continuing.

Punishment can set a bad example. Still another disadvantage of punishing athletes is that there is the real possibility that this negative tone may filter through the entire team. When players see their leaders acting in a disparaging, derogatory, or hurtful way toward members of the team, they sometime take this as a signal that this is how members of this team are expected to treat one another. Coaches who intentionally or unintentionally model sarcasm, cruelty, and ridicule of others as being an acceptable form of team interaction run the risk of players treating one another with a similar level of disrespect.

Negative Consequences of Using Physical Activity as Punishment

Despite the many problems associated with any form of punishment, the physical nature of athletics seems to make the use of extra physical activity as a punishment particularly attractive to coaches in all sports and at all skill levels. Our profession (and our close cousins, the "gym" teachers) relies so heavily on punishments that involve push-ups, sit-ups, down-ups, running laps, running sprints, leg-raisers, etc. that we have become caricatures of ourselves — constantly portrayed as authoritarian bullies who routinely punish their athletes' every offense with excessive amounts of physical exercise. Like most of our coaching techniques, we learned that the use of physical activity as punishment was a perfectly legitimate — even appropriate — means by which to train athletes. Few of us have ever stopped to consider the negative consequences associated with this time-honored tradition. It's important to begin by underscoring that coaches who punish their athletes by assigning additional physical exercise are setting themselves up to reap all the evils previously discussed that tend to accompany any form of punishment:

- Works for a limited time and only when you're present
- Wastes valuable practice time that could be spent on quality instruction
- Increases "fear of failure" and reduces necessary "risk-taking" behaviors
- Creates an unpleasant and de-motivating environment
- Increases performance anxiety which can hurt performance
- Decreases athlete self-confidence
- Rewards unwanted behaviors

As if all these aren't reasons enough to avoid punishing our athletes, there is one additional limitation of punishment that only shows itself when the punishments we choose to administer involve the performance of additional physical activity — it tends to make our athletes view physical activity as something negative and to be avoided at all costs. Just think about it. Our clear intent here is to make our athletes perceive this act of physical activity such an unpleasant experience they will do whatever it takes to avoid having to do it again in the future. If we weren't able to cultivate such a negative view of physical activity, we couldn't use it as punishment. This view of physical activity as something to be avoided that we rely on to change behavior can result in some serious problems for our athletes in the future.

It's a coach's job to promote lifelong healthy behavior. According to the National Institutes of Health (1998), over 97 million adults in the United States are either overweight or obese — largely because they don't exercise enough — and being overweight or obese is a serious matter. It increases the risk of high blood pressure, diabetes, heart disease, stroke, respiratory problems, certain forms of cancer, and a number of other serious health problems (Flegal 2005). What do the terrible diseases and conditions associated with being obese and overweight have to do with coaches punishing their athletes with physical activity? Plenty. If, year after year, coaches force athletes to run or "drop and give me twenty" (push-ups) after every miscue, how might those athletes come to view physical exercise at the end of 10, 15 or 20 years? How eager will they be to voluntarily engage in similar activities for the rest of their lives? Although it's difficult to draw a direct connection between coaches using physical activity as punishment and athletes getting sick and dying years later, the Centers for Disease Control and Prevention were convinced that there was a strong enough link to issue the following unequivocal warning to all of us: "Using physical activity as a punishment risks creating negative associations with physical activity in the minds of young people" (Center for Disease Control and Prevention 1997, 12). If that isn't convincing enough, when the National Association for Sport and Physical Education (NASPE) published the second edition of its *National Standards for Sport Coaches* (NASPE 2006) it specifically condemned the use of physical activity as punishment. In Standard 26 of this document, the preeminent national authority on sport and physical education specifically tells us that it is essential that "the coach understands principles of motivation and develops and maintains a repertoire of positive strategies for helping athletes maximize their success and enjoyment of sport ... [and] coaches should never use physical activity or peer pressure as a means of disciplining athlete behavior" (NASPE 2006, 17).

Using physical activity as punishment can lead to injuries. Any level of physical activity can result in injury and coaches and athletes accept this as a normal risk associated with participating in sports. However, forcing athletes to engage in extreme levels of exercise as punishment for poor performances or disciplinary violations simply increases these risks. Fortunately, these punishments rarely results in serious injury or illness — but they can. This is particularly a problem when the physical activity is administered to the point of exhaustion, when environmental conditions (i.e., heat and humidity) are extreme, when the athletes are inadequately hydrated, or when the athlete has an aggravating health condition such as exercise-induced asthma or cardiomyopathy (enlarged heart). Common sense should tell us that any time we force athletes to engage in physical activity that causes them to vomit, experience dizziness, or collapse due to exhaustion, we are getting dangerously close to creating a life-threatening situation. Far more likely are the less-severe, but totally preventable injuries that sometimes occur when physical activity is used as punishment such as cramping, pulled muscles, and injuries resulting from a lack of coordination that often accompanies physical and mental exhaustion.

Punishment Is Not Conditioning

It's essential that coaches understand there is a huge difference between requiring physical activity in an attempt to enhance stamina, cardiovascular fitness, or strength and imposing physical activity merely to punish an athlete for committing a performance or disciplinary error. Although bouts of conditioning and punishment may incorporate some of the same forms of exercise (running, push-ups, etc.) they are in no way related. Unfortunately, many coaches have come to use these terms interchangeably. Perhaps they just feel embarrassed to use the "P-word" even though that's' exactly what they're doing. These coaches euphemistically inform their athletes that their poor performance will result in "extra conditioning." Of course that's a lie. The extra physical activity will not be undertaken for the purpose of improving physical condition. It will be done for only one reason — to punish the players for making mistakes. Whenever coaches feel tempted to mix these terms, they need to think about the interesting case of former University of Michigan football coach, Rich Rodriguez. It's well-known that in 2010, the University of Michigan football program was sanctioned for violating NCAA rules. In fact, that was one of the reasons Rodriquez was fired a year later (Bacon 2012). What isn't as well-known is that some of the violations came about because Coach Rodriguez and his staff confused *punishment* they imposed on their athletes with *conditioning*. According to the official infractions report, the school was found guilty of violating NCAA legislation when "strength and conditioning coaches who monitored and conducted some voluntary athletically related activities occasionally used additional conditioning activities as a disciplinary measure when they required football student-athletes to participate in such activities as a punishment for missing class ... the institution's compliance staff advised the football coaching staff ... that such activities were impermissible, yet the strength and conditioning staff conducted them anyway" (NCAA 2010, 5–6). There is no doubt that coaches need to make sure athletes are in the proper physical condition to perform their sport at the highest level. This conditioning, however, should not be contingent on mistakes — performance or disciplinary. If additional conditioning is truly needed, it's needed regardless of the quality of the performance and should be realistically incorporated into the normal flow of practice. If additional conditioning is not needed — don't do it.

Punishment Is Not Discipline

Another important distinction that must be made is that between "punishment" and "discipline." To have discipline is to follow a prescribed set of rules governing conduct or activity. These rules can be imposed by others or from within. In fact, the highest form of discipline is self-discipline —

where an individual follows an inner set of rules governing his or her behavior. Some coaches take great pride in being a "strict disciplinarian." That's fine; discipline is an essential part of sport. The mistake these self-described disciplinarians often make, however, is to think that in order to instill discipline in their followers (turning them into "disciples") they need to develop a ruff, tuff, negative coaching style that relies on frequent doses of punishment.

Changing Behavior Without Punishment

As we mentioned at the beginning of the chapter, coaches must be able to eliminate, or at least reduce, the mistakes their athletes are making while, at the same time, inspiring them to continue executing the proper elements of their performances. All too many coaches think the only way these changes can be made is by adopting a negative coaching style that relies on yelling, screaming, ridiculing or punishing their athletes. Even though it requires a little more patience and thoughtfulness, there are several ways of correcting athlete errors without resorting to such harsh coaching methods. One thing we need to consider in order to effectively alter our athletes' behavior is whether the error committed was one of performance or discipline.

Correcting performance errors. Coaches are, of course, always trying to eliminate mistakes committed by their athletes during the execution of motor skills. Common errors such as mishandling or misplaying the ball, missing an open shot, or failing to block out an opponent will infuriate even the most patient of coaches. When this happens, it's only natural to lose control of our emotions and react with a less-than-positive form of error correction. But there is a far more effective way to correct performance errors such as these — the "feedback sandwich." This three-step process consists of putting our "meat of the message" between two genuine, supportive statements. The reason it works so well is that in most cases our athletes already feel pretty bad about their poor performance. They know they weren't supposed to strike out; miss the tackle; double-fault on their serve; or kick the ball out-of-bounds. If we then start screaming and yelling about the mistake they've just made, they will simply protect themselves by tuning us out. All those brilliant points we are about to make fall, quite literally, on deaf ears. By using a negative style of error correction we have rendered ourselves useless and irrelevant. A more effective way to correct performance errors is to use what is called a "feedback sandwich" and here's the three-step process:

(1) Give honest, positive reinforcement for something the athlete has done correctly. It may seem strange to begin error correction by focusing on what they've done right, but athletes need to know (and we need to remind ourselves) that most of their performance was perfectly fine. It's just that one or two small errors made the whole thing appear totally wrong. Acknowledging the positive aspects of their performance increases the likelihood that athletes will do those things correctly again next time. More importantly, when we begin with a positive statement, it makes athletes willing to listen to what we have to say. Once we have their attention, it's time to slip in the "meat" of our message.

(2) Give future-oriented instruction. Athletes don't typically need their coaches to tell them when they have made an error — that's usually painfully obvious. What they need above all else is a coach who can tell them how to avoid making the same mistake in the future. The key here is specifying one simple change they should make next time. We certainly don't want to overload them with several suggestions at once or focus too much attention on the error that was made. We often forget that there is nothing an athlete can do to change what's happened in the past. Life doesn't come with a rewind button. The more we rant and rave about a mistake and what "should have been done" the more it just frustrates the athlete and wastes time that would be better spent addressing the only thing that is in their power to doing something about — how they perform the *next* time.

(3) Give general encouragement and support. The final step in the feedback sandwich involves letting the athletes know we have confidence in their ability to perform the skill properly. If we can't honestly say that, we are setting them up for almost certain failure. If necessary, we should consider adjusting their responsibilities (and our expectations) so that we are only asking them to perform tasks they are truly capable of accomplishing.

Although the feedback sandwich is an excellent way to create a respectful and enjoyable athletic experience, don't think of it merely as a "feel-good" encounter. The real value is that it is the best way to correct mistakes and enhance learning. And isn't that what a coach's job is all about?

Correcting disciplinary errors. Mistakes in execution aren't the only kind of errors coaches need to eliminate. As frustrating as performance errors might be, our athletes will sometimes commit a type error that is more likely to arouse our feelings of anger and outrage more than frustration — errors that are purely disciplinary in nature. Athletes violating team rules, coming to practice late or without proper equipment, missing the team bus, or involving themselves in horseplay will understandably cause a coach's blood to boil. Again, our immediate reaction is to "come down hard" on anyone who engages in these behaviors that demonstrate disrespect for themselves and the entire team. Although it might make us feel better to scream or run them until they throw up, it won't be nearly as effective in eliminating the bad behavior as it will be to calmly remove something the athlete truly values. Here's an example: Let's assume your star player comes to practice 10 minutes late. A lot of coaches will have the athlete do something like run for 10 minutes as punishment. This might sound reasonable enough but it's really not all that effective. First, as we've discussed, it relies on physical activity as punishment. Second, it's a waste of time — especially if the running takes place during practice when the athlete and his or her teammates should be developing skills. Finally, it's not that meaningful. Sure, the offending athlete may not enjoy running but in 10 minutes it's over and done with. Here's a better way to make sure the unwanted behavior is never repeated: When the player arrives 10 minutes late, calmly and respectfully indicate that he or she won't be playing for the first 10 minute of the next game — regardless of its importance. That's it. The rules have been enforced, there's not been a lot of negativity and the athletes can begin practicing immediately. The player who was late will also spend almost every waking minute until game-time thinking about what he or she has done. Unlike simply running the player for 10 minutes, the removal of something very precious — in this case playing time but it could be anything — will assure that you never have to deal with this problem again.

Instilling team discipline by taking away things our athletes want. At first glance, it may appear that by taking away playing time we are punishing the athlete for misbehavior. Not really. Remember, punishment is defined as "the infliction of pain or discomfort upon a subject for failure to conform to a predetermined course of action" (Chaplin 1975, 434). Here we are not "inflicting" (giving) pain of discomfort. Instead we are merely removing something they greatly value and once had. This may seem like a minor distinction but, when used to eliminate unwanted disciplinary errors, it doesn't carry nearly as many of the negatives typically associated with punishment (e.g., there is no misuse of physical activity, no wasted practice time, etc.). Many coaches (not to mention parents and fans) are unwilling to take away playing time to extinguish inappropriate behavior. This reluctance generally stems from two somewhat related concerns: (1) the real possibility that restricting an athlete's playing time might negatively impact the team performance, and (2) other members of the team who did not behave improperly will unfairly suffer from such a loss. The first concern — we might lose — is a definite possibility but coaches can be so preoccupied with winning at all costs that they fail to take an opportunity to teach the entire team the valuable lifelong lesson that all behaviors have consequences. The second concern is also not legitimate if we consider that the very definition of a "team" means that all our behaviors — for better or worse — impact everyone else on our team. This is most easily seen in performance errors. When one team member is out of position or misplays the ball in such a way that the team loses *everyone* on the team — even those who did not commit an error — suffers the loss. That's what being part of a *team* means.

The quote at the beginning of this chapter demonstrated that being a successful and respected coach — even in the rough, tough, "manly" game of professional football — does not mean we have to resort to negative tactics to correct or motivate our athletes. As Coach Dungy let his teams know right from the beginning, "I don't yell a lot... When I get mad I usually talk at the same volume I'm talking now. And when I get really mad — I whisper. So if my voice at this level won't get your attention, and you believe you need someone to yell at you to correct you or motivate you, then we'll probably need to find you another team to play for so you can play your best" (Dungy 2007, 105).

"The More You 'Fire Up' Your Athletes, the Better They'll Perform"

I don't believe in team motivation. I believe in getting a team prepared so it knows it will have the necessary confidence when it steps on a field and is prepared to play a good game.

— Coach Tom Landry[1]

Isn't it odd that we've somehow arrived at the point where coaches feel the need to resort to all sorts of pre-game antics to bring out the best performances in their athletes? Perhaps we are influenced by reading grotesque stories like that involving former Mississippi State football coach Jackie Sherrill who, prior to the 1992 season opener against the University of Texas, "emotionally prepared" his team for their eventual 28–10 upset over the nationally ranked Longhorns by ordering the castration of a bull on his team's practice field (Merron 2003). Or maybe the notion comes from hearing of bizarre coaching techniques such as that reported in *The Washington Post* describing how Aron Bright, an Indiana high school wrestling coach, explained to his school board that the reason he had bitten the head off a live sparrow was to "inspire his team" (McCombs, 2002). Now maybe I'm missing something, but the last time I checked, football players are rarely called on to castrate bulls on opening day and athletes — even high school wrestlers — don't show tremendous improvement after receiving instruction in the finer points of biting the heads off little birds.

These particularly gory and sensational cases aside, every day thousands of coaches give thousands of pep talks to thousands of athletes — all in the hope of somehow magically inspiring them to perform otherwise unattainable feats of strength, stamina, speed, and determination. But where do coaches come up with the idea that motivating their athletes with "fire and brimstone" tirades is appropriate — or that it even works? Like most of our coaching behavior, we learn it from one another.

Apparently most of us weren't listening when legendary coaches like Tom Landry were offering their opinions of motivational speeches such as the one we used at the beginning of this chapter: "I don't believe in team motivation. I believe in getting a team prepared so it knows it will have the necessary confidence when it steps on a field and is prepared to play a good game." We were far more likely to have been listening to — and believing in — the ubiquitous rah-rah speeches of "master motivators" such as former Notre Dame football coach Knute Rockne. After all, how many times have we been exposed to the emotional movie portrayal of his "win one for the Gipper" halftime speech delivered during the 1928 Army-Notre Dame game or his rousing "we're going inside 'em and outside 'em" speech that is played before every nationally televised Notre Dame football game? Interestingly enough, however, when it came to pep-talks, it seems that even the legendary Knute Rockne wasn't really what most of us would consider a true "Knute Rockne-type" coach.

Consider the following excerpt from an obscure letter Rockne wrote to the "Father of Sport Psychology," Coleman Griffith, at the end of the 1924 season:

> I do think our team plays good football because they like to play and I do not make any effort to key them up, except on rare, exceptional occasions... I try to make our boys take the game less seriously than, I presume, some others do, and we try to make the spirit of the game one of exhilaration and we never allow hatred to enter into it, no matter whom we are playing [Rockne 1924].

Can it be? Did Knute Rockne, the very personification of the fiery pep-talk himself, just say he *rarely* tried to "key up" his players before a game; did his best to get them to take the game *less* seriously than most other coaches; and made a sense of sheer exhilaration — *not hatred* — the cornerstone of this violent game? To counter any claim that "Rock" may have been merely telling Professor Griffith what he thought the famous psychologist wanted to hear, we can confirm the fact that the "real" Rockne rarely used pep-talks to motivate his athletes. One of his players — three-time letter winner and two-time All-American, Paul Castner, pointed out that "[Rockne] himself said that one talk a year was enough and I don't believe that he gave many of the emotion-packed talks that the myth has him giving every game" [Sperber 1993, 280].

Despite the serious reservations both Landry and Rockne — the two all-time giants of coaching — had about the value of stirring up excessive emotions prior to a competition, most of us are more inclined to pattern ourselves after our personal mentors who were absolutely convinced of the positive impact a rousing pregame or halftime pep-talk can have on performance. Regardless of whether we follow the lead of Landry and Rockne or our own coaches, it's important to understand what science can tell us about the relationship between the emotional arousal our athletes experience and the way they perform. Although several scientific theories have been set forth to explain how various levels of excitement affects our athletes' performance, three have particular relevance to the way we coach. Let's dispense with their formal scientific labels and more descriptively refer to them as the "Adrenaline Rush" theory, the "Goldilocks" theory, and the "What You Think is What You Get" theory.[2]

The "Adrenaline Rush" Theory

Coaches are obviously in the "result business"—getting their athletes to perform at the highest level possible. In this quest for ultimate performance coaches are sometimes tempted to resort to pretty much any trick, technique, or tear-jerker they think might have a chance of jacking up their players' performances. Although it's a bit unusual to run across coaches who actually believe they have to tear the testicles off a bull or chew the heads off small animals to fire up their team, anyone who has spent any time whatsoever in a locker room — or in a movie theater — has probably seen a coach preparing a team in accordance with this theory.

Arousal and performance according to the "Adrenaline Rush" theory. As the name implies, coaches who feel the need to pump up the adrenaline surging through the veins of their athletes prior to competition adhere to the widely-accepted belief that there's a straight-line relationship between athletes' excitement levels and their performance. Simply put, the more athletes are emotionally charged up, the better they'll perform (Spence and Spence 1966). Figure 10.1 shows a picture of the straight forward connection these coaches — and many of their athletes — assume exists between emotion and performance. The common wisdom underlying most coaches' unwavering acceptance of the "Adrenaline Rush" theory goes something like this: When athletes are feeling very low levels of emotional or physical arousal (excitement, activation, energy, etc.) they are so uninterested and uninvolved in what they're doing that their performance is very poor (i.e., low arousal equals poor performance). As we might expect, getting the athletes a bit more excited, energized, and enthused about the task at hand will result in a noticeable improvement in the quality of their performance (i.e., moderate

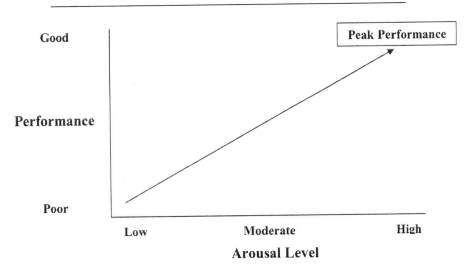

Figure 10.1: Proposed Relationship Between Emotional Arousal and Performance According to the "Adrenaline Rush" Theory.

arousal equals moderate performance). Finally, as the athletes are increasingly pumped up to the point where they are experiencing enormous amounts of emotional and physical excitement, they will exhibit the highest levels of performance of which they are capable (i.e., high arousal equals peak performance).

The enduring regard coaches have for the "Adrenaline Rush" theory is probably due, in part, to its overall simplicity and the mere fact that it seems to make a lot of sense to a lot of people. After all, who hasn't heard the remarkable tales of mothers lifting automobiles off their trapped infants as a result of an emotionally-induced adrenaline rush? Doesn't it only seem logical that this same kind of superhuman physical exertion is something that coaches could put to great use in enhancing athletic performance? The sad news is, just because coaches tend to find the idea of "higher arousal means better performance" intuitively appealing, it does not necessarily mean it truly reflects the way emotion influences athletic performance — and for the most part it doesn't.

Coaching implications. Unfortunately, a young mother using a momentary rush of adrenaline to rescue her baby has little in common with the basic elements of a successful athletic performance. First of all, her mission is of very short duration — probably a couple of seconds at most. Athletes, on the other hand, are often required to sustain a high performance level for minutes or even hours at a time. Adrenaline alone doesn't stay in the system long enough to keep our athletes functioning at their peak for any extended period of time. Secondly, lifting a car off a child is a pretty clear cut event. There isn't a lot of thoughtful analysis involved. You either pick the car up, or you don't — that's it. Compare this to a successful athletic performance that usually requires properly focused attention to detail, recognition of complex patterns and cues, retrieval of strategies, quick and precise decision-making, perfect execution and integration of both gross and fine motor skills, and a constant reevaluation of an ever-changing environment (Landers and Arent 2010). This all leads to exactly what Coach John Wooden said regarding excessive emotion, "Unless you're attempting to run through a brick wall, excessive emotion is counterproductive" (Wooden 1997, 125). Unless they're coaching weightlifting or some other short duration, explosive, closed-environment sport, most coaches have probably found, like Coach Wooden, that "Mistakes occur when your thinking is tainted by excessive emotion" (Wooden 1997, 124). Which brings us to our discussion of the "Goldilocks" theory.

The "Goldilocks" Theory

We all remember the children's story of "*Goldilocks and the Three Bears*" and how a tired and hungry little girl named Goldilocks enters the home of the three Bears (Papa, Momma, and Baby) while they're taking a walk to let their breakfast porridge cool off. While they're gone, Goldilocks tastes their breakfast, and tries out their sitting chairs and beds. She finds, in turn, that Papa Bear's porridge is far too hot, his chair far too high, and his bed far too hard. She's similarly dissatisfied with Momma Bear's possessions. Her porridge is too cold, her chair too wide, and her bed too soft. However, she discovers, to her pleasure, Baby Bear's breakfast is "just right" (and she ate it all up), his chair is "just right" (and she sat on it so hard she broke it), and yes, even his bed is "just right" (and that's where she was when the Bears returned home).

Arousal and performance according to the "Goldilocks" theory. So what does a fairy tale have to do with the relationship between emotional arousal and athletic performance? Plenty — because it's actually a story of individual differences, discovering what works best for each person, and moderation. By looking at Figure 10.2 we can see that according to the "Goldilocks" theory, too little arousal is associated with a very poor athletic performance — for basically the same reasons as we discussed in the Adrenaline Rush theory. Also, just as we saw in the Adrenaline Rush theory, as athletes become more aroused — to a relatively moderate level — their performance steadily improves. But it's at this point that the Goldilocks theory radically departs from Adrenaline Rush theory. Recall that in Adrenaline Rush theory, the more and more aroused an athlete gets, the better and better the performance. So the main job of a coach is to fire up every athlete to the highest level of emotional arousal possible — thereby assuring their best performance. However, just the opposite is predicted in the Goldilocks theory. According to this theory, when arousal levels become too high, there is a dramatic drop off in performance. Just like Goldilocks in the children's story, our athletes can experience "too little" emotional arousal (and a poor performance), "too much" emotional arousal (and a poor performance) or, of course, the exact amount of emotional arousal that is "just right" for peak athletic performance given their individual personality, their experiences, and the requirements of their sport (Landers and Arent 2010).

Coaching implications. You might think coaches would be eager to accept the "Goldilocks" explanation of the way emotional arousal impacts athletic performance. After all, it has received far more scientific support than the alternative "Adrenaline Rush" theory (Cox 2012) and every coach has witnessed athletes turning in a poor performance because they were either under- or over-aroused. But putting this nifty little theory into prac-

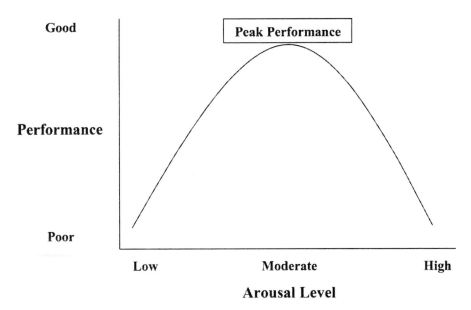

Figure 10.2: Proposed Relationship Between Emotional Arousal and Performance According to the "Goldilocks" Theory.

tice is a lot more complicated than simply gathering the team around us and giving them one of our prepackaged "one size fits all" inspirational speeches. That's because every one of our athletes is a unique person, performing in a unique situation, and each, therefore, requires a unique message that is specifically tailored to his or her motivational needs.

First, there are the handful of athletes who are not excited enough to perform at their highest levels. They'll perform best if they're "jacked-up" a bit and our traditional pep talk might be just the thing they need. But there are also the athletes who are already feeling too excited or nervous to perform well. The last thing in the world these poor souls need is a pep talk — but we usually give them one anyway. Finally, there are at least a few athletes who have emotionally prepared themselves "just right" and are ready to perform at their highest level. The best thing we could do for these athletes is simply leave them alone — but we usually don't.

To gain the full benefit of this theory coaches have to get to know each of their athletes personally and understand whether a particular person is feeling "too much," "too little," or "just the right" amount of arousal. Then,

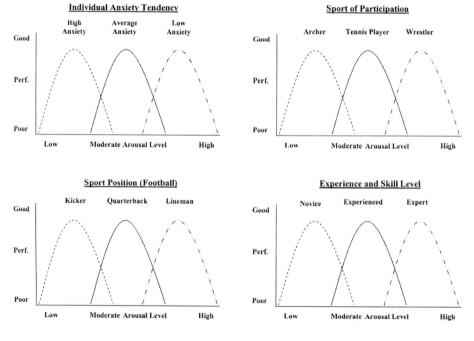

Figure 10.3: Individual Athlete Arousal Requirements for Peak Performance According to Personal Anxiety Level, Sport of Participation, Sport Position, and Sport Experience and Skill Level.

based on the individual needs of the athlete, the coach has to provide a different motivational message to each and every member of the team. As you can imagine, this is no easy task. The four illustrations in Figure 10.3 give us a sense of just how difficult it is for a coach to make sure every athlete on a team has the precise amount of emotional arousal he or she needs to turn in a peak performance. Just some of the factors that need to be considered are the athlete's individual predisposition toward becoming overly anxious, the sport involved, the position played within the sport, and the athlete's overall skill level. Only then does the coach have a chance of pumping up athletes who need to be pumped up — while calming down those who need to be calmed down.

Given the practical limitations involved in finding and addressing every athlete's ideal emotional need, it's no wonder that coaches — even those who disagree with the "one size fits all" approach of the Adrenaline Rush theory — shy away from complete implementation of the Goldilocks theory. But fortunately there is an even better alternative.

Learning a Valuable Lesson from the Athletes at the Olympic Training Center

In the summer of 1985 my colleagues at Michigan State University and I were invited to start a psychological skills training program for the athletes attending USA Hockey Development Camps at the U.S. Olympic Training Center in Colorado Springs. Athletes attending these camps were generally considered among the top teenage hockey players in the country and were, in fact, being groomed to play on various national and elite teams including the biggest of them all — the U.S. Olympic Hockey Team (several did ultimately make the Olympic team and a number of others went on to have successful NHL careers).

Because of the important role emotional preparation plays in hockey performance, we conducted a number of sessions where we discussed the need for elite athletes to control their emotional arousal in order to play their best. During these sessions we spent most of our time focusing on the Goldilocks theory because it was (and generally still is) the most widely accepted theory as to how emotions impact athletic performance. In fact, we, as the so-called "experts" in the field of sport psychology, were so convinced that "Goldilocks" was such a great way to prepare for athletic competition, we talked about little else. At one point we were so confident that we had made such a strong case for "Goldilocks" that we asked several players to come to the chalkboard and draw the relationship they personally thought best represented the way their emotions affected their hockey performance. What a disaster. We were convinced that most, if not all of them, would draw some sort of curved line indicating that both too little — and too much — arousal hurt their performance. Unfortunately, nearly every player who went to the board drew something more like Figure 10.4.

Now we had a real problem. All the scientific literature dismissed the "Adrenaline Rush" theory as a plausible explanation for how arousal affects performance and yet many of the best young hockey players in the country had publicly stated that they were absolutely convinced that when they were totally "pumped" they played better. We were so flustered by this unexpected finding that we dismissed it as players buying into a scientifically debunked myth simply because their coaches and parents had "brainwashed" them over the years into believing it was true. We were wrong — and we knew it — we just didn't have a better explanation. That is, until we got back to our library at the University. Motivated by our frustrations at the Olympic Training Center, we spent the next couple months trying to figure out how we could have been so wrong. Almost everything we had read up to that point had indicated that there was very little reason to think the "Adrenaline Rush" theory had anything to do with the way athletes performed. But the players themselves — and most of their elite-

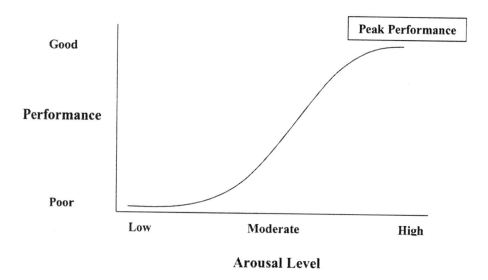

Figure 10.4: Relationship Between Arousal and Performance as Perceived by Elite Hockey Players.

level coaches — weren't having any of it. Finally, we stumbled on the missing piece of the puzzle.

Almost immediately on our return from the Olympic Training Center, we noticed two groundbreaking articles had just been published in the sport science literature (Apter 1984; Kerr 1985). These two articles pieced together bits of the "Adrenaline Rush" theory with pieces of the "Goldilocks" theory and added a completely new element — the athletes' feelings about the arousal they're experiencing — and, in the process, laid out a totally new theory regarding the way emotional arousal impacts athletic performance. Better yet, this new way of thinking provided us with a perfect explanation for what the hockey players were trying to tell us was an easy way their coaches could get the best performance from every one of their athletes — by simply making sure the game always remains fun and never perceived as a threat.

The "What You Think Is What You'll Get" Theory

The Adrenaline Rush and Goldilocks theories are only concerned with one thing — how the total amount of emotional arousal affects performance. Both theories basically suggest that if we had a way of hooking our athletes up to some sort of "arousal meter" we could accurately predict how they would perform. The "What You Think Is What You'll Get" theory is likewise keenly interested in the overall amount of arousal our athletes are experiencing. It, however, makes one very important distinction that the other two theories overlook — not all emotional activation is equal. Sometimes the high emotions we experience make us feel exhilarated and excited; other times they make us feel nervous and scared.

Arousal and performance according to the "What You Think Is What You'll Get" theory. We all know that approaching a task with a sense of positive exhilaration, excitement, and energy will generally result in a high quality performance (causing even more excitement and energy). That's true in athletics, academics, our careers, our interpersonal relationships, and pretty much everything else we do. But of course the opposite is also true. Being emotionally overwhelmed with negative feelings of anxiety, apprehension, and angst will almost always result in a disastrous performance (causing additional anxiety and apprehension). If we approach a task thinking we're going to have fun and perform well, we probably will. On the other hand, if we start thinking about everything that could go wrong, it's a pretty safe bet that a lot of it will. In other words, "What You Think Is What You'll Get."

So let's put all the pieces of the "What You Think Is What You'll Get" theory together by examining Figure 10.5. Athletes who look forward to an event as a positive, exciting opportunity to have fun, display their skills, and successfully meet a challenge (the solid line in Figure 10.5) will likely feel somewhat dissatisfied and bored when they are not emotionally aroused (imagine an elite tennis pro competing against an unskilled novice). As their emotional arousal increases, however, they begin to feel more and more energized and exhilarated — and their performance improves.

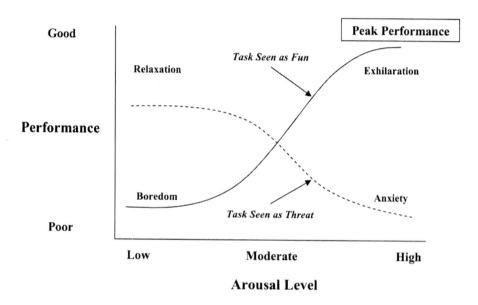

Figure 10.5: Proposed Relationship Between Emotional Arousal and Performance According to the "What You Think is What You'll Get" Theory.

The exact opposite occurs when athletes view the upcoming task as a physical or psychological threat, a chance to embarrass themselves, or a chance to disappoint others (the dotted line in Figure 10.5). As long as they are not highly aroused, they feel somewhat relaxed. Their performance is acceptable — but not great. As their arousal increases, however, they become more and more anxious and worried about their performance which, as we would expect, causes their performance to deteriorate.

Notice that the solid line in Figure 10.5 is virtually identical to the lines our elite hockey players at the Olympic Training Center drew when asked how arousal affects their performance (Figure 10.4). After all, these guys were some of the best hockey players in the world. There's nothing they loved more than playing hockey — they were very good at it and they knew it. They approached every competition with positive energy and enthusiasm because to them, it was just another opportunity to have fun, do what they loved best, and demonstrate their considerable talents. Other, less confident, hockey players might have been more inclined to fret about not performing well in an important game or high-level tryout and experience feelings more like those depicted with the dotted line.

Another related characteristic that elite athletes tend to share is that the "best of the best" in nearly every sport seem to take their game to the next level when they're under the most pressure. It seems that they love nothing more than to be in a "sudden-death" overtime game. Consider the performances of Derek Jeter, Michael Jordan, Tiger Woods, Mariano Rivera, Larry Bird, Magic Johnson, and Joe Montana when they were in their prime. Aside from being terrific athletes, each had that "something extra" that allowed them to perform their best when the pressure was almost unbearable — even for the spectators. With teammates and opponents wilting under the pressure they would take over when the game was on the line. Each of these great athletes wanted to take the last shot, have the ball hit to him, come in with the bases loaded, or call their own number when it's 4th and 15. That doesn't mean they were always successful but they viewed every challenge as an amazing opportunity rather than a chance to fail. As a result, they not only survived — but thrived — on emotional arousal that would make the rest of us crumble.

Coaching implications. The interesting thing about the "What You Think Is What You'll Get" theory is that the way an athlete perceives the situation can flip-flop on a moment's notice. Whether an upcoming performance is seen as an incredible opportunity or an impending disaster is often the result of intentional and unintentional signals sent by the coaching staff. Even our well-intentioned pre-game reminders such as "This is the most important game you'll ever play" or "Today, failure is not an option" or "Everybody's counting on us today" often have the affect of replacing our athletes' positive feelings of enjoyment, exhilaration, and energy with nagging thoughts of distress, disappointment, and doubt.

The message is clear. If we allow our athletes to focus on the possibility of failure, they'll end up failing. If, on the other hand, we constantly emphasize the fun and excitement of competition, the exhilaration they feel will increase the chances they'll perform at their highest level possible.

This is a good time to reconsider the Knute Rockne quote we introduced earlier. At that time it may not have made much sense but with what we now know, it's easy to see that at least some of Rockne's success was probably due to his use of coaching methods that totally conformed to the "What You Think is What You'll Get" theory. Here again, were his major points:

- "Our team plays good football because they like to play"
- "I do not make any effort to key them up"
- "I try to make our boys take the game less seriously than, I presume, some others do"
- "We try to make the spirit of the game one of exhilaration"

Notice that each of Rockne's points is designed to emphasize fun, enjoyment, and exhilaration while downplaying the gravity of the situation.

Replacing Pep Talks with "Prep" Talks

Although our well-intentioned pep talks often do more harm than good, we still need to make sure our athletes are prepared to perform at their best. So instead of our typical pep talk, here's what we should be doing before the big game:

Make sure everybody's having fun. Your athletes won't be worried about their performance if they're having fun. You and your entire staff need to downplay the importance of winning and emphasize effort, energy, and enjoyment — the building blocks of winning.

Remind all athletes of the progress they've made. This is a great time to remind the players of everything they've practiced and how much they've accomplished. Athletes of any age often don't realize how much progress they've made and how much their hard work has paid off.

Focus on specific goals and strategies. Helping everyone set performance goals will get them to think about the things they can control. By focusing their attention on specific parts of their performance, we can keep our athletes from being overwhelmed by the excitement of the game.

By making sure our athletes are always having fun, improving their skills, and focusing on their performance rather than the outcomes of their performance we can increase the chances that they will enter what many people call the "flow experience" associated with peak performance (Csikszentmihalyi 1990; Jackson and Csikszentmihalyi 1999). We'll discuss "flow" in more detail in the Myth No. 11 chapter but, for the moment, it's sufficient to say that in the flow experience, performance improves because we are "neither bored nor threatened, we feel in control of ourselves and our environment" (Martens 2012, 108).

We started our discussion of pep-talks with what many coaches might think to be an absurd quote from Coach Tom Landry who guided the Dallas Cowboys to an NFL record 20 consecutive winning seasons, 13 Divisional championships, five NFC titles, and to Super Bowl victories: "I don't believe in team motivation. I believe in getting a team prepared so it knows it will have the necessary confidence when it steps on a field and is prepared to play a good game." This quote makes it perfectly clear that Coach Landry understood that his players were far more likely to play up to their capabilities if he replaced pep talks with "prep talks" and that we can't make up for poor preparation with a rousing pep talk just moments before the big game. If we've prepared our athletes properly, they won't need one — if we haven't, it's too late to worry about that now.

"Trophies, Medals, Ribbons, and Money Are Good Ways to Motivate Athletes"

Conventional carrots include money, of course, as well as advancement, awards ... or a more prominent role on the team or in the organization. Carrots come in many forms. However, I believe the strongest and most meaningful motivators are not necessarily the materialistic, but the intangible.

— Coach John Wooden[1]

Many of us believe that giving external rewards as "incentives" is an excellent way to increase our athletes' motivation to participate and persevere in sports. Unfortunately, the way we allocate these rewards often results in our unknowingly doing more to diminish our players' desire than enhance it. Because how we reward, when we reward, and why we reward our athletes can either increase or decrease their intrinsic motivation, it's essential that we understand the finer points of how giving external rewards impacts internal motivation.

Results from more than 800 research papers written over the past 40 years (Vallerand 1997) suggest that if we reward our athletes (or anyone else for that matter) with external, tangible inducements for doing something they already find pleasurable — such as participating in sports — they often become so caught up in collecting the rewards we're offering they forget about the very things that attracted them to sports in the first place — having fun and becoming competent at an activity they enjoy. Once our external rewards are removed (and all external rewards given for participating in sports will eventually be removed) so is their main reason to continue playing (Deci, Ryan, and Koestner 2001; Kohn 1993; Lepper and Henderlong 2000).

As we'll see, however, enhancing our athletes' internal desire to participate in sports is far more complicated than vowing to "just say no" to all forms of external rewards. When used in a limited and thoughtful manner, external rewards can be extremely powerful motivational tools (Cameron and Pierce 1994). Unfortunately, the down side is that like all powerful tools, when used indiscriminately or inappropriately, they can sometimes cause more harm than good.

Although there are ways we can provide rewards to our athletes that will actually enhance their motivation levels, a lifetime of witnessing the negative affects external rewards often have on athletes' intrinsic motivation led Coach Wooden to arrive at the conclusion we set forth as an introduction to this chapter, "Carrots come in many forms. However, I believe the strongest and most meaningful motivators are not necessarily the materialistic, but the intangible" (Wooden and Jamison 2010, 167–8). And we'll take the Coach's astute observations even further.

Why We Do the Things We Do

One of the most important lessons we all learn as children is that there are certain things in this world we must do in order to get the rewards, or avoid the punishments, of others. We *must* go to school; we *must* clean our room; we *must* share our toys; we *must* eat our peas. When we fail to do these things, we soon discover that other people either stop giving us the things we want (e.g., our allowance, the keys to the car, their love and approval, etc.) or they purposefully give us what we don't want (e.g., a spanking, a stern lecture, ridicule and disrespect, etc.). By acting, and then observing the positive and negative consequences our behaviors elicit from others, we quickly come to realize that doing what other people want us to do is sometimes a good way to get them to give us what we value while avoiding the things we would rather not have (Lepper, Greene, and Nisbett 1973).

Of course not everything we do is motivated by what we think others will give us in return for our actions. When we choose to take a long walk on the beach, read a good book, listen to our favorite music, or relax with a leisurely soak in the tub, we are not particularly concerned with whether or not other people will approve of what we're doing. We engage in these activities solely for our own personal enjoyment. And so it is — or at least should be — with sports.

There are two motivations in sports, which is yours? A perfect depiction of internal motivations in sports can be seen in a series of television commercials that were part of a national advertising campaign put together a few years ago by the New Balance athletic shoe company (PR Newswire Association 2005). One of these 30-second spots shows clips of runners of nearly every age, gender, race, ethnicity, and physical condition (New Balance 2005a). As they run, several words or phrases appear next to them... *"Zero ... Nothing ... Not a Cent ... Zilch ... Nada."* A young runner then looks directly into the camera, smiles, and says, *"I've made no money running."* And the tag line appears on the screen... "For Love or Money?"

Another ad in the campaign shows a number of young, but obviously less-than-elite, long distance runners gutting it out as they approach the finish line (New Balance 2005b). All the while a background voice says, "No agents are waiting" ... "No reporters are waiting" ... "No T.V. cameras" ... "No endorsement deals" ... "No victory parades" ..."There are two motivations in sports. Which is yours?"Again, the tag line appears on the screen... "For Love or Money?"

Last, but certainly far from least, is the ad the shoe company made just for us — the coaches (New Balance 2005c). Several of our peers, from various sports, are seen going about some of the routine tasks with which we have all become familiar — cleaning and stacking equipment, taping ankles, scribbling instructions on a whiteboard, counseling athletes, observing practice, and arranging hurdles on a track. As we watch, one coach speaks for most of us when he says, "Never interviewed on SportsCenter" ... "Never jumped to a bigger school" ... "Never broke a contract" ... "Never threw a chair" ... "Never, never forgot it was a game" ... "Never forgot they are kids" ... "There are two motivations in sports. Which is yours?" On the screen we again see the now-familiar tag line that perfectly illustrates the difference between internal and external motivations for participating in sports... "For Love or Money?"

Do we win "Silver" or lose "Gold"? It's particularly interesting to contrast the way the New Balance ads emphasize the intrinsic, personal satisfaction that can be achieved through sports with the "in-your-face" combative approach espoused by the most dominant player in the athletic apparel industry — Nike. Although the ubiquitous "swoosh" and "Just Do It" slogan can be seen as merely advocating a focused pursuit of personal excellence, it is also possible that a far less generous interpretation can be offered. By imploring all of us to "Just Do It," Nike is perpetuating the proposition that the external rewards that come from winning (gold medals, endorsement contracts, public adulation, etc.) are the things that drive us to compete. For example, it's pretty hard to misinterpret the less-than-admirable "win at all costs" messages contained in Nike's controversial "Search and Destroy" advertisements unveiled during the Centennial Olympic Games in 1996

(McCarthy 2003). One of the huge black-and-white billboards the company strategically situated in the host city of Atlanta left little doubt as to which of the "two motivations in sport" was foremost in the minds of the Nike-sponsored athletes, as they somberly put their competitors on notice, *"I'm not here to trade pins."* As insulting to the spirit of sportsmanship as such trash-talking commercials may be, perhaps even more disrespectful to the athletes themselves, were Nike's direct attacks on the Olympic Creed which states, "The most important thing in the Olympic Games is not to win but to take part.... The essential thing is not to have conquered but to have fought well."[2] Of course Nike is not about to have any part of such sentimental claptrap. To them, athletics is about winning and losing. The company's disdain for the Olympic Creed was pretty obvious when they put up another larger-than-life poster at the Games that snarled, *"If I say I'm just thrilled to compete, blame my interpreter."* Finally, even Nike crossed the line. They decided that right in the middle of the Olympics, it was perfectly appropriate to air a 30-second television ad which concluded with the assertion, *"You don't win Silver; you lose Gold."* Keep in mind this commercial was viewed by millions of people who had just witnessed top athletes pitting themselves against the toughest competition in the world. Just to participate, they had pushed themselves through thousands of hours of practice, pain, and politics. Of the 11,000 or so Olympians in Atlanta, a select few had achieved something almost no other human being will ever experience — the thrill and satisfaction of winning of an Olympic Medal. Now, in the midst of their well-deserved celebration, a billion dollar, mega-corporation had the audacity to tarnish their accomplishment by dismissively announcing to the entire world... *"You don't win the Silver, you lose Gold"* (Elliott 1996). Public reaction to the shoe company's direct attack on the Olympic ideal was swift and overwhelmingly critical. For example, the demeaning ads prompted *USA Today* columnist Erik Brady to publish a scathing commentary in which he posed the rhetorical question, "And what of the bronze? The ad doesn't say, but the tone suggests something along the lines of shooting the laggards in the back" (Brady 1996). As might be expected, Olympic silver medalists took particular offense to a bunch of shoe salesmen ridiculing them for "losing the Gold" medal. Amy White, who as a fifteen-year-old, won the 1984 Olympic silver medal in the women's 200-meter backstroke, voiced the outrage felt by many Olympic medalists when she called the sneaker company's ads a "slap in the face" to anyone who hadn't won a gold medal (McCarthy 2003). Even the *Calvin and Hobbes* cartoon below pokes fun of the "win-at-all-costs" attitude that huge companies like Nike are instilling in the minds of many of our athletes (and coaches).

Figure 11.1: "Winning is Everything" Attitude Fostered by Commercials Targeting Athletes and Fans. (CALVIN AND HOBBES ©1993 Watterson. Dist. By UNIVERSAL UCLICK. Reprinted with permission. All rights reserved.)

So the distinction between internal and external rewards in sport is pretty much as simple as that. As depicted in the Nike and New Balance sneaker ads, we (and our athletes) are sometimes driven to behave in a certain way because of how we think others will react toward us and other times because we merely find it enjoyable. It would be an oversimplification, however, to think that everything we, or our athletes, do is motivated by *either* intrinsic *or* extrinsic rewards. In the real world, the way we act is often the result of a complicated mix of what we enjoy doing *and* how we think others will react. But this is also where things get a bit tricky for coaches and parents.

Effect of External Rewards on Internal Motivations

We all know that it's sometime necessary to "incentivize" people to perform tasks for which there is little or no intrinsic value. Rare is the child (or adult for that matter) who looks forward to sweeping the driveway or scrubbing out the toilet because of the sheer pleasure they will receive from performing the task. If they do these chores at all, it's usually only after they are made to understand that in order to satisfy other people (who control rewards and punishments) it's sometimes necessary to do things even if they don't find them inherently pleasurable. Fortunately, when it comes to sports, we usually don't have to bribe people to participate.

Physical activity as an end in itself. Although kids quickly learn the value of meeting other peoples' expectations, they all come "hard-wired" to move their bodies around in all kinds of ways. It's an essential first step in exploring and controlling their environment. Like little "Energizer Bunnies," they spend their days running, hopping, skipping, jumping, spinning, dancing, flopping, rolling, and twisting — just for the fun of it. At least initially, their purpose isn't necessarily to please others; it's to experience the inner joy they get from the movement itself. Sports are also something kids often do for fun. A national survey of over 8,000 boys and girls participating in agency- and school-sponsored sports found that the three main reasons kids choose to be part of a sport team is to have fun, to be with their friends, and learn new skills (Ewing and Seefeldt 2002). Unfortunately, in our well-intentioned efforts to motivate our athletes to the highest levels possible, we sometimes introduce powerful external rewards in the hope of providing "motivational supplements" to the inherent enjoyment the athletes are experiencing. We mistakenly think that although naturally occurring pleasures (such as having fun with friends) may be a sufficient reason for our athletes to participate in sports, we can enhance their motivation levels further by giving "super" rewards like trophies, excessive attention and adulation, or a college scholarship. If we don't pay close attention to the way we give these external rewards, we may end up replacing our athletes' original reasons for playing. It's possible, for example, that instead of playing primarily "to have fun," our athletes will begin playing to get another trophy; instead of playing "to be with their friends" they may begin playing to continue experiencing the extra attention and adulation they get from family, friends, and coaches; instead of playing "to learn new skills" they begin playing in the hope of being offered a college scholarship. In each of these instances, notice how perfectly legitimate internal rewards can be replaced by the rewards others are willing to give.

The parable of the old man, the noisy kids, and turning play into work. Mark Twain once said that "Work and play are words used to describe the same thing under differing conditions." In the second chapter of *The Adventures of Tom Sawyer*, he spells out precisely what those two "differing conditions" are: "Work consists of whatever a body is obliged to do, and Play consists of whatever a body is not obliged to do" (Twain 1876, 32). An example of the way an activity can be transformed from play into work merely by replacing internal rewards with external rewards is seen in a Twain-like story[3] that originally appeared in a side piece accompanying an article entitled "Intrinsic Motivation: How to turn Play into Work" in the 1974 issue of *Psychology Today* (Greene and Lepper 1974):

> He lived alone on a street where boys played noisily every afternoon. One day the din became too much and he called the boys into his house. He told them he liked to listen to them play, but his hearing was failing and he could no longer hear their games. He asked them to come around each day and play noisily in front of his house. If they did, he would give them each a quarter. The youngsters raced

back the following day and made a tremendous racket in front of the house. The old man paid them, and asked them to return the next day. Again they made noise and again the old man paid them for it. But this time he gave each boy only 20 cents, explaining that he was running out of money. On the following day, they got only 15 cents each. Furthermore, the old man told them he would have to reduce the fee to five cents on the fourth day. The boys became angry and told the old man they would not be back. It was not worth the effort, they said, to make noise for only five cents a day [Casady 1974, 52].

At first glance it might be hard to see how this far-fetched story has anything to do with our athletes' motivation. But now think back to all the times we've heard about professional athletes threatening to sit out an entire season because they've been asked to take a salary cut — or even forego a huge salary increase. Just a few years earlier, these millionaire athletes were perfectly content spending the entire day playing the game they loved for its own sake. But they no longer come to the ballpark to experience the joy their sport once provided. Instead, they show up because they are, as Twain would say, "obliged" to do so by a written legal contract requiring them to *work* in order to receive huge external rewards in return. Just like the annoying kids in the story, athletes who exchange the internal rewards of *play* for the external rewards they receive for "services rendered" may no longer find it worth the effort to continue playing for the measly million dollars a year they are now being offered.

How Athletes Perceive the Rewards We Give

If giving our athletes external rewards *always* resulted in either lower or higher levels of internal motivation, our lives would be pretty simple. If, for example, the rewards we gave always lowered motivation, we would obviously refrain from giving theses rewards for any reason whatsoever. On the other hand, we would certainly be wise to dole out rewards at every possible opportunity if we were certain they would result in enhanced motivation. Unfortunately, like so many things in the real world of coaching, the research suggests that the best answer to the question of whether rewarding our athletes will end up supplementing or substituting for their own internal motivation is, well, "it depends" (Cameron and Pierce 1994).

Do our rewards provide information or manipulate behavior? Every time we reward our athletes for something they've done, we are sending the message that we approve of and value their actions. The rewards we give might be as simple as a "thumbs up" or as complex as several paragraphs of legally binding incentives written into a multiyear performance contract. Regardless of the form they take, it appears that there is one sure way to tell whether the rewards we give will enhance or eliminate our athletes' internal motivation to participate — whether they are interpreted as being given with the intent of providing the athletes with relevant *information* regarding their competency or merely as our attempt to manipulate and *control* their behavior. Whenever our rewards are perceived as providing information about the quality of a performance (i.e., "the reward the coach is giving me tells me I'm a competent athlete") it is likely to enhance internal motivation. The exact same reward, however, can sometimes be viewed as nothing more than a "bribe" being given to bring about a certain behavior (i.e., "the reward the coach is giving me is designed to control the way I act"). When that happens, it will almost certainly reduce internal motivation. The athlete begins to think, "I am not doing this because I want to but because it's the only way I can get rewarded." A perfect example of how a valuable reward can sometimes be interpreted as an attempt to manipulate behavior was offered by perhaps the most highly recruited high school basketball player in history — Earvin "Magic" Johnson. When asked if he had ever received any outrageous (and illegal) inducements to attend a particular college, Johnson responded, "I received my share of offers for cars and money. It immediately turned me off. It was like they were trying to buy me, and I don't like anyone trying to buy me" (Weinberg and Gould 2011, 145). Apparently Johnson perceived these outlandish offers more as the recruiters' attempts to control his behavior (persuade him to enroll in their college) than a true recognition of his previous basketball accomplishments. On the other hand, the greatest hockey player of all time, Wayne Gretzky, received just about every external reward imaginable without ever losing his love for the game. On the dust jacket of his father's book, Wayne writes, "Hockey is so much fun. You know, maybe it's just as well that I live in a penthouse. If I lived at street level in Edmonton, the winter would come and I'd look out the window at the kids playing road hockey, and before you know it I'd be out there with them and there would go my game that night" (Gretzky and Taylor 1984). Apparently, "The Great One" didn't view the numerous tangible and intangible rewards he received as obvious attempts to manipulate his behavior; merely as recognition of his remarkable accomplishments on the ice.

Athletic scholarships: Acknowledging competence or manipulating behavior? By examining athletes' diverse reactions to a reward commonly given in sports — the athletic scholarship — we can easily see how something that is often considered an honor given on the basis of athletic competence, might also be interpreted solely as an attempt to influence behavior. The original investigation into the effects athletic scholarships have on internal motivations arrived at the rather surprising conclusion that college football players who had been given scholarships did *not* enjoy playing as much as non-scholarship players. Equally unexpected was the counterintuitive discovery that the internal desire to play football actually *decreased* each and every year a scholarship was given (Ryan 1977). When the research was repeated a couple years later, it confirmed the initial findings that scholarship football players indeed reported lower internal motivation than their non-scholarship teammates. But this time the researchers extended their study to include athletes participating in what are generally considered "non-scholarship" sports—and that allowed them to see something truly interesting. Both male wrestlers and female athletes who had been given scholarships, unlike the football players, actually reported having higher levels of internal motivation than their non-scholarship teammates (Ryan 1980). Although these results seem to muddy the waters regarding of the impact rewards have on internal motivation, the researchers proposed that the key factor wasn't the scholarships (the rewards) themselves that undermined or enhanced internal motivation but rather the athletes' *perception* as to why the scholarships had been given. The explanation went something like this ... on a college football team nearly everyone receives the same scholarship—superstars and benchwarmers alike. Therefore, receiving this reward provides an individual player with very little information about how he is actually performing. At the same time, it's important to note that when this study was conducted (and until 2012), "NCAA legislation permit[ted] the nonrenewal or reduction of athletics scholarships for any reason" (NCAA 2008, 1). Therefore, in many programs, a scholarship football player receives periodic messages (sometimes subtle, sometime not-so-subtle) that failure to conform to a coach's orders can result in the removal of the scholarship. Simply put, as long as the player does whatever the coaching staff demands, both on and off the field, he will continue to be rewarded—just like everyone else on the team. Football players eventually begin to think of themselves as playing their sport in order to receive the external reward of a college scholarship rather than for the internal pleasures associated with the game itself. This situation is, of course, quite different for athletes participating in traditionally non-scholarship sports. Relatively few of these athletes receive scholarships. When they are given, they usually go to the better performers. Therefore, when the scholarship is given in a non-scholarship sport such as wrestling or many women's sports, it carries with it a great deal of information regarding the athlete's competence level (i.e., "Only the most competent members of the team get this reward therefore, I must be a highly competent athlete") rather than a thinly veiled attempt to control the athlete's behavior (i.e., Everybody on the team gets this reward regardless of how good they are as long as they conform to the coaches' demands"). Because scholarship recipients participating in non-scholarship sports are less likely to see their scholarships as mere "carrots" being dangled in front of them to manipulate their behavior, they also tend to think of their participation must be driven by their internal motives rather than the desire to obtain external rewards. As we can see, the exact impact external rewards have on internal motivation depends, in large part, not on the reward itself but on why athletes think they've received the reward. But that's not the only way an athlete's perception of a coach's behavior can influence his or her internal motivation.

Getting Your Athletes "Into the Zone" with the Proper Use of Rewards

Almost every athlete and coach understands what it means to be "in the zone." The phrase has come to describe that mysterious mental "sweet spot" where performances become smooth, effortless, and automatic. It's also where the body's intuition — rather than conscious thought — controls all action. Although the brain feels oddly disengaged, there is still the sense of being totally absorbed in the performance, and every movement is inexplicably perfect and precise. Athletes in every sport — from water polo to weightlifting — have experienced this strange, almost "out-of-body" sensation. Most describe it as an incredible distortion of time and space. It's not unusual, for example, to hear basketball players talking about the basket being "the size of a garbage can" or baseball hitters saying a pitched ball appears "as big as a grapefruit" or automobile racers saying they can see themselves in a tunnel where the 200 mph cars around them appear to be barely moving. An excellent description of what it feels like to be "in the zone" comes from one of the greatest players in NBA history, Hall of Famer Bill Russell:

> Every so often a Celtic game would heat up so that it became more than a physical or even mental game, and would be magical. That feeling is difficult to describe, and I certainly never talked about it when I was playing. When it happened I could feel my play rise to a new level... At that special level all sorts of odd things happened.... It was almost as if we were playing in slow motion. During those spells I could almost sense how the next play would develop and where the next shot would be taken... My premonitions would be consistently correct... These

were the moments when I had chills pulsing up and down my spine [Russell and Branch, 1979, 155–7].

Not surprisingly, getting into the zone has become the Holy Grail of almost all performers. Almost every musician, artist, actor, writer, and of course, athlete, would do just about anything to possess the ability to transport themselves to this magical place. But there is the cruel irony about "the zone." The more intently it is pursued, the more elusive it becomes. As Monica Seles, the former #1 tennis player in the world, observed, "once you think about being in the zone, you are immediately out of it" (Krug 1999).

Stumbling into — and out of — the zone. The strange thing about being in the zone is that although most athletes have been there, neither they, nor their coaches, have any idea what got them there or how to find their way back. They simply view the experience as some cosmic accident and hope they will be fortunate enough to stumble back into it again in the future. That's where the researchers come in because researchers are convinced that nothing happens purely by accident. So in the mid 1960s, a graduate student at the University of Chicago named Mihaly Csikszentmihalyi began observing and interviewing artists who sometimes became so totally absorbed in their creative activity they would go for long periods of times without food or drink. Even more amazing was his discovery that these artists had no concern whatsoever about what others might think of their work. Their intense focus was driven solely by the internal pleasure they received from the activity itself— not the thought of the profits or adulation it might bring. After watching the artists' complete immersion in their task, Csikszentmihalyi developed a model of what he would call the "flow experience" and athletes and coaches today refer to as being in "the zone" (Csikszentmihalyi 1975; 1990; 1997; Jackson and Csikszentmihalyi 1999). Extending his observations to peak performers in other areas, Csikszentmihalyi soon noticed that being in a "flow state" (i.e., "in the zone") was something that seemed to only happened when there was a near-perfect match between the skills a person possessed and the challenges they faced. When the demands of the task exceeded their skill level, there was a tendency for the performers to become overly anxious about their performance and fall out of the "flow zone." On the other hand, when their skills surpassed the requirements of the task to the point performance became too simple, they soon found themselves uninterested and bored — and once again fell out of the zone. To illustrate his point, Csikszentmihalyi (1990) used an example of a hypothetical novice tennis player by the name of "Alex." Like all beginners, Alex possesses few tennis skills when he picks up a racquet for the first time. His challenge at this point is simply to hit the ball over the net. Although this isn't a very difficult task, his skills are rather limited so the challenge he faces and the skills he possesses are perfectly matched. If he intently focuses on the task at hand, he's typically successful and intrinsically rewarded for his efforts. This situation is represented in Figure 11.2 by "A_1" (Alex at time 1). Alex is in a position to experience a "flow state" because his skills match the demands he faces. But Alex won't stay in that flow state for very long. Either his skills will eventually improve enough that merely hitting the ball over the net becomes boring (as seen in A_2) or he might begin to volley with a somewhat more skilled player (A_3). Not being able to successfully compete against the better player is likely to cause Alex to feel a bit overwhelmed and anxious about his performance. Once again, he falls out of the flow zone. Notice that the only way Alex (or our athletes) even has a chance to remain in the zone—and be neither bored nor anxious when playing tennis—is to continually match his ever-improving skill level with an ever-increasing challenge (A_4). Therefore, to help our athletes "get in the zone," our first step is to make sure the tasks we ask them to perform are a good match for their skills—not too easy, not too difficult. But there is even more we can do to help our athletes perform at their optimal level.

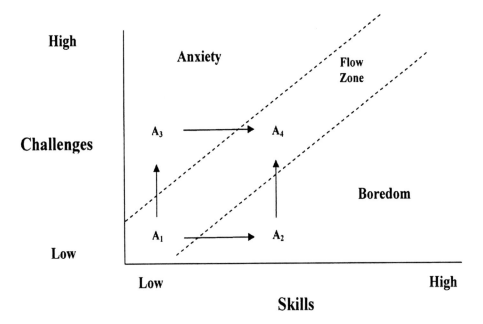

Figure 11.2: *Flow: The Psychology of Optimal Experience* by Mihaly Csikszentmihaly. Copyright ©1990 by Mihaly Csikszentmihaly. Reprinted by permission of Harper-Collins Publishers.

Guidelines for enhancing internal motivation and flow. Helping our athletes get into a flow state is nothing more than a logical extension of what we should be doing every day to make sure their performance is always driven by the internal rewards that come naturally from taking part in sports — not the external rewards they might receive from others. There is little doubt that athletes who feel either bored or anxious while performing are going to find it very difficult to be internally motivated or get into the zone. It's a coach's job, therefore, to make sure all athletes are placed in positions that maximize their skills. If we don't push them to accept new challenges, they'll soon become bored. If, on the other hand, we push them too far beyond their current capabilities, we risk making them feel anxious and nervous about their performance. As coaches, we can do several things to give our athletes the best opportunity to develop internal motivation and, if all goes well, regularly experience the tremendous sensation of flow. We've discussed each area in detail elsewhere in this book but now we can see that they all come together to build internal motivation in our athletes (Amorose and Horn 2000; Hollembeck and Amorose 2005):

• Provide our athletes with every opportunity to take an active role in game and performance-related decisions. When athletes feel they have control over their own performance they tend to develop internal motivations (see the Myth No. 2 chapter).

• Make sure our athletes are always setting clear, realistic, and controllable goals for themselves. Setting effective goals not only lends structure and direction but allows the athletes to think about what is truly important to them (not necessarily to others). A daily goal that emphasizes performance as opposed to outcome will also focus their concentration on the internal rewards they can receive through sport participation (see the Myth No. 5 chapter).

• Give positive, information-based rewards to all our athletes. Remember that some of the most meaningful rewards an athlete can receive are the personal reinforcements for a job well-done. A simple "good job," a smile, a nod, or a pat on the back tells our athletes that we appreciate their effort (see the Myth No. 11 chapter).

• Stay positive and use the "feedback sandwich" when performance errors need to be corrected. Starting the error correction process with positive reinforcement for what is being done correctly is a great way to motivate our athletes to keep trying even when they're making mistakes (see the Myth No. 9 chapter).

• Take time to organize and plan every practice. A smooth running practice will allow our athletes to concentrate on what they're doing rather than what we're doing. This ability to focus on the task will improve their motivation and increase the chances they will get into a flow state (see the Myth No. 8 chapter).

• Set aside time for fun. What is really the point of sport participation if it's not fun? Athletes perform better and are more likely to be internally motivated when they're having fun. Remember, young athletes think the three most important reasons they get involved in sport are to have fun, to be with their friends, and to learn new skills (see the Myth No. 10 chapter).

It's important that we help our athletes understand that sport can provide them with many internal and external rewards. Equally important is the recognition that becoming concerned with external rewards tends to put the performer at the mercy of others. Athletes who are judged to be successful by the standards of others will be given every tangible reward imaginable — but only as long as they continue to perform at a high level. The purest and longest-lasting motivations can never be taken away or manipulated by others — they come from within. It was the lasting value of these incorruptible internal rewards that led Coach Wooden to observe, "Carrots come in many forms, However, I believe the strongest and most meaningful motivators are not necessarily the materialistic, but the intangible" (Wooden and Jamison 2005, 167–8).

MYTH NO. 12

"To Be the Best, Athletes Need to Commit Themselves to a Single Sport"

The first questions I'll ask about a kid are, "What other sports does he play? Is he a big hitter in baseball? Is he a pitcher? Does he play hoops?" All of those things are important to me. I hate that kids don't play three sports in high school. I really, really don't favor kids having to specialize in one sport.

— Coach Pete Carroll[1]

Can you imagine letting your athletes engage in a sport activity that over 60,000 pediatricians say should be avoided because it can cause physical and psychological damage? No? Well that's exactly what the American Academy of Pediatrics says we're doing when we encourage our children to specialize in a single sport throughout the entire year (American Academy of Pediatrics 2000).

There was a time when families could mark the season by the type of athletic equipment strewn across the family room floor. Every summer they tripped over bats, balls, and gloves; in the fall it was probably helmets, shoulder pads and spikes; in the winter it was more likely to be sticks, pucks, and skates or basketballs, kneepads, and sneakers. Throw in the occasional golf bag, soccer ball, tennis racquet, or swimsuit and everyone knew that the kids were on their way to becoming well-rounded athletes — and people. Coach Carroll's quote at the beginning of this chapter serves as a good illustration that despite an increasing consensus that young athletes have to specialize in a single sport in order to have a shot at the "next level," some of the coaches who are known for their ability to locate and recruit the best talent into the most elite programs in the country purposefully search for athletes who have *not* specialized in one sport. And he certainly makes his view on the topic of specialization perfectly clear, "I hate that kids don't play three sports in high school... I really, really don't favor kids having to specialize in one sport" (Stack Magazine 2007).

But times have changed (Hecimovich 2004). Youth sports are now more often seen as proving grounds for up-and-coming "superstars" who, if we're lucky, will pay off like an overdue slot machine. Even if Junior can't become the entire family's "meal ticket" perhaps he or she will at least help pay for college by landing an athletic scholarship. But it's about time for a reality check.

Statistics show our kids are more likely to become brain surgeons, college professors, lawyers, and astronauts than money-making athletes (Farrey 2008). But it's this unrelenting dream of athletic stardom that propels moms and dads by the thousands to enroll their children — some barely out of diapers — in never-ending seasons of a single sport where they often participate in more competitions than the average professional athlete. And that's where we, as coaches, are in the unique position to provide some much-needed guidance.

It's our job to encourage skill development at the highest level while tempering the natural exuberance parents and athletes sometimes experience — but there's the problem. We often shirk our responsibility to serve as a check on these unrealistic expectations, by encouraging — some might even say pushing — our talented athletes to specialize in a single sport. Worse still, we usually do so without any idea of the true costs and benefits associated with single-sport specialization. But we shouldn't be too hard on ourselves. The whole notion of single-sport specialization is such a recent phenomenon that we haven't had time to really judge many of the long-term advantages and disadvantages associated with concentrating year-round on a single sport. What we do know, however, is that whenever a young athlete participates in a single sport there are bound to be tradeoffs. And coaches, more than anyone else, need to educate themselves about the potential costs and benefits associated with single-sport specialization in order to help parents and athletes make informed choices.

Potential Advantages of Single-Sport Specialization

It should come as no surprise that the main reason coaches and parents urge their young athletes to concentrate on a single sport rather than gain a broader range of experiences from participating in several different sports throughout the year is to enhance their skill level in that one sport of their choosing. We have considerable scientific evidence supporting the common sense notion that if you want to become highly skilled at a task — any task — it requires thousands of repetitions (Moran 2004). Most research, in fact, indicates that somewhere in the neighborhood of 10,000 hours of practice is required to become highly proficient at most sport skills (Baker, Côté and Abernethy 2003; Starkes 2000). And make no mistake, there are plenty of financial incentives for those special few who have developed their athletic skills far beyond those of their peers.

Athletes performing at the highest level of competition, whether that takes the form of an Olympic medal or the professional sport contract, will be handsomely rewarded for their efforts. Although we all know that elite athletes make a lot of money, few of us can really comprehend how much is actually at stake. Here's a real-life example that clearly illustrates the kind of money top athletes are chasing: In 2008, despite being at the end of his career and just days prior to being implicated in illegal steroid use by the Mitchell Report (Mitchell 2007), Andy Pettitte signed a one-year, $16 million Major League Baseball contract. If, like me, you have a hard time wrapping your head around eight-figure annual salaries, just think of it this way — Pettitte made roughly as much money throwing a baseball for the New York Yankees that one summer as the average American household earns in 320 years (roughly the time that has passed since the Salem Witch Trials and nearly 100 years before the United States became a country). Add in a few million more in endorsements, personal contracts and perks and it is it any wonder that so many parents are willing to do just about anything to give their kid a shot at the brass (or gold) ring? And you don't have to make millions in order to profit financially from athletics.

As the cost of tuition rises, parents are looking for alternative ways to pay for their kids' college education. One of the ways they are choosing is to invest in year-round training in the hopes that their son or daughter's will be skilled enough to land a "full-ride" athletic scholarship at the college of their choice.

So let's do the math. Even our most talented athletes will need to devote somewhere in the neighborhood of 20 hours of their time each week to deliberate and focused practice within their sport — for a minimum of 10 straight years — in order to acquire the skills they need to perform at the highest levels of national or international competition. Remember, this doesn't include time they have to spend traveling to and from competitions, conditioning their bodies, or analyzing game film — it's just the time they need to spend deliberately practicing their sport skills (Baker, Côté and Abernethy 2003). When we further consider that these young athletes are going to school and doing homework for six or seven hours each day during the week, it's plain to see that this level of commitment is impossible without sacrificing participation in other sports or extracurricular activities. There's just no time.

There we have it. The numbers don't lie. Unless kids (not to mention their parents and coaches) are willing to set aside roughly a thousand hours a year in practice time, it's unlikely they'll ever truly be contenders in the "superstar sweepstakes." It therefore makes perfectly good sense for coaches and parents who want to give their kids a real competitive advantage to push them into participating year-round in a single sport. Or does it?

Potential Disadvantages of Single-Sport Specialization

Will devoting thousands of hours to practicing a single sport improve a child's performance? Of course, but that's not really the question well-intentioned coaches and parents should be asking. Two far more important questions would be, "Are there any physical, psychological, or social drawbacks associated with children focusing all their energies into a single sport?" and "If there are likely to be physical, psychological or social costs, do they outweigh the potential benefits the child might receive from any expected performance improvements?"

Physical costs associated with year-round single sport participation. One of the concerns the American Academy of Pediatrics (2000) has about specializing in a single sport is the increased likelihood of physical injury. When young athletes participate in the same sport on a year-round basis, they subject their undeveloped bones, muscles, ligaments, and tendons to the same stresses again and again, ultimately resulting in tendonitis, shin splints, and stress fractures. This "repetitive stress" is why, for example, a young baseball "phenom" is far more likely to injure his throwing arm if he pitches for several baseball teams all year long than if he divides his time between sports that each place different stressors on the body (e.g., baseball, basketball, soccer, and tennis). Long-term repetition of the same movements place children's immature bodies at significant risk of injury and, when you add in the use of improper mechanics or techniques due to poor coaching, you have a perfect recipe for disaster. That's why a public service campaign sponsored by two organizations devoted to the health of young athletes — the American Academy of Orthopaedic Surgeons and the National Athletic Trainers' Association — asks all coaches, parents, and administrators who advocate year-round single-sport participation for children to consider the pointed question, "What will they have longer, their trophies or their injuries?" (Stenson 2005).

Psychological costs associated with year-round single sport participation. It's pretty easy to see how repeatedly performing the same sport movement can eventually wear out a young athlete's body. Equally devastating, but far more difficult to gauge, is how playing the same sport day after day, month after month, year after year can eventually wear down a young athlete's passion for the game. Coaches and athletes often call this drop in performance caused by overtraining "staleness" but sport psychologists refer to it as "burnout"—and describe it as "an emotional/physical exhaustion, reduced sense of accomplishment, and sport devaluation" (Raedeke and Smith 2001, 283). Burnout in sport can be caused by many things including performance-related stress and anxiety (Smith 1986), a feeling that the overall costs of participation are beginning to outweigh the benefits (Weiss and Weiss 2003), or a feeling on the part of the athlete that others (parents, coaches, sport organizations, etc.) have taken over complete control of their lives (Coakley 1992). The important thing to notice here is that intense training in the same sport throughout the entire year can dramatically increase the chances of a young athlete experiencing all of these potential causes of burnout.

Social development costs associated with year-round single sport participation. It's sometimes easy to forget that some of the most valuable experiences a young athlete can gain through sport participation come from interacting with—and learning from—a diverse group of other kids and adults. However, when we allow our athletes to specialize in one particular sport, they tend to interact with the same kinds of kids again and again. Sure, they may be playing on several different teams but many of the other players are the same they had played with before. After all, those other athletes are often specializing in that sport too, so they are simply making the rounds with all the other specialists. When basketball players only come in contact with other basketball players, tennis players only come in contact with other tennis players, or gymnasts only come in contact with other gymnasts, there is undoubtedly less to be learned from social interaction with others than if the same athlete participates yearly in all three of these sports.

Societal costs associated with year-round single sport participation. When we concentrate on the physical, psychological, and social development costs associated with year-round single sport participation we are mainly concerned with the negative affects specialization can have on the individual athlete. Another important, yet often overlooked, societal cost of sport specialization has to do with the decreased availability of sporting opportunities for any kids who aren't the most athletically gifted or who are simply not willing to devote themselves to a single sport. Many varsity coaches are starting to encourage — if not outright insist — that their athletes dedicate themselves to year-round training in order to be favorably considered for a position on the team. Spring practice and summer workout camps are "unofficially required" to make the football team; "spring-ball," "summer-ball," and "fall-ball" has become the expectation for any baseball or softball player who wants to show the coach they're willing to dedicate themselves to their sport; participation in AAU basketball leagues all summer long in addition to the typical basketball season is the only way to impress potential college recruiters; attendance at summer hockey camps are mandatory if a player wants to be selected for a national team; and the list of year-long commitments to a single sport go on and on. Of course the coaches' rationale here is pretty transparent ... if athletes engage in their chosen sport on a year-round basis they will probably develop skills that will allow them to be a greater asset to their team — and their coach. As a volleyball tournament director in California put it, "It's no longer a myth: If your kid wants to make a high school team, he has to play club ball. They're getting the training and the attention that the normal rec leagues are not providing" (Cary 2004, 50). When this year-round commitment becomes the formal or informal expectation for participation we're left with most, if not all, of the spots on a given team's roster being set aside for athletes who have been willing to devote themselves to year-round participation in one sport. But what happens to all those kids who would like the experience of participating in a variety of sports? What happens to all those kids who simply don't want to invest such a large portion of their time in one sport? Unfortunately these kids are increasingly being left behind with nowhere to play because they're unable to compete with the new generation of "single sport specialists" that their coaches, parents, and administrators have created (Farrey 2008). And even when an athlete does devote himself or herself to a single sport the odds are still stacked against them making a professional roster or even landing a college scholarship.

The Harsh Reality of Financially Profiting from Sports

Although it would really be great to think that your athlete can parlay his or her sport specialization into a career — heck, even a college scholarship — we have to live in the real world. And there's probably no organization better equipped to give a high school athlete the real-world odds of participating in athletics at the collegiate level (with or without a scholarship) or making it in the pros than the National Collegiate Athletic Association (NCAA). A quick glance at Table 12.1 reveals at least part of the bitter truth that only a tiny fraction of high school athletes will ever even participate in intercollegiate athletics — let alone have a legitimate shot at the pros. Unfortunately, even this unlikely prospect of participating at the college level is still only half the story. Many parents, athletes, and even coaches, operate under several misconceptions regarding the availability of college scholarships.

Table 12.1: Odds of High School Athletes Playing in College or the Pros

Student-Athletes	Men's Basketball	Women's Basketball	Football	Baseball	Men's Ice Hockey	Men's Soccer
Odds of Advancing From High School to NCAA (all Divisions)	3.2 in 100	3.6 in 100	6.1 in 100	6.6 in 100	10.7 in 100	5.7 in 100
Odds of Advancing From High School to the Pros	3 in 10,000	3 in 10,000	8 in 10,000	60 in 10,000	10 in 10,000	4 in 10,000

Myth #1: Talented high school athletes will receive four-year athletic scholarships. We often hear reports of hundreds of colleges and universities engaging in mortal combat just for the privilege of signing a particularly outstanding recruit to a national letter of intent. Because these top athletes are in such high demand, we naturally assume that they will ultimately be guaranteed a four year athletic scholarship to the college or university of their choice. Not necessarily. Under rules that were adopted by the NCAA back in 1973, *all* athletic scholarships, at *all* NCAA institutions were limited to one year — renewable solely at the discretion of the school's scholarship committee. In 2012, the NCAA passed legislation that would give the Division I institutions the option to offer scholarships guaranteed for more than a single year (Hosick 2012). However, there are two important aspects of this recent change that should be noted. First, it only gives Division I schools the *option* of offering multiyear scholarships. It in no way requires such long-term guarantees. Second, the legislation passed with 62.12 percent of the NCAA institutions voting against the option (62.5 percent was required to kill the legislation). Furthermore, although recently pass legislation now requires the college to notify athletes in writing of the opportunity for a hearing when their scholarships will not be renewed for the following year, there is still no guarantee of renewal. To get a sense of how flimsy a college's commitment is, just listen to how the NCAA Student-Athlete Well-Being Subcommittee puts it, "NCAA legislation permits the nonrenewal or reduction of athletics scholarships for any reason" (NCAA 2006, 1).

Myth #2: Athletic scholarships are "full-ride" and will pay most college expenses. Colleges are limited in terms of how many scholarships they can offer in each sport. Therefore, aside from those given in Division I football and basketball, most scholarships are actually "partials"—one full scholarship that is split up and shared by several athletes. These partial scholarships can range from a few hundred to a few thousand dollars a year. The benefit of dividing scholarships is that more athletes get at least a little money for college. The down side, unfortunately, is that most parents and athletes who are expecting to get the entire cost—or even a substantial portion—of a college education paid for through an athletic scholarship are going to be very disappointed.

Myth #3: All NCAA college athletic programs offer athletic scholarships. With all the colleges and universities around the country it might appear a rather simple task to find a place that will give a good athlete at least a partial scholarship. The problem with that logic is twofold: (1) NCAA Division III colleges (usually the smaller schools) aren't even allowed to provide athletic scholarships, and (2) there are more Division III colleges (about 430) than either Division I (342) or Division II (282) institutions. Add to this the fact that even within Division I and II, schools don't necessarily field teams in all NCAA-sanctioned sports—and even when they do there are not typically enough scholarships for everyone on the team.

What Professional Athletes Say about Participating in Multiple Sports

Coaches and parents who are trying to convince others—and sometimes themselves—of the tremendous benefits of single-sport specialization frequently cite the well-chronicled biography of arguably the greatest golfer of all time—"Tiger" Woods. They are quick to point out that Earl Woods bought his son Eldrick Tont Woods (yep, that's Tiger's real name) his first club for Christmas—five days before his first birthday—and had him taking private lessons with golf pro and instructor, Rudy Duran, by the time he was four (Woods 1997; Duran 2002). They further make the case that although Tiger dabbled a bit in a couple other sports, he spent virtually his entire childhood focused on a single sport. And the payoff was that he not only became the best athlete in the world at that sport, he turned out to be a reasonably well-rounded, successful person too. And they're right. Tiger Woods has become a shining example for everything positive that can happen if your kid dedicates himself or herself to a single sport.[2] In his book *Game On,* ESPN correspondent and journalist Tom Farrey implies that the "Tale of the Tiger" might actually be the worst thing that ever happened to youth sports because, "Tiger Woods has slapped a Good Housekeeping Seal of Approval on these efforts, as a model athlete and the kind of son any parent could be proud of" (Farrey 2008, 18). But the question coaches and parents are rarely asking is how many kids have been — and are being — raised to be "the next Tiger" only to find out too late they can't make the cut. Interestingly, if we listen to most other exceptional athletes we can't help but recognize that Tiger is simply an all-too-obvious exception to how most great athletes are made.

As a coach or parent what would you do if it became apparent that your young basketball sensation has what it takes to be the NBA's next Kobe Bryant or LeBron James? Would you allow him or her to spend large chunks of the year playing soccer — like Kobe did, or football — like LeBron did? What kind of sport participation would you recommend for a kid who wants to dominate the world of tennis? Would you suggest he or she does what Roger Federer and John McEnroe did and play soccer for part of the year? Or perhaps it would be better to get involved in basketball like Andy Roddick? Would you try to encourage a future Alex Rodriguez to play football or a potential Tom Brady to try his hand at baseball? They both did exactly that (Mason 2008).

Just listing the names of exceptional multiple-sport athletes would fill this entire book but here are a few we may want to consider whenever we think it's essential for young athletes to devote themselves to a single sport: Jim Thorpe, Babe Didrikson, Jim Brown, Deion Sanders, Michael Jordan, John Elway, Jackie Robinson, Steve Garvey, Danny Ainge, Kirk Gibson, Bo Jackson, Dave Winfield, Marion Jones, and the list goes on and on. These fantastic athletes are not only recognized as some of the best athletes in the history of sport, they participated in — and excelled at — some of the highest levels of competition in more than one sport at one time. Perhaps more amazing still is the fact that so many top professional athletes attribute much of their success to the very fact they played more than one sport.

Soccer, in particular, has been credited in the development of some of the greatest basketball players in the NBA. Kobe Bryant, for example, has said, "When you grow up playing soccer, you obviously carry that over to other sports. I think it has helped me tremendously" (Witz 2008). And Bryant isn't the only basketball star who used his experiences on the soccer pitch to enhance his basketball skills. Eight-time NBA All-Star power forward Dirk Nowitzki played soccer while growing up in Germany; NBA finals MVP, Tony Parker, played the game as a child in France; and two-time MVP Steve Nash was an outstanding youth soccer player in Canada. Nash is even reported to have said that after so many years of playing soccer, it almost felt he was taking unfair advantage of his basketball opponents by using his hands (Witz 2008).

Some of baseball's greatest players have also drawn on their participation in other sports to enhance their prowess on the diamond. Hall of Famer Tony Gwynn, for example, credits his tremendous hand-eye coordination to playing the point guard position in basketball (Farrey 2008) and Cal Ripken, Jr. attributes much of his later success in baseball to the fact he was a three-sport athlete into high school. Specifically, Ripken says playing soccer enhanced his footwork and balance and basketball helped him develop his explosiveness and quick movements. The payoff Ripken received from participating in sports other than baseball is undoubtedly one of the main reasons he advises his own son, Ryan, to "put down your glove" as soon as the spring baseball season is over (Cary 2004).

Although Kobe Bryant, Steve Nash, Tony Gwynn, and Cal Ripken Jr. all readily admit they wouldn't have been as good without their multiple-sport experiences, Dallas Cowboy quarterback Tony Romo goes even further — he's convinced that he wouldn't even be playing football at all if he had concentrated on only one sport. That's because if forced to choose — as many coaches today demand — Romo would have selected basketball or soccer and would have never had the chance to develop his football skills. As he puts it, "I would have never been able to do what I'm lucky enough to do — play football" (Sonner 2008).

Finally, let's consider the case of the greatest hockey player who ever lived — Wayne Gretzky who starred in both baseball and lacrosse as a kid (Schwartz 1999). In his book *Gretzky: From the Backyard Rink to the Stanley Cup,* Wayne's father offers us some insight as to how the young "Great One" trained for future stardom, "In public school he played baseball, soccer and basketball and ran track and cross country. He also played for city teams in hockey, lacrosse, and baseball, ran track, played golf and did weight training three times a week" (Gretzky and Taylor, 1984, 52). Would a kid with Wayne Gretzky's exceptional hockey talents be allowed to participate in so many different sports and activities if he was coming up through the system today?

It's obvious that many of the greatest professional athletes consider their participation in various sports to have played an essential role in their overall athletic development. They readily admit that their all-round performance would have suffered had they been forced to specialize in a single sport early in their careers. But what about the opinion of elite-level coaches? Do they likewise see the value of kids participating in a variety of sports?

What Professional and College Coaches Say about Participating in Multiple Sports

As coaches, we need to admit that we sometimes have a conflict of interest that might make us more inclined to encourage our best athletes to specialize in a single sport (as long as it's *our* sport of course). After all, it's our job to put together a successful athletic program and the more time our players devote to developing skills that are specific to our sport, the better they will probably perform. And the better our players perform, the more likely it is that we will have a successful (at least in terms of wins and losses) team. As if this burning desire to field the best team isn't enough of a conflict of interest, many coaches "moonlight" by running sports camp, elite (travel) clubs, or by giving private instructions in the off season. Again, it's to our advantage, financially and professionally, if we can convince top athletes to commit to spending their entire year under our tutelage. But the difficult question we need to ask ourselves is not whether this kind of year-round participation in a single sport is good for us or our program, but whether it will ultimately be in the best interest of the individual athlete. It's obviously a tough call so it might be interesting to see what a couple of highly successful coaches at the college and professional level think about single-sport specialization.

Entering the 2009 season, NFL and former University of Southern California Trojan head football coach, Pete Carroll, owned the highest winning percentage (85.4 percent) of all active coaches of Football Bowl Subdivision programs. Among his many accomplishments, Coach Carroll's Trojans were ranked #1 in the country for 33 consecutive weeks by the Associated Press, had two (one shared) National Championships, and had been Pac-10 Champion or Co-Champion for a record seven consecutive years. We can accurately assume from his coaching achievements Carroll knows a thing or two about player development. During his nine-year tenure at USC he turned out three Heisman Trophy winners, 25 First-Team All-Americans, and had 53 of his players drafted into the NFL — including 14 first round picks. As a three-sport standout himself, it's not surprising that Carroll has a strongly-held opinion regarding the importance of multiple sport participation — an opinion that directly impacts his recruiting decisions:

> I really, really, don't favor kids having to specialize in one sport. They don't have to, to excel. Even here [at USC] I want to be the biggest proponent for two-sport athletes on the college level. I want guys that are so special athletically and so competitive that they can compete in more than one sport here at SC. I think all of that is part of the makeup of the guy that you get. So to me it's really important that guys are well-rounded and have this tendency for competitiveness that they have to express somewhere. So yeah, I'm all for that and I take a lot of stock in that [Stack Magazine, 2007].

So it's pretty hard to believe that Pete Carroll — for years the head coach of one of the truly premier college football programs in the country — thinks our young athletes will be disadvantaged by playing several sports. On the contrary, he's even more likely to be interested in recruiting players with multiple sport experiences. And he's not alone.

On June 12, 2009, the Pittsburgh Penguins under their first-year head coach, Dan Bylsma, invaded Joe Louis Arena in Detroit and beat the venerable Red Wings 2–1 in Game 7 to capture the Stanley Cup Championship. Bylsma, a former player with the Los Angeles Kings and the Mighty Ducks of Anaheim (where he was also an Alternate Captain), had been named the Penguins head coach in mid season in an attempt to stem a downward spiral that placed even the possibility of a playoff berth in serious jeopardy. During his first 25 games, however, his young team rocketed to an 18–3–4 record — the second best start in NHL history for a rookie coach. Over the years, Dan and his father, Jay, have teamed up to author four books. Their first two books *So Your Son Wants to Play in the NHL* (Bylsma and Bylsma, 1998) and *So You Want to Play in the NHL* (Bylsma and Bylsma, 2001) were written to provide young athletes and their parents practical, first-hand advice about chasing their dream of becoming a professional athlete. To get a sense of what Dan and Jay think of specializing in one sport, let's take a look at their answers to some questions on the Q & A section of their companion webpage (www.DanBylsma.com) that specifically address the topic:

Question # 3: "What are good ways to train for hockey in the off season? Also what age do you recommend a player start to train?"

> DAN REPLIES: I never trained specifically for hockey in the off season until I got to college. My dad thought it was best to hang up the skates and think about other sports. I learned that there was carryover from sport to sport. Soccer, for

example, was very good training to keep in shape, learn how to use your feet to handle the ball (good for handling the puck with your feet in hockey), and the strategy of the game is the same. I think playing other sports helped me to play hockey better because I became a better athlete playing those other sports. I think playing other sports also kept me from burning out in hockey.

Question # 7: "My Mite aged son (8) played a regular 25 game schedule, 3 games at state the tournament, then 11 games with an AAA team, and now wants to play in a 20 game fall league. He maintains a two to one practice to game ratio, and loves every minute. But, how much is too much?"

> DAN REPLIES: How much is too much? It all depends on what your family's values are. If your family's goal is to try to produce the one kid in one million (that's about the odds of all the kids in the world who play amateur hockey) to make it to the NHL, the schedule you outlined is probably not enough but burnout becomes a serious risk. If your family's goal is to develop a well-rounded athlete, he should play all the sports at age eight and until he's 12–13. That is, hockey in the winter, baseball in the spring, soccer in the summer, and golf in the fall, then back to hockey.

Question #52: "Dan: I am an above average 13 year-old hockey player. I was wondering what are some things I can do in the off-season to get better."

> DAN REPLIES: I recommend you play other organized sports if you have the chance ... baseball, golf, lacrosse, soccer, etc. Playing other sports do three things for you: they help you develop as an athlete (and as a person), you learn other skills that will carry over to hockey, and playing other sports will sharpen your desire to get back to hockey in the fall.

Dan's responses leave little doubt as to what the Head Coach of the 2009 Stanley Cup Champion Pittsburgh Penguins thinks of specializing in a single sport at a young age. And there's also little doubt as to how he got those views. His father (who happens to be my neighbor and graciously comes into my coaching classes on occasion to chat with the students) puts it this way:

> And while my experience is with hockey, I am aware that this kind of intensity pervades most of youth sports with travel leagues, player ratings, etc. It's yet another sign the apocalypse is upon us. There are only two reasons why kids should be involved in youth sports: to teach them life lessons and for them to have fun. To participate in sport to generate a professional athlete is counterproductive at best and often destructive.... The conventional wisdom in our country is to become successful you must start kids very young, play ever more games, play year around, and concentrate on one sport. And the youth sports establishment perpetuates this mantra despite the abundant evidence to the contrary [Bylsma, 2000].

To Specialize or Not, That Is the Question: Practical Advice for Coaches and Parents

Coaches and parents can usually rely on hard scientific evidence to help them make the tough choices about how they can best help their athletes benefit from sport participation. Unfortunately, when it comes to deciding whether a particular athlete should specialize by limiting his or her sporting activity to one sport or take part in multiple sports, science is of little help. Regardless of which position you take, we can find several scientific studies that suggest the exact opposite. As Pittsburgh Penguin head coach Dan Bylsma indicated in his response to Question 7 above, it all depends on what your values are. If your primarily interest in helping the child under your care develop a specific set of skills in the hopes of propelling him or her to a college scholarship or professional career, specialization is probably the answer — assuming they don't burn out or get injured somewhere along the way. On the other hand, if you are more interested in letting the child experience a wide variety of sport situations that might help them learn important life lessons while developing transferable skills from other sports, multiple sport participation is the way to go. Since the answer isn't obvious, let's at least try to identify some general guidelines that might help us make this important decision.

Long-Term Athlete Development (LTAD) model. Parents who are trying to determine the type of athletic activities appropriate for their children might find it useful to consider the Long-Term Athlete Development Model, a general 5-Step "rule of thumb" developed by Istvan Balyi (2001) an expert on performance training who has worked with several Canadian national teams and serves as a high performance consultant at the IMG Academies in Bradenton, Florida. According to the LTAD model there are five stages of athletic development that we need to consider when trying to determine when single-sport specialization is appropriate:

- **Stage 1 — Learning the FUNdamentals (ages 6–10)**
Give the kids the chance to learn basic movement skills in an athletic setting that is organized and structured but, above all else, fun. Let the kids practice the "ABCs of athleticism" — Agility, Balance, Coordination and Speed.
- **Stage 2 — Training to Train (males ages 10–14; females ages 10–13)**
Once the kids have the body control and fundamental movement skills needed in all sports, they can begin working on general sport skills. Games and activities should allow kids the chance to improve their bodies' flexibility, endurance, and quickness.

- **Stage 3 — Training to Compete (males ages 14–18; females ages 13–17)**

In this stage, kids need to take the movement skills they've developed and apply them to competitions. They should try their best to win but focus mainly on learning how to apply their skills in competitive games.

- **Stage 4 — Training to Win (males over age 18; females over age 17)**

Because athletes have mastered basic movement and sport skills they can now learn to perform their skills in highly competitive situations. Winning and losing now becomes very important. Because the athlete's skills are fully developed, the emphasis can now shift to high-level performance in all competitions.

- **Stage 5 — Retirement and Retraining**

This stage refers to the activities performed once an athlete has retired from competition. During this, the final stage of athlete development, former athletes move into sport-related careers.

It's easy to see that the whole notion of sport specialization is inconsistent with the LTAD model until the athlete reaches puberty in Stage 3. It's also important to note that delaying single-sport participation until early adolescence is in complete agreement with the first recommendation of the Committee on Sports Medicine and Fitness of the American Academy of Pediatrics which says, "Children are encouraged to participate in sports at a level consistent with their abilities and interests. Pushing children beyond these limits is discouraged as is specialization in a single sport before adolescence" (American Academy of Pediatrics 2000, 156).

Asking the right questions will usually give you the right answer. It's easy for coaches and parents to get caught up in the hype surrounding sport specialization. With all the talk about varsity teams to make, college scholarships to pursue, professional careers to be advanced, fortunes to be had, and coaching reputations to be enhanced, there is a tremendous temptation to encourage our young athletes to devote their time and energy to becoming an expert in a single sport. After all, the thinking goes, that's what's going to give them the edge they need to compete with all those other sport specialists out there. But you may also have legitimate concerns about injuries, burnout, and disappointment that can result from over-specialization. What's a coach or parent to do? Generally, there is one fail-safe method to increase the chances of making the right decision — just ask the right questions. Here are the first 10 questions we all might want to consider when faced with this decision:

1. Does the youngster love participating in this sport more than all others? First and foremost we have to make sure it's the child's choice and not ours. We can put a lot of subtle pressure on kids who usually want nothing more than to please the most important people in their lives — parents and coaches.

2. Has the child already gone through their adolescent "growth spurt"? If not, we can't predict what sport they may be best suited for once they mature. What happens, for example, when our tiny gymnast's body becomes better suited for volleyball or our stocky little goaltender grows to a lanky 6 feet 10? If their early sport experiences were limited to gymnastics or hockey, they might find it difficult to make the transition to other, more interesting or appropriate, sports.

3. Has the child participated for more than one season in more than one sport? If they haven't experienced other sports, how do they — or we — know the sport they are about to specialize in is really the best fit for them? Tiger Woods notwithstanding, most 4-year-olds don't have enough experience to make a career choice.

4. Does the child have the "proper" amount of talent to benefit from specialization? Specialization really isn't needed if the young athlete doesn't possess a certain amount of natural ability. On the other hand, if the youngster is exceptionally talented, specialization may not be needed either. For obvious reasons it's best not to rely on our own judgment here. We need to consult the opinions of unbiased experts.

5. Would you consider specializing in this sport to have been worthwhile even if the young athlete never lands a college scholarship or signs a pro contract? There are a lot of things that can prevent even the most talented athletes from becoming that one or two percent of the population fortunate enough to make money — even in small amounts — from sport. Dreams are fine but reality has to guide our real-life decisions.

6. Do you have access to the best coaches and trainers to work with kids this age? What good is it to train specifically in one sport if the training isn't the best? Many coaches — even elite coaches — don't have the skills, knowledge, or temperament to work with physically and emotionally immature children. And if we are the one who is going to be providing the specialized training, we're probably not in any position to make that decision.

7. Have you seriously considered the time and money the entire family will have to spend to support this child's sport specialization? Total dedication to a single sport is a big commitment — and not only for the athlete. Often special training, membership on regional travel teams — even moving away from home — are necessary to realize every advantage of sport specialization. Families sometimes spend thousands of dollars a year on specialized sport training for a child. And often overlooked is the impact the "special athlete" in the family has on his or her siblings. Will everyone else be expected to forego their needs just so "the little star" can travel to tournaments and camps?

8. Has the child developed emotionally, socially, and academically enough to devote so much time to a single activity? Specializing in a single sport can take away time with friends, time for other extracurricular activities, and time needed for schoolwork. It takes a great deal of discipline for kids to not resent watching all their friends being given the chance to grow up "normally" while they focus solely on their sport.

9. Have you considered what you would do if, in a couple of years, the child says he or she doesn't want to (or can't) compete in this sport anymore? After spending thousands of hours and/or thousands of dollars on the best coaches, camps, and equipment, how would we react if the athlete simply says he or she has "had enough" and wants to do something else? Would we be reluctant to let them quit simply because we've invested too much to let them do anything else?

10. Have you considered how much you have to gain personally from the child specializing in a single sport? Coaches and parents stand to reap great social and personal (not to mention financial) rewards if their athlete or child develops into a great athletic talent (think Earl Woods, Rudy Duran, Bela Karolyi, etc.). We need to make sure that our encouragements to focus on a single sport are not, in any way, based on our own personal needs.

If we can honestly answer "yes" to each and every one of these 10 questions, it may be appropriate to consider what single-sport specialization has to offer. If not, our young athlete is probably at least a few years away from committing to one sport.

Finally, whenever we find ourselves tempted by the exaggerated promises of fame and fortune that can be achieved through single-sport participation, we—and the young athletes we serve—will find it useful to reflect on the insightful observation President Theodore Roosevelt passed on to his son, Ted, when he learned the boy was trying out for the football team at Harvard: "Athletic proficiency is a mighty good servant, and like so many other good servants, a mighty bad master" (Bishop 1919, 63).

MYTH No. 13

"The Worst Thing About Coaching Is Dealing with Parents"

I don't have much personal experience with loud/critical/pushy parents because I was lucky enough to have two parents who were quiet, very affirming, and only asked that I do my best—and did so in private and never scolded or berated me in public. But I've seen a lot of other parents whose behavior at games would have embarrassed me if I were their kid. It's not a pretty sight.

— Coach Dan Bylsma[1]

As if coaches don't already have enough to do, the "experts" are now telling us to spend even more of our precious time with the one group of people many of us believe are responsible for most of the problems in kids' sports today—parents. But that's exactly why we need to do it.

For more than three decades the experts have been telling us that if we would simply spend about the same amount of time we typically devote to a single practice session to "coaching" parents, we will make our lives a lot easier and our young athletes' sport experience far more enjoyable (Martens 1978). On the other hand, if we make the common mistake of doing everything we can to avoid parents in the hopes they will magically "go away and leave us alone" ... well, they won't ... and they shouldn't. As Coach Bylsma's quote at the start of this chapter points out, parents come into the sport setting with every personal characteristic imaginable. Some are loud and critical while others are quiet and affirming. Despite their differences, the one thing we can always be assured of is they are all doing what they truly believe in their hearts is what's best for their children. And parents—like coaches—are duty-bound to make sure their kids are receiving what they think is the best possible care and instruction—at home, at school, in the community, and on the playing field.

171

Even though parents and coaches are supposedly working toward the same goal, they don't always agree on the means and methods by which that goal should be achieved. In fact, some of the most disturbing events in all of sport have occurred as "all hell broke loose" when parents and coaches should have been working together for the betterment of their kids. The following are just a few examples of complete coach-parent meltdowns.

Reading, MA, July 5, 2000: A pickup youth hockey game becomes — even by hockey standards — unusually chippy and rough. One parent verbally confronts another who is acting as an informal coach and referee. Angry words are soon replaced by flying fists. In the end, the father who was ironically objecting to the violent level of play slams the head of the coach into the floor so many times and with such force that the medical examiner testifies it nearly severs his head from the rest of his body. Several young athletes watch in horror as the entire event unfolds. The victim never regains consciousness and dies in the hospital the next day [Butterfield 2002].

Centennial, CO, February 1, 2002: Two days after a Massachusetts man is sentenced to serve 6 to 10 years in prison for killing another parent in the previously described fight over excessive roughness in youth hockey play, a disagreement over the same issue erupts into an all-out melee among more than a dozen hockey parents. The altercation becomes so intense that the game has to be postponed and four parents — one of whom is an off-duty police lieutenant — are charged with disorderly conduct [Sink 2002].

Livingston, NJ, April 10, 2004: The mother of a Little League baseball player gets upset when the boy's coach won't give her a team hat and t-shirt for her son who was not at practice. The coach says he wants to first offer the hat and shirt to players who attended the practice. Unfortunately, he also can't resist making snide comments about her husband's (a former team coach) ability as a coach. The mother goes home and tells her husband who immediately heads to the practice field, grabs the coach by the neck and punches him in the face a couple of times. After parents separate the pair, the still-infuriated father picks up an aluminum baseball bat and uses it to bash the coach in the head, leg, and arm [USAToday.com 2004].

Philadelphia, PA, October 22, 2006: A group of parents attending a "Little Guys Conference" peewee football game begin "hollering and cursing" at a substitute coach. The verbal abuse escalates into pushing and shoving and a brawl breaks out. One of the parents feels he's losing the fight and pulls a .357 magnum from his belt and points it at the coach. The entire parent-coach fracas takes place in front of the 5- and 6-year-old football players [Santoliquito 2006].

Springfield, MA, March 9, 2012: A group of 10–12-year-old basketball players exchanging post-game handshakes are knocked to the ground by an irate father of a losing player as he rushes to attack the winning coach. The man strikes the sixth-graders' coach in the face and body with his fists and then bites off part of his left ear. Several youngsters are left on the floor crying as bystanders pull the father off the coach. The coach's ear was reattached at a local hospital after the game [McCarthy 2012].

Although these kinds of "over-the-top" physical altercations between parents and coaches seem to be increasing, they are still — at this point anyway — extreme examples of what can happen when the relationship between parents and coaches breaks down. Far less sensational — but much more prevalent — are the disagreements between parents and coaches that have become a routine — even expected — part of coaching.

If we stop to think about it, the inherent volatility of youth sports makes it almost inevitable that conflicts will develop between parents and coaches. By their very nature youth sports regularly bring together immature, emotional children; overprotective, unrealistic parents; and over-pressured, under-prepared coaches. These explosive ingredients are then mixed and agitated in a boiling cauldron of publicly observable and critically evaluated performances. Is it any wonder that such a potent concoction often ends up with parents and coaches (and sometimes even kids) at each other's throats — either figuratively or literally?

If you're one of those coaches who thinks your sport would benefit from the total exclusion of parents, think again. Parents are — or at least should be — the foundation of any successful athletic program. So it's up to us, as coaches, to do everything we can to help parents willingly become our allies rather than enemies. And it's not nearly as hard as it sounds. Just think back on all the disagreements you've witnessed (or experienced) between coaches and parents. It's a pretty safe bet that most of these disputes resulted from — or were at least aggravated by — a lack of communication between the warring parties. Spending a little time helping parents better understand the goals of our program, our personal coaching philosophy, and the responsibilities we all have to provide kids with the best possible experiences, will pay off many times over throughout the season.

The Importance of a Parent-Orientation Meeting

By taking time from our busy schedules to meet "face-to-face" with our athletes' parents, we're demonstrating our recognition and respect for the legitimate concerns parents have regarding their kids' involvement in our sport. When conducted properly, there are at least 10 important things a preseason meeting can help us accomplish:

(1) Establish a positive and productive line of communication between the two most important set of people in the lives of our athletes — their parents and their coaches.

(2) Assure the parents that — like them — we have the best interest of their children at heart.

(3) Collect essential medical, health, and emergency information.

(4) Inform parents about the types and severity of injuries that are common in our sport.

(5) Communicate the guiding philosophies — our own philosophy as a coach and that held by the sponsoring organization or agency — that will govern all team-related decisions.

(6) Provide important logistical information about the day-to-day operations of the team.

(7) Establish basic "ground rules" covering the required, encouraged, and prohibited behaviors that are expected of everyone involved with the team — coaches, parents, and athletes alike.

(8) Establish agreed-upon goals for the team.

(9) Initiate an ongoing social contract among everyone involved with the team that can be used to "remind" those who later engage in inappropriate behavior.

(10) Recruit willing parents to volunteer to help with important team tasks.

Although the exact format of a preseason meeting is largely a matter of personal preference, many coaches can be intimidated — and reluctant to conduct the meeting — simply because they don't know exactly where to begin. To let coaches see how simple and straightforward a preseason meeting really is — and to make sure the important elements aren't overlooked — here is a basic outline for a preseason meeting agenda (Martens 2012).

Introductions. The obvious place to begin our parent orientation session is by taking about 10 minutes to introduce ourselves and our assistant coaches to the parents (and to give the parents a chance to introduce themselves as well). Parents will appreciate hearing about why we decided to be a coach and why they should feel at ease allowing us to work closely with the single thing in this world they value more than life itself— their children. Because parents are entrusting us with their dearest possession, we need to let them know what makes us qualified to assume this important responsibility. When organizing the introduction portion of our parent-orientation session it might help to think about the things we would like to know about a teacher or coach who was going to work with our children. Here, for example, are some questions we might have:

- Why does this person want to coach my kids? (Coaching can sometimes be a demanding and thankless job. What's in it for this coach?)

- What type of experience does the coach bring to this position? (Does this coach know enough about the sport at this level to help my kids develop essential skills and enjoy the game?)
- Does the coach have any formal training as a coach or teacher? (Does this coach really know how to interact with and teach kids at this level?)
- Will this coach treat every player on the team fairly? (Even though athletes will have different abilities and skills, will the coach have "favorites" who are given preferential treatment?)
- Is the coach trained to deal with medical emergencies? (If my child is injured, will this coach be able to take appropriate action)?

Coaching philosophy. Once we've introduced ourselves, explained why we think coaching is such an important job, and indicated why we're qualified to be a coach, it makes sense to elaborate a bit more (maybe another 10 minutes or so) about our coaching philosophy — how and why we've decided to coach the way we do. Make no mistake; the way we coach is always a deliberate choice. We choose to be critical or compassionate, aloof or approachable, stormy or stoic. And there is ample evidence that any and all of these coaching traits can contribute to our success — or failure. Every coaching decision we make — from distributing playing time and determining positions, to the way we structure our practices, to the way we interact with athletes, parents, and officials — is a direct reflection of our coaching philosophy. That's why it's important to help parents understand how we view the world. Table 13.1 is a little self-examination we should all take to gain a better sense of our coaching philosophy. Once we understand ourselves as a coach, we'll be in a better position to tell others — in this case our athletes' parents — what they can expect from us.

Table 13.1: Discovering Your Coaching Philosophy.

By considering what is important to you as a coach, you'll be able to uncover your basic coaching philosophy. Although there are no right or wrong answers, it is important you justify your responses.

1. What is the main purpose of sport at the level you are coaching? Please explain your answer.

2. To what extent do you agree with the following statement "I will sacrifice a game — or even a season — before I'll sacrifice an athlete's physical or psychological well-being"? Please explain your answer.

3. On this team, playing time and position played will be determined on the basis of...

_____

4. In order for me to consider myself a successful coach this season, I feel...

_____

5. The one thing, above all else, I owe every athlete on this team is...

_____

6. The one thing, above all else, every athlete on this team owes me is...

_____

7. The one thing, above all else, I owe every athlete's parent is...

_____

8. The one thing, above all else, every athlete's parent owes me is...

_____

9. At the end of the season, the one thing that would make me proudest would be...

_____

10. At the end of the season, the one thing I hope every athlete says about me is...

_____

When you've completed your self-assessment, go back and try to figure out what your responses, when taken as a whole, say about you as a coach. If you feel a bit uncomfortable about what you've just learned about yourself, consider how you need to change. If, on the other hand, you're comfortable with who you are as a coach, you're ready to share this philosophy with your athletes' parents.

Demonstration. Being able to effectively demonstrate the proper performance of a sport skill is a coach's "stock-in-trade." Although you probably expect to demonstrate skills to your athletes, you may not realize that showing parents how you help your athletes learn new sport skills during the parent orientation meeting is a good way to accomplish several important objectives. First, the parents will get to see, with their own two eyes, that you really know your sport. Your credibility as a coach will skyrocket if you can just show the parents you have a solid grasp of how to teach the basic skills required in your sport in an age-appropriate way. By proving you can give an effective demonstration you've shown the parents that you know how to teach complex motor skills to their children. Demonstrating the execution of a fundamental sport skill in front of the parents might also provide the parents with a better understanding of how at least one basic element of their child's sport is correctly performed. Depending on the sport you're coaching, some parents may already have a pretty good understanding about how the game is played. However, if the sport is one they didn't learn when they were growing up, they may need you to provide them with a "crash course" in the fundamentals of the game. It shouldn't come as a great surprise that many of our athletes' parents don't know the first thing about lacrosse, soccer, gymnastics, snowboarding, rowing, or martial arts. You might be surprised, however, by how many adults have never been correctly instructed the basics of even popular spectator sports like golf, tennis, hockey, football, basketball, and baseball. Because conflicts between parents and coaches are often rooted in a lack of understanding regarding the technical and tactical skills required in the sport, simply taking a little time at the beginning of the season to educate the parents might help you avoid some future problems. Finally, having the parents try to perform even the most basic skills in their child's sport is often an "eye-opener" for them in terms of how difficult the sport really is. This humbling experience will generally keep "know-it-all" parents from trying to convince you, other parents, or their kids that they are experts at this sport. Once they give it a try, they quickly see that much of what their kids are doing is not nearly as easy as it looks from the sideline.

Potential risks. As coaches, we need to understand — and help parents understand — that there are inherent risks associated with participating in any sport. Obviously, in relatively slow-paced, individual sports like golf, archery, or bowling, the risk of serious physical injury — although still possible — is minimal. On the other hand, fast-paced, contact and collision sports like hockey, football, basketball, or lacrosse place athletes at considerable risk for relatively minor injuries (cuts and bruises, muscle, tendon, and ligament injury, etc.) and can, on the rarest of occasions, result in catastrophic permanent injury or even death (Radelet, et al. 2002). Unfortunately, some coaches are hesitant to talk honestly with the parents about injuries their children might sustain while participating in their sport. Perhaps they think that telling parents about the risk of injury will cause needlessly worry and, in some cases, even scare the parents so badly that they will refuse to permit the child to participate in the sport. Although it's always possible that parents will overreact when informed of the physical risks their children face, we need to remind ourselves that withholding the truth from our athletes' parents certainly won't make the athletes any safer; nor is it likely to produce the trusting and respectful relationship we hope to foster. The best course of action is to openly and honestly discuss the risk of injury by putting it in the proper context. It's a good idea, for example, to reassure the parents that most sport injuries are relatively minor and you have specifically designed your practices and the systematic conditioning of the athletes to reduce the likelihood these injuries occur in the first place. In addition, you need to emphasize your complete and total commitment to providing their children with as safe a playing environment as possible (e.g., by inspecting all playing surfaces before each practice and competition, examining the protective equipment for wear, tear, and proper fit, and eliminating hazardous horseplay). This is also a great time to reiterate your training in emergency medical care and the fact you have developed — and routinely rehearse — an emergency practice plan with your team. Legal decisions across the country have consistently supported the contention that coaches have a legal (as well as ethical) duty to inform athletes (or their parents) of the risks associated with participating in their sport (Cotten and Wilde 1997). Therefore, if our athletes are ever seriously injured, the courts will immediately check to see if there is evidence that we adequately warned the participants of the risks involved in our sport. Although warning athletes and parents will not necessarily keep us from being sued — or in some cases even losing the lawsuit — it's almost certain that if we fail to warn parents of the potential risks their sons and daughters face by participating in our sport we are far more likely to be held legally and financially liable if a terrible injury occurs. Protecting ourselves from astronomical legal expenses may seem reason enough to warn parents of the potential risks their children face by playing our sport, but the real reason we set aside time to discuss risk during our parent orientation session is that it's the right thing to do. Parents are well within their rights to expect us to inform them of the likelihood of their child sustaining an injury while participating in our sport. It's only when they've been given this information that the parents can grant their *informed* consent to allow their children to participate.

Program information. This is the "nuts-and-bolts" of our program. To reduce the chances of conflicts arising from simple misunderstandings, it's a good idea to not only address these topics briefly during the parent orientation session, but to provide "hard copies" of this information in the form of handouts or on your personal or program webpage. The following list presents the type of the information we typically need to share with parents:

- How often, when, and where does the team practice?
- How long is the season?
- How many contests will there be? When and where will they be held?
- What rules govern the transportation of athletes to and from competitions and practices?
- How do you decide who competes in certain positions or events and the amount of playing time each athlete receives?

- How frequently does the team travel, and who pays the expenses?
- What equipment does each athlete need to purchase?
- Where is equipment available, and how much does it cost?
- What insurance requirements are there, if any?
- How, when, and where can parents communicate with you or your assistants?
- Are medical examinations necessary for the players to compete?
- Who decides when an athlete is ready to return to play after an injury?
- Are there any nutritional or hydration needs for athletes in this sport that should be considered?
- Are there any specific eligibility requirements?
- What can parents do at home to facilitate the athlete's physical development or learning of sport skills?
- How and when should the parents contact you — and how do you intend to contact them when necessary?

Behavioral expectations. We've now arrived at the part of the parent orientation session most coaches dread but it's also the part that will go a long way in determining how enjoyable the season is for the coaches, the parents and — most importantly — the athletes. In fact, it's no exaggeration to say that these 15 to 20 minutes will very likely make or break your entire season. It's crucial that everyone affiliated with the team, in any capacity, fully understands their unique and essential role. Equally important, of course, is an appreciation for the behavioral expectations that are associated with that role — and the consequences that come from failing to meet those expectations. To simplify our discussion it might be helpful to think about it this way: By the end of the parent orientation session it's important that everyone agrees with the basic premise that there are three distinct roles on this team: (1) athlete, (2) coach, or (3) parent. In addition, there are specific behaviors within each of these roles that will be: (1) required, (2) encouraged, or (3) prohibited. These three roles and the three categories of behavioral expectations can be presented to the parents in the form of the chart such as the one shown in Table 13.2. Notice that the examples of behaviors in each category are just there to get you started. Depending on your sport, the age of the athletes, and the issues you've experienced in the past, you can make each section of the chart as detailed as you wish. You may even want to put together a single page covering each type of behavior. The important thing here is that parents aren't made to feel as if they are being singled out in your discussion of appropriate and inappropriate behaviors. *Everyone* associated with this team — including coaches — are expected to act in a way that will benefit all athletes and help the team accomplish its stated goals. It's only fair to warn you (but you probably saw it coming) that this is the portion of the parent orientation session where most of the disagreements generally occur. Make sure you can justify why each behavior in your chart has been classified as required, encouraged, or prohibited. The last thing in the world we want to do at this point is get into a shouting match with the parents. We need to resist the temptation to argue our case with the parents

	Team Role		
	Athlete	**Coach**	**Parent**
Required Behaviors	• Attend all practices and competitions (or notify the coach in advance) • Immediately notify the coach whenever an injury occurs	• Treat every athlete with the utmost dignity and respect • Inspect all playing surfaces and equipment before every competition and practice	• Attend the parent orientation session prior to the season • Complete a parental consent form and emergency treatment authorization card
Encouraged Behaviors	• Support and encourage teammates when they've made mistakes • Pay attention to (and comply with) all coaching instructions	• Structure practices and games to make the sport fun and exciting for all athletes • Allow athletes to assume as much responsibility for team decision-making as possible	• Provide supportive comments to all players from both teams • Help your child practice sport skills at home
Prohibited Behaviors	• Arguing with officials and coaches or taunting other athletes • Participating in (or encouraging) the hazing (initiation) of teammates	• Arguing with or confronting a parent or official • Using any form of tobacco or alcohol in the presence of athletes	• Taunting or arguing with any coach, player, or official • Hollering out instructions to the players during the competition

Table 13.2: Team Roles and Behavioral Expectations.

and simply listen carefully to their concerns while stating the reason these behavior policies are in place. It often helps to relate the policies back to your coaching philosophy and the philosophy espoused by the sponsoring organization. Emphasize that coaches and parents must work together — as partners — to make sure all the kids on the team have a safe, enjoyable sport experience. If a parent or two still doesn't agree with the behavioral policies that have been established for everyone affiliated with the team, offer to discuss it with them in a respectful, quiet, and private manner after the session. If there are parents who still don't "get it," suggest that they just "give it a try for a week" and you'll be happy to talk with them about it again at that time.

Question-and-answer period. Be sure to set aside a few minutes at the end of the parent orientation session for questions and answers. Despite our best efforts to prepare a thorough and complete session, there's no way we'll be able to anticipate all the concerns and questions the parents will have. Perhaps some of their questions will be on issues we think we've adequately covered. We can't let this upset us. Maybe we didn't explain ourselves as clearly as we could have the first time. It's important to keep in mind that the only goal of this session is to facilitate communication and understanding and it really doesn't matter how many times we have to cover the same material — as long as everybody is on the same page in the end. Another thing that can keep us from becoming frustrated with a particular parent is to remind ourselves that if one parent asks a question, it's probably a safe assumption that several others have similar concerns. When it's all said and done, the degree to which our parent orientation session is successful is not based on whether we have "out-debated" or "shouted-down" all the parents, but that the parents understand how they can act to best serve the needs of all athletes on the team.

Closing remarks. When the session is over, remember to thank the parents for taking time from their busy schedules and mention how encouraging it is to see so many parents interested in providing the best sport experience for their children. Reinforce how import it is that parents and coaches are always "pulling in the same direction" to benefit the kids and that you'll always be interested in their comments and suggestions — as long as they are offered in an attempt to improve the experiences of *everyone* on the team (not just their son or daughter). This also allows us to reinforce how parents can get in touch with us if questions or concerns arise during the season. Finally, offer to stay after the session for a few minutes to continue the discussion with anyone who wants to discuss any additional topics (make sure you've set this time aside in your schedule before offering to stay).

Hints for conducting a parent-orientation meeting. As is the case with nearly every aspect of coaching, close attention to detail can make the difference between the success and failure of your parent orientation session. Here are a few suggestions that are almost certain to make your session a big hit with the parents:

• *Encourage a league or school administrator to attend your parent orientation session.* Just having an official of the sponsoring organization present at our parent orientation session will automatically boost our credibility with the parents. Without uttering a single word the administrator is sending a clear message that the organization is backing us to the hilt. There's no point in disgruntled parents trying to "go over our head" because the league is totally supportive of our coaching policies and procedures. In addition, questions might arise during the session that can best be responded to by an organizational representative.

• *Provide some light refreshments.* There's no need to overdo it here. A couple of pizzas, a big bag of chips and a liter or two of soda pop will do just fine. Throw in a bag or two of cookies from the local grocery store and you're in business. It's not really about what you bring as much as simply showing the parents you appreciate them stopping by and you recognize that some of them may have had to forego dinner just to be there. You might even be able to convince the sponsoring organization to foot the bill. Either way, it's a pretty small price to pay to make the parents feel welcome and positive about being at this important session.

• *Use concrete examples.* One of the easiest ways to get parents discussing appropriate (and inappropriate) behavior is to give them some real-world examples of coaches and parents behaving badly (like those presented at the beginning of this chapter). Putting parents into small groups and giving them a chance to discuss the inappropriateness of the behaviors and the opportunity to suggest more productive ways of dealing with these issues will usually get parents thinking about their own behaviors — without directly confronting them. Most of us find it a lot easier to recognize bad behaviors on the part of others than ourselves, and parents are certainly no exception.

• *Lighten things up with a little humor.* Because of potential conflicts and disagreements that can arise from some of the content, it's not unusual for parent orientation sessions to quickly start to take on the tone of critical, finger-waging, lectures — which we all find about as pleasant as being force-fed a cupful of castor oil. When this happens, parents naturally begin to get defensive and simply tune us out. Fortunately, there are ways to get parents to have a laugh or two at the way they sometimes behave by showing humorous video clips such as those produced by Hockey Canada (Hockey Canada 2002; 2003). The six 30-second videos are part of the *Relax, It's Just a Game* public service announcement (PSA) campaign designed to raise awareness and promote discussion of inappropriate adult behavior by showing how ridiculous some parents sound when they put excessive pressure on their kids. There are basically two sets of videos. The first set (Hockey Canada 2002) depicts as series of role-reversals where kids are watching their parents engage in routine tasks (a dad being pulled over for a traffic violation, a mom shopping at the grocery store, and a dad playing golf with his buddies). Throughout each scene, the kid is constantly yelling instructions and criticizing the parent's every move. The tag line that appears at the end of each clip is, "What if kids pressured us the way we pressure them?" The other set of videos (Hockey Canada, 2003) show parents acting overly competitive during inane children's activities such as a "potato sack" race, a game of "hide and seek," or a birthday party game of "pin the tail on the donkey." After we see the parents behaving foolishly the screen goes blank and a tag line comes on asking the viewer to consider the question, "If it's wrong here, what makes it right at the rink?"

• *Recruit parents to help with important team tasks.* Many coaches have already discovered the advantages of involving parents in team activities. First, parents can serve as assistant coaches, scorekeepers, equipment managers, or just another set of eyes and ears to help keep our games and practices organized, efficient, and safe. Equally important is the "off-the-field" help parents can provide by chaperoning team outings or taking turns bringing snacks, drinks, and ice (for keeping cool or soothing those inevitable bumps and bruises) to practices. As useful as these tasks are, perhaps the main reason we need to recruit parents to help us with the team can be found in the old adage, "The Devil finds work for idle hands to do." Parents who truly feel the need to play an active role in their children's sport participation will find a way to be involved — whether it's appropriate or not and whether we like it or not. By seeking them out in advance and offering them "a really important job" we at least have given ourselves a fighting chance of channeling their natural involvement into more productive behaviors. If we keep our potentially disruptive parents busy performing important tasks, they simply won't have as much time to create problems for our team.

Working with Parents to Support Our Athletes

A successful parent-orientation meeting is one of the best ways to start the season on a positive note but it's only just that — a start. We need to continue to foster good communication with parents throughout the entire season. One of the main reasons coaches and parents find themselves at loggerheads is that they both tend to lose sight of the fact that amateur sport is (or was at least designed to be) conducted solely for the benefit of the athlete(s)—not for the benefit of coaches, and not for the benefit of parents. To emphasize that point, let's remind ourselves of a famous Coach Wooden quote, "I did not refer to UCLA as 'my team' or the athletes as 'my players'" (Wooden 1997, 123). It's clear the Coach understood that each and every one of his actions had to be in the best interest of the athletes.

As we know, sometimes a picture is worth a thousand words. The rela-

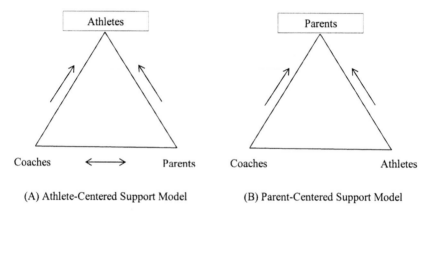

(A) Athlete-Centered Support Model   (B) Parent-Centered Support Model

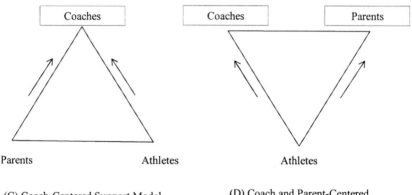

(C) Coach-Centered Support Model   (D) Coach and Parent-Centered
                                                Support Model

Figure 13.1: Models of Coach/Athlete/Parent Support.

tionships depicted in Figure 13.1 illustrate how the three main characters in most sport settings — athletes, coaches, and parents — can support one another. These support triangles are an synthesis, elaboration and extension of models first set forth in Hellstedt's "Coach/Parent/Athlete Triangle" (1987) and McPherson's "Little League Triangle" (1978).

In the first triangle (Model A), notice that the coaches and parents are working together to provide a solid base of support for the ongoing development of the athlete. This is the way sport is "supposed" to be. In the real world, however, we often see one of the other, more dysfunctional, models of support.

Model B shows parents as the center of consideration with both coaches and athletes working to satisfy the needs of the parents. In this model, it's all about the parents. A successful athlete is often seen by the parents as either a "meal ticket," a "retirement plan," or as indicator of their self-worth as parents. The coaches in this model are merely used as "a means to an end." They are present to make certain the athlete develops the technical and tactical skills necessary for success — nothing more, nothing less. It's not unusual for parents to simply dispose of and replace these coaches on a whim, whenever they feel he or she is not providing the athlete with the proper skills to get them to the "next level." This type of "Parent-Centered" relationship has been described in detail by tennis great Andre Agassi in his bestselling book *Open: An Autobiography* (Agassi 2009) and in the bizarre story of former Oakland Raiders quarterback Todd Marinovich which has become the classic tale of parental exploitation and manipulation of young athletes (Looney 1988).

Model C is basically the reverse of Model B. Here everyone is working to support the coach's needs. Parents are generally viewed as troublesome meddlers who, at best, need to be tolerated or, better yet, completely ignored. Athlete development in this model is viewed as a way to advance the reputation or career of the coach. A prime example of a coaches who demand center stage are perhaps the most famous Olympic coaches in the world, Bela and Martha Karolyi, whose abusive and demeaning coaching tactics were revealed in Joan Ryan's expose of the hothouse world of figure skating and gymnastics (Ryan 2000).

Finally, Model D is perhaps the most dysfunctional of all support models. Notice that it is turned completely upside down with the athletes providing total and simultaneous support to *both* their coaches and their parents. In many ways this is an appalling blend of Model B and Model C. Here, both the parents and the coaches are using the athletes as tools to fulfill their own selfish interests. Athlete exploitation is the primary feature of

Model D and can be found in a variety of sports. Again, the egotistical Bela Karolyi sometimes teams up with greedy and self-centered parents to take advantage of athletes in order to advance each of their own personal agendas. Gold medal winning gymnast Dominique Moceanu's memoir *Off Balance* depicts both her coach, Karolyi, and her father, Dumitru, demanding that she provide them with the fame and fortune they craved. It got so bad Dominique even had to legally separate herself from her parents after they stole and squandered her sizable earnings (Moceanu 2012).

Although it may sometimes seem as if parents are a major problem in sport today, that's simply not the case. It's a good thing parents are concerned about their kids and involved in their activities. Sure, some parents go way too far in terms of their involvement, but even then, we often have only ourselves to blame. By refusing to take time to build a strong working relationship with parents — for the betterment of the athletes — we often end up aggravating minor misunderstandings. A portion of Coach Bylsma's depiction of his own parents should serve as the athlete development model we are working toward, "I was lucky enough to have two parents who were quiet, very affirming, and only asked that I do my best — and did so in private and never scolded or berated me in public" (Bylsma and Bylsma 2001, 131).

Myth No. 14

"Great Players Are Likely to Become Great Coaches"

Do not equate professional expertise with your ability to teach it. There's a big difference between knowing what you're doing and knowing how to teach what you want done — in ALL areas.
— Coach John Wooden[1]

Coach Wooden's strong admonition that we resist the temptation to equate personal expertise with an ability to teach it may sound like just so many hollow words until you consider that this man was the first person ever to be inducted into the Basketball Hall of Fame as *both* a player (1961) and a coach (1973). Not only does his tremendous achievements as a athlete and a basketball coach give him the "street creds" to back up such a statement, it's a topic he is more familiar with than you might imagine — or than he'd like to admit.

Johnny Wooden developed a reputation as a schoolboy "phenom" while playing for Martinsville High School in the heart of the basketball-crazed state of Indiana. Although his hometown had a total population of only 4,800, more than 5,200 screaming fans would regularly pack the high school gym on East Morgan Street to see the powerfully-built farm boy lead his "Artesians" to three consecutive state title games — winning it all his junior year (Wooden 1997; 2004). Wooden went on to be a three-time All-American guard at Purdue, leading his team to a national championship in his senior year. At the time of his graduation, Wooden was considered by many to be the best basketball player in the country.

Like today, coaching positions at the time were often filled by hiring top athletes. It was (and still is) commonly thought that a great player possessed the knowledge and skills necessary to become a great coach. As a result — even in the midst of the Great Depression — Wooden's reputation as an outstanding athlete easily landed him a job coaching high school football, basketball, baseball, and track in Dayton Kentucky. But despite his extraordinary skills as a player, he knew next to nothing about the art and science of coaching. As Coach Wooden honestly concedes:

> If pressed, school officials would have told you that Johnny Wooden, a three-time All–American and Big 10 scoring leader while a member of the national champion Purdue Boilermakers basketball team, was on the Dayton faculty ... because he knew all about coaching and leadership. They were wrong.... With all that experience and know-how as a player, I thought I understood basketball pretty well — and I did. Unfortunately, I didn't know beans from apple butter about teaching it [Wooden 2005, 3; 93].

With this quote, the basketball legend who would later be recognized by many — including ESPN and *The Sporting News* — as the greatest American coach of the 20th Century (Nater and Gallimore 2006; D'Alessio 2009) is telling us two important things: (1) great athletes are often assumed to possess comparable skills in the area of coaching and leadership, and (2) even though he had been one of the top athletes of his day, he was totally unprepared to teach the game he had mastered as a player. And Coach Wooden isn't alone in having difficulty making the transition from great athlete to great coach.

The Surprisingly Mediocre Coaching Careers of Top Athletes

Just think about how many true sport superstars have turned out to be dismal failures when they tried to do what, at least on the surface, seems like a pretty straightforward task — simply teach others how to do the one thing they, themselves could do better than almost anyone else in the world. Hall of Famers like Ted Williams and Frank Robinson (baseball), Isiah Thomas and Wilt Chamberlin (basketball), Bart Starr and Norm Van Brocklin (football), and Wayne Gretzky and "Boom Boom" Geoffrion (hockey) struggled mightily when they tried their hand at coaching in the leagues they once dominated as players.

That's not to say that exceptionally talented athletes never succeed in becoming a great coach. Former Los Angeles Dodger and New York Yankee Manager Joe Torre, for example, ranks fifth in all-time managerial wins, and guided the New York Yankees to ten American League East Division title, six American League Pennants and four World Series titles. Unlike most great head coaches or managers, Torre had also been a nine-time Major League All-Star and the 1971 National League MVP during his days as a player. Similarly, at the college level, the 1966 Heisman Trophy winner,

Steve Spurrier, became a coaching legend with his success — including a National Championship — as the head coach at his alma mater, the University of Florida. Pat Summitt, the winningest college basketball coach in the country was also an elite college basketball player who captained the first Women's Olympic basketball team in 1976. But despite these notable exceptions, it's remarkable to consider the general lack of success some of the best athletes have as coaches — especially when compared to the outstanding coaching careers of, well, let's just say "far less talented" athletes.

The Surprisingly Mediocre Athletic Careers of Most Top Coaches

While many things contribute to the overall success of a coach, it's rather apparent that playing at an elite level has virtually no bearing on coaching productivity. In nearly every sport, most of the top coaches have relatively little or no personal playing experience.

Although we may never agree on who was the all-time best coach in the National Football League, there are a few names that would undoubtedly appear somewhere near the top of everyone's list: Vince Lombardi, Bill Belichick, Bill Parcells, Chuck Noll, Bill Walsh, Don Shula, Marv Levy, John Madden, Joe Gibbs, Mike Holmgren, George Allen, Paul Brown, and the list continues. What's interesting about this "Who's Who" of football coaches is the general absence of any star athletes. Noll and Shula were average players in the NFL for a few years but most of the others never played as much as a single down of professional football. And football isn't the only sport where many of the best coaches had little playing experience.

Since its inception at the end of the 1973–74 season, only five men have been honored multiple times with the Jack Adams Trophy — signifying the Coach of the Year in the National Hockey League. Of the five multiple recipients, Jacques Lamaire (1994 & 2003) is the one truly outstanding hockey player while Pat Quinn (1980 & 1992) bounced around as a journeyman player for several NHL teams during his career. The remainder, Jacque Demers (1987 & 1988), Scotty Bowman (1977 & 1996), and Pat Burns (1989, 1993, & 1998), never laced up a pair of skates for an NHL game. In fact, Burns — the only three-time winner — has as the exact same number of NHL Coach of the Year awards as games played in the Ontario (Junior) Hockey League.

And let's not overlook the mediocre playing careers of some of the most successful baseball managers. While the names Earl Weaver, Jim Leyland, Tommy Lasorda, Sparky Anderson, Bobby Cox and the Hall of Famer Walter Alston will always be remembered for their managerial skills that led to a total of 12 World Series Championships, their talents were not nearly as impressive when they stepped "between the lines." Weaver and Leyland didn't play in the majors at all, Lasorda finished his 26 game big-league pitching career with a dismal 0–4 win-loss record and an ERA of 6.48, Anderson batted an anemic .218 during his single season with the Philadelphia Phillies, Cox hit .225 in just over a year with the Yankees, and Alston — who would later lead the Dodgers to four World Series Championships between 1955 and 1965 — struck out in his only major league at bat and committed an error on one of the two opportunities he had in the field.

The point here is not to argue that great athletes can never *become* great coaches. John Wooden is living proof to the contrary. What is important to remember is that merely being a great athlete will never *make* anyone a great coach. It's pretty apparent that what turned Coach Wooden from what he readily admits was "a good player — a bad coach" (Wooden 2004, 55) into the "Coach of the Century" was his insight to recognize why good athletes often fail as coaches and what they can do to *learn* to teach the game properly.

Why Great Athletes Often Don't Make Great Coaches

Although it's impossible to precisely pinpoint what it is that causes so many great athletes to struggle as coaches, there are plenty of plausible explanations. It may be that truly great athletes develop their skills to the point that they no longer even think about what they are actually doing. Another possibility is that great players sometimes have a hard time relating to lesser-skilled athletes who seem incapable of performing at a level that was almost second nature to the old coach. Finally, some elite athletes suffer from the delusion that their athletic prowess is evidence that they already know just about everything there is to know about their sport — including how to coach it.

Great athletes perform on "automatic pilot." A combination of extraordinary natural ability and years of practice and repetition can result in exceptional athletic performance — even of very complex skills — with little or no conscious thought or attention. We marvel, for example, at how elite basketball players like Kobe Bryant or LeBron James can dribble a basketball — behind their backs and between their legs — while constantly analyzing the position of teammates and opponents alike as they dash and dodge nonstop around the court. We are amazed that Tom Brady and Peyton Manning seem to have developed a "sixth sense" that tells them when their pass protection is breaking down. But can these incredible athletes teach mere mortals how to execute these tasks they, themselves, seem to perform almost without thinking? Probably not. In fact, can they even describe exactly what it is they're doing? Probably not. And that may be because they're actually *not* thinking about what they're doing. They are operating in what performance scientists refer to as the "autonomic" stage of learning (Fitts and Posner 1967) but coaches like to call "muscle memory." For what our muscle memory metaphor lacks in pure precision it more than makes up for in elegant simplicity. It's almost as if the muscles remember exactly what to do on their own, thus freeing up the real brain to consider more complex or rapidly changing environmental cues. Accomplished athletes can simply flip the "automatic pilot" switch for their well-learned motor movements and attend to other, more pressing, matters. Although learning to execute sport skills with a certain degree of "unconscious competence" may be required for top-level athletic performance, coaches are unlikely to find it helpful when trying to teach the skill to others. And this may not be the only personal trait that is an asset to an athlete but a liability for a coach.

Great athletes can get frustrated and impatient with learners. Elite athletes are, by definition, extremely competent people — at least in their sport. They often possess an inordinate amount of physical ability, a highly competitive nature, and work ethic few can match. As coaches, we purposely seek out individuals who possess huge amounts of talent, desire, and drive because we recognize these traits as the foundation of athletic greatness. Ironically, these unique characteristics that are the essential building blocks of athletic performance are apt to be stumbling blocks in the coaching profession. Coach Wooden, for example, describes how the very skills that had served him so well as a player betrayed him during the early part of his coaching career:

> Coaching basketball presented its own challenges, many of which I wasn't prepared for. I not only saw my temper flare up, but I was too critical, impatient, eager to fill players full of information, and quickly irritated when they couldn't absorb it. Since everything had come easily for me as a player, I didn't understand why these young men couldn't do the same [Wooden 2004, 55].

Although it's hard to believe, even the stoic Coach Wooden was completely overcome by the constant frustration and impatience he felt when teaching the simplest skills to novice athletes:

> I pushed harder and talked louder. Harder and louder were my teaching techniques... My impatience precluded good teaching. I am embarrassed to say that during my second week of practice as Dayton's football coach I got involved in a fracas with one of the players, a fight, because my teaching skills were so green and my fuse — my patience — so short [Wooden 2005, 95].

Can you imagine? The mild-mannered John Wooden, of all people, in a fist fight with one of his high school athletes. This one story, more than any other, illustrates the way athletic talent, competitiveness, and striving for perfectionism — all valuable traits in an athlete — can undermine the efforts of even the best coaches.

Great athletes sometimes assume they already know how to coach. Many exceptional athletes — and those who hire them as coaches — suffer from the false assumption that the ability to perform a skill properly will directly correlate with the ability to teach it to others. Oddly enough, however, it's not unusual for the "stars" of a team to know less about how their sport is properly played — and taught — than their less talented teammates who ride the bench. After all, really good players spend most of their time playing. Whether it's in practice or competition, they are always in the heat of the battle. But almost all of this "doing" is confined to their own narrow area of responsibility and can thus make it difficult for them to appreciate what others — coaches and teammates — are doing, thinking, or feeling. Simply put, they fail to develop a sense of the big picture. Poorer players, on the other hand, have plenty of time — often far more than they would like — to observe, listen, and learn from those around them without the constant "distraction of doing." Of course, most athletes don't see it that way. In my coaching education classes, for example, I often begin by shocking the students when I tell them that "the more you 'know' about sports, the more you're likely to struggle in this class." That's largely because successful sport experiences leave us with the false impression that we know a lot more than we really do. This is why, on the very first page of this book, we began with the quote from Soto Zen master Shunryu Suzuki (1970): "In the beginner's mind there are many possibilities, but in the expert's there are few." and why Coach Wooden always posted a sign in his office reminding him (and others) that "It's what you learn AFTER you know it ALL that counts" (Wooden 2004, 109). Great athletes would undoubtedly be far better coaches if they would frequently remind themselves how little they truly know about coaching their sport.

Becoming a Great Coach: The National Standards for Sport Coaches

If, as we've seen, athletic prowess isn't the key of coaching competence, what is? What criteria should those in positions of hiring, supervising, and evaluating coaches be considering as true indicators of coaching potential and performance? And finally, what should we, as coaches, be using to assess our own technical proficiency and to guide our ongoing professional development? Although it may sound like an impossible task to develop a set of agreed-upon standards of competence that are equally suitable for *all* coaches, at *all* levels, and in *all* sports — it's already been done. And they're sitting there just waiting for coaches, athletic directors, recreation leaders, school boards, and parents to put them to good use.

In 1995, the National Association for Sport and Physical Education published the first set of national standards outlining what administrators, athletes, and the general public should expect athletic coaches — at all levels of competition and in all sports — to know, to value, and be able to do (NASPE 1995). Ten years later, a panel of experts from the United States Olympic Committee (USOC), the National Federation of State High School Associations (NFHS), and the National Association for Sport and Physical Education (NASPE) revised these competencies and organized them into eight broad categories or "domains" of expertise that should be expected of all coaches. Although the exact knowledge, values, and behaviors will differ based on the sport and level of competition, all coaches need to meet specific minimum standards regarding: (1) Philosophy and Ethics, (2) Safety and Injury Prevention, (3) Physical Conditioning, (4) Growth and Development, (5) Teaching and Communication, (6) Sport Skills and Tactics, (7) Organization and Administration, and (8) Program Evaluation. The 40 specific Standards that fall within these domains are set forth in the NASPE publication, *National Standards for Sport Coaches: Quality Coaches, Quality Sports* (2006). By examining the formal rationale for establishing each of the coaching domains, it's easy to see why these National Standards must be met by *all* coaches at *all* levels and in *all* sports.

Domain 1: Philosophy and Ethics. "It is imperative that the coach establishes a coaching philosophy that focuses on the safety, development, and well-being of the athlete. As a key leadership figure, the coach must model and teach appropriate behavior in all aspects of coaching and maintain ethical conduct during practices and competitions" (NASPE 2006, 7).

Domain 2: Safety and Injury Prevention. "The coach is often the first and only responder in the event of an accident or injury and should be properly trained in injury prevention and first responder emergency care. The coach must recognize high-risk situations, as well as unsafe equipment, facilities, and environmental conditions in order to ensure the safety of the athletes and make necessary modifications to the playing environment should unsafe conditions exist" (NASPE 2006, 9).

Domain 3: Physical Conditioning. "Sport requires proper physical preparation in order to perform safely and effectively. The coach is responsible for implementing research-based, developmentally appropriate drills and teaching techniques that support athlete development while maintaining safety. The coach should encourage healthful decisions by the athlete to promote healthy lifestyles and low-risk training practices" (NASPE 2006, 11).

Domain 4: Growth and Development. "The coach should be knowledgeable about the age and skill levels of their (sic) athletes. By recognizing the patterns of cognitive, motor, emotional, and social development, the coach can create effective learning environments that allow athletes to progress and improve at different rates. The coach should be properly trained to recognize the need to modify practice and competitive strategies to accommodate the athlete's readiness for competition" (NASPE 2006, 13).

Domain 5: Teaching and Communication. "The coach must plan and implement organized practices so that athletes have a positive learning experience. In addition to understanding the fundamentals of the sport, the coach should use a variety of systematic instructional techniques to provide a positive learning environment and maximize the potential of each athlete. Furthermore, the coach needs to be aware of his or her own expectations of an athlete's potential and how it impact athlete performance" (NASPE 2006, 14).

Domain 6: Sport Skills and Tactics. "The art and science of coaching includes developing skills of all team members into an efficient and successful group. Knowing how to utilize athletes' abilities to maximize meaningful participation and team success relies on up-to-date understanding of specific sport skills and game tactics" (NASPE 2006, 18).

Domain 7: Organization and Administration. "The coach is an integral resource in the overall administration of the sport program. The coach provides information regarding the needs of the athlete, serves as a key communicator of program goals and policies, and facilitates compliance with established program policies. Program accountability and public trust depend a great deal on the coach's administrative skills" (NASPE 2006, 19).

Domain 8: Evaluation. "The coach needs to be able to make accurate and timely decisions regarding aspects of the sport program. Planning program goals start with a careful analysis of player ability and program needs. Evaluation becomes a critical part of player and staff recruitment and retention as well as of maintaining program accountability Systematic evaluation ensures that the sport program runs smoothly and efficiently and that the goals and objectives of the program are the focus for the coach, athlete, and team" (NASPE 2006, 21).

Practical assessment of coaching competence. It's pretty hard for anyone to make the claim that coaches don't need to possess the knowledge, hold the values, and exhibit the behaviors articulated in the *National Standard for Sport Coaches*. The only problem is there's no way for busy coaches, administrators, and parents to objectively assess if a particular coach (including themselves) actually conduct themselves in accordance with these standards. So here are 30 simple, straight-forward, "yes or no" questions you can ask yourself—or coaches you employ—to get a general sense of their (or your) "coaching competence."

Table 14.1: Rating Yourself (and Others) as a Coach.

Introduction: Too often coaches are evaluated solely on wins or losses. That's often not fair to the coach or their athletes. The following 30 questions are designed to give administrators and parents a better way to judge the competency of their coach by objectively assess essential and desirable coaching behaviors. It also provides coaches with an easy way to engage in on-going self-evaluation. Simply put, by doing—or not doing—these 30 things, coaches are demonstrating the level of commitment and respect they have for their athletes, their communities, their sport, and themselves.

Safety Skills

1. Is the coach certified to handle medical emergencies (e.g., certified in First Aid/CPR, American Red Cross Sport Safety Training, etc.)?

   YES (essential). *It's no exaggeration to say that this type of formal emergency medical training can literally be a matter of life or death to your child.*

2. Does the coach carry an appropriately stocked first aid kit to every practice and game?

   YES (essential). *What good is a first aid kit if you don't have it with you when you need it? The exact contents may vary by sport but a list of essentials can be found on the web or by asking a health care provider.*

3. Does the coach carry a signed "medical treatment consent form" and "contact information" (parent's/guardian's phone numbers, name of physician, relevant medical conditions, etc.) for every player to every practice and game?

   YES (essential). *These forms (often printed on both sides of a large index card) should be completed at the parent orientation meeting (see item #10) and kept in a watertight plastic bag in the First Aid kit (see item #2). They authorize medical care specialists to treat an injured child when a parent/guardian cannot be contacted. They also provide essential health-related and contact information to make sure the child gets the fastest, most appropriate, treatment possible.*

4. Does the coach give the athletes frequent water breaks?

   YES (essential). *All athletes need hydration and rehydration. Children, in particular, have less effective thermo-regulatory systems and therefore often don't consume enough fluids to meet their needs during intense physical activity. Requiring frequent water breaks (flavored sports drinks will be an incentive to get kids to drink more) can prevent life threatening heat-related illnesses.*

5. Does the coach frequently inspect the equipment (e.g., helmets, facemasks, shoes, racquets, bats, pads, etc.) used by the players for proper fit, protective condition, and normal wear-and-tear?

YES (essential). *Ill-fitting, inappropriate, or damaged equipment can't serve the purpose for which it was intended — keeping athletes as safe as possible.*

6. Does the coach inspect all playing surfaces for potential hazards prior to every practice and competition?

YES (essential). *Injuries often occur because of dangerous playing conditions. Before every practice and competition, the coach should systematically survey all playing surfaces and surrounding areas to make sure there are no environmental threats to the athletes' safety.*

7. Does the coach always remain at the practice location until all players have left the area?

YES (essential). *Unless the athletes are adults, coaches are legally (and ethically) responsible for their athletes' safety until everyone has departed the playing location. Serious injuries can result from typical "horseplay" that takes place when unsupervised children are waiting to be picked up after practice. Without an adult present, children are also more vulnerable to dangers posed by others.*

8. Does the coach, in any way, encourage the use of "performance-enhancing" substances (e.g., caffeine, nutritional supplements, cold medications, etc.)?

NO (essential). *Coaches who advocate the use of performance-enhancing substances are setting a bad example. They are basically telling their athletes that they don't inherently "have what it takes" so they must resort to chemical aids to boost their performance. In the presence of a well-balanced diet, supplements are often a waste of money and should only be taken when recommended by a physician. Remember, nutritional supplements are not regulated by the Food and Drug Administration. There is often little or no evidence that they are beneficial or even safe. Supplements may be especially harmful to children.*

9. Has the coach satisfactorily completed a general "coaching education" certification course such as the National Federation of State High School Associations (NFHS) "*Fundamentals of Coaching Course,*" the American Sport Education Program (ASEP) "*Professional Coaches Education Program,*" or a sport-specific (soccer, ice hockey, etc.) coaches certification program)?

YES (desirable). *Completion of an approved coaching education program is an indication that the coach — and the program administrators — are committed to providing your child with the safest and best coaching environment possible. Information about the NFHS can be found at: http://www.nfhslearn.com/ and information about ASEP can be found at http://www.asep.com*

Organizational Skills

10. Does the coach conduct a "parent-orientation" session prior to the start of the season?

> YES (essential). *A parent orientation session allows potential problems to be addressed in a calm atmosphere before they become "personal" issues. Organizational and coaching philosophies, behavioral expectations, rules, regulations, and scheduling can be shared with parents before the season, thereby resulting in fewer misunderstandings. This is also a great opportunity to recruit parent volunteers and collect vital health and emergency information (see item #3).*

11. Does the coach have a written seasonal plan (outlining skills that will be taught at various points throughout the season)?

> YES (desirable). *Developing new sport skills often requires previous knowledge and ability. If skills are not introduced and learned in the proper order, performance — and enjoyment—suffers. Sequencing skills in advance of the season makes coaching and learning more efficient and fun.*

12. Does the coach have a written plan for each practice (outlining skills that will be taught at various points throughout the practice session)?

> YES (desirable). *As John Wooden often said, "failure to prepare is preparing to fail." Teachers are taught the importance of creating daily lesson plans. Coaches are, of course, teachers too. Rarely do we find that the best practices are developed on the way to the practice field.*

13. Do the players tend to stand around a lot during practices waiting to take their turn?

> NO (desirable). *An advantage of planning for the season (see item #11) and planning for individual practice sessions (see item # 12) is that practices can be organized to maximize learning. Children's short attention spans require coaches to keep them involved, active, and on task during the entire practice. Few things are more boring than standing around watching others play. When children are bored, they aren't learning and they tend to generate their own "entertainment" which can result in disciplinary problems.*

14. Whenever possible, does the coach let the players get involved in making team decisions (e.g., skills to be worked on in practice, team strategies, team rules and discipline, etc.)?

> YES (desirable). *Sport exists for the kids—not the coaches, not the administrators, and not the parents. Consistent with their age and maturity levels, children should be given ownership of their sport activities. When the athletes are included in team decisions, it's more likely they'll abide by them. Bringing them into the decision-making process is also a great way to help the youngsters develop a sense of personal and team responsibilities.*

Sportsmanship Skills

15. Would you think it's acceptable for your son, daughter, students, or athletes to act the way the coach does toward officials, parents, other coaches, teammates or opponents?

> YES (essential). *Children are impressionable and readily emulate the behavior of the adults around them. Coaches must always model appropriate interpersonal behaviors — both on and off the field of play.*

16. Does the coach argue with, or berate, game officials?

> NO (essential). *Officials are an essential part of the game. At the youth sport and interscholastic level, officials aren't highly paid professionals. They do us a favor by making our games possible. Youngsters tend not to remember an official's decision nearly as long as they remember a parent or coach's response to it.*

17. Does the coach insist that her/his players demonstrate "good sportsmanship" at all times?

> YES (essential). *One of the most heartening sights in all of athletics is to see a coach reminding his or her players of the need to be good sports regardless of the outcome. Meaningful congratulatory handshakes and genuine acknowledgements of appreciation to the other team and officials for making the game possible are the true signs of a well-coached team.*

18. Does the coach instruct his/her players on how to "bend the rules" without getting caught?

> NO (essential). *Sport is a perfect setting in which to teach young people personal integrity and ethical behavior. Coaches who imply by word or deed that it's acceptable to "get away with anything you can" are sending the wrong messages to our next generation of citizens.*

19. Does the coach ever use "inappropriate language" around the team (e.g., cursing, swearing, degrading or demeaning names for minorities, females, etc.)?

> NO (essential). *Inappropriate language is always unacceptable. Many well-known coaches who are admired for being the strictest "disciplinarians" seem to be the least capable of disciplining themselves when it comes to language and behavior. Temper tantrums and foul or inappropriate language are not the signs of a self-disciplined coach.*

20. Does the coach ever use tobacco (in any form) around the team or arrive at practices or games smelling of alcohol?

> NO (essential). *Coaches are role models. Those who choose to use tobacco, alcohol, or any other chemical substance have an obligation to make certain their athletes will never see them engage in these activities.*

Effective Teaching Skills

21. When "cuts" have to be made, does the coach sit down and tell each player personally that she/he is being cut from the team, why they're being cut, and how they can improve in areas where they are currently deficient?

YES (essential). *Few events in a young person's life are more traumatic and devastating than being cut from an athletic team. Eliminating players should only be done when absolutely necessary and no other option exists! If done at all, coaches have the responsibility to let each player know how he or she can improve in the specific areas that caused them to be removed from the team.*

22. Does the coach understand the fundamental tactics and strategies of the sport (in accordance with the level of participation)?

YES (essential). *Youth sport and interscholastic coaches need not be technical experts in their sport. They do, however, need a basic understanding of tactics and strategies that will enable them to properly teach the sport to their athletes.*

23. Does the coach demonstrate new skills and drills effectively?

YES (essential). *Effective demonstration is every coach's "stock-in-trade." Athletes, particularly children, learn from watching others. Very little motor learning will take place if a coach cannot show (or find someone else to show) the proper execution of important sport skills.*

24. Does the coach take partial responsibility when there is poor player performance?

YES (desirable). *It is very easy for a coach to simply blame an athlete for a performance error. Good coaches know that it is their job to teach proper execution of sport skills. Teaching, however, cannot exist in the absence of learning. If a player fails to learn, what exactly is it that the coach has taught?*

25. Does the coach yell, scream, embarrass, or belittle players (in competitions or in practices)?

NO (essential). *Sport skills are not taught through intimidation and fear. Improvements in learning and performance are fostered by encouragement and technical instruction not ridicule. Criticism not only makes participation unpleasant, it interferes with an athlete's ability to focus on the task and ultimately results in them taking fewer performance risks—something that will almost always results in a poorer athletic performance.*

26. Does the coach use physical activity (e.g., running sprints, running laps, push-ups, sit-ups, etc.) as punishment?

NO (essential). *It is often said that a major benefit of sport is that it helps athletes develop an appreciation for lifelong physical activity. If, however, they are made to run or do push-ups every time they make a mistake, we are using the very thing we are trying to promote as punishment. These punishments also are unpleasant, a waste of valuable practice time, and don't actually show the athlete how to improve their performance. Running for punishment is not the same as running to improve conditioning.*

27. When correcting performance errors, does the coach start by telling the athletes what they've just done correctly, and then follow that with future-oriented instruction?

YES (desirable). *It seems natural to begin by telling a young athlete what he or she has done wrong. The problem is, however, most of the time they are already feeling pretty bad about their performance. Starting by telling them what they did right puts them in a better frame of mind and gets them listening to the coach when he or she begins instruction. It also reinforces the things they've done correctly so they don't lose that part of the performance the next time.*

28. Does the coach emphasize goals such as "winning this game," "winning the championship," "making it to the playoffs," or "beating a particular opponent"?

NO (desirable). *These seem like good goals but an individual athlete has little or no control over these outcomes. Even if they perform at their highest level, these things won't necessarily happen. A better approach is to focus on individual preparation and performance at the highest levels possible. That's usually all we can control.*

29. Does the coach make sure every player gets an opportunity to enhance his/her skills by providing meaningful practice and competition experiences for everyone on the team?

YES (essential). *Skill development should be one of a coach's main concerns. This applies to every member of the team—not just the starters or the few who are most likely to help the team win. A good coach makes certain that every player on the team gets better throughout the season.*

30. Does the coach set aside time during every practice to simply "have fun"?

YES (desirable). *The main reason children participate in sports is to have fun and be with their friends. If that's what they are hoping to experience, coaches should find a way to make it a regular part of every practice. It's really very simple. Sports are supposed to be fun. If they aren't, what is the purpose of participating?*

"Bonus" Question

Do the athletes look forward to playing for this coach again next year?

YES (essential). *This simple question is likely the single best indicator of overall coaching effectiveness.*

The Real Secret of Great Coaching

In the quote at the beginning of this chapter, Coach Wooden spoke from personal experience when he warned us that when it comes to coaching, we should never "equate professional expertise with your ability to teach it. There's a big difference between knowing what you're doing and knowing how to teach what you want done" (Wooden 2005, 102). And there's certainly no evidence that suggests great athletes make the best coaches — some do, some don't. Even so, athletic directors, school boards, parents, and recreation leaders are still often convinced that hiring a great athlete will increase the likelihood they are hiring themselves a great coach. In fact, as we've seen throughout this chapter, being a great athlete may, in some ways, present unforeseen obstacles for a coach. The only real way to become a great coach is to learn the knowledge, values, and behaviors that all coaches should possess. *The National Standards for Sport Coaches* (NASPE 2006) give all coaches, at all levels, the direction they need when training to be a good coach.

"Hazing Is an Innocent Sport Tradition That Helps Teams Bond"

The young guys are part of our football team. They certainly need to get themselves acclimated in a lot of different ways, and our veteran players are in charge of welcoming them to the NFL in a real positive way... There's not going to be anything that's demeaning in any way that a rookie has to do. We just don't believe in that.
— Coach Jason Garrett[1]

Does your team initiate its new players? Before being accepted as full-fledged members of your team are athletes forced to eat or drink large amounts of disgusting, potentially dangerous concoctions, endure sexual humiliations, physical or emotional assaults — or worse? Are you sure? What makes you think you would know even if these things did happened? Unfortunately, your answers are likely to be similar to those given by most coaches and parents — until some of us painfully discover otherwise.

Hazing is a term given to actions expected of someone joining a group that humiliate, degrade, or cause emotional or physical harm. Although this broad definition may include activities some consider relatively harmless, make no mistake. Hazing can cause permanent emotional distress, serious physical injury — and in extreme cases, death.

As coaches we need to understand that the odds are alarmingly high that several members of our team will be involved — as perpetrators, enablers, bystanders, or victims — in a hazing incident at some point during their athletic careers. And by choosing to "turn a blind eye" to what many coaches mistakenly believe are innocent bonding rituals, we become responsible for any hazing that takes place on our team. When we intentionally or unintentionally allow our athletes to be ritualistically humiliated, degraded, or harmed, we are certainly not fostering the type of team climate that Dallas

Cowboy's Head Coach Jason Garrett is attempting to create with his quote at the beginning of this chapter, "Our veteran players are in charge of welcoming them to the NFL in a real positive way... There's not going to be anything that's demeaning in any way that a rookie has to do. We just don't believe in that" (MacMahon 2011).

Protecting Our Athletes—and Ourselves

When we became coaches we accepted a position of trust. Parents, administrators, and the broader society we serve have every reason to expect that we will do everything humanly possible to safeguard the physical and emotional well-being of all our athletes. Whenever we fail to provide any athlete with a safe environment—on or off the field—we are violating this, the most sacred, tenet in coaching. The only way we can protect our athletes—and fulfill our responsibilities as a coach—is to educate ourselves about the dangers hazing poses and the myths that allow it to persist. We also need to recognize that there are practical actions every coach must take to eliminate hazing. There's no need to sugarcoat this. Any refusal to be proactive in eliminating any and all hazing practices puts our athletes at risk. And all coaches who are willing to put their athletes at risk can—and should—be dismissed from this position of trust and be held legally accountable for their (non)actions.

When it comes to hazing, what we don't know certainly can hurt us—and our athletes. To illustrate the point, let's examine one of the most horrific hazing incidents to surface in the past few years (Wahl and Wertheim 2003). As you read the details of this case, the devastating emotional and physical trauma inflicted on these undeserving victims of hazing will be readily apparent. But look closer. Notice the irreparable damage a hazing incident such as this can cause to an otherwise respected coaching staff, a successful athletic program, a distinguished educational institution, and an entire community.

Hazing: A High School Football Example

Over the course of several days and nights during a five-day pre-season training camp, freshman high school football players were repeatedly attacked and tortured by their older teammates. Some of the younger boys were beaten so severely with plastic garbage bags filled with ice that it left welts and bruises on their faces, chests, arms, and legs. Worse still, while their coaches slept peacefully in a separate cabin, at least three of the older teammates duct-taped some of the rookies to their beds and, after putting heat-producing mineral ice on broomsticks, pinecones, and golf balls (simply to enhance the pain), used those items to sodomize the younger players while the rest of the boys in the cabin watched (Kolker 2003; Lipkins 2006).

The fact that these high school athletes were sexually assaulting their younger teammates only became public when two of the victims were forced to seek medical attention because they were still bleeding from their rectums three weeks after the attacks (Lipkins 2006; Wahl and Wertheim, 2003). One of the players suffered injuries so severe he required surgery to repair the damage (Kolker 2003; Wahl and Wertheim 2003).

Upon their return to school the victims were forced to endure what experts call "a second hazing" (Lipkins 2006). They were subjected to verbal taunts of being "football faggots," "butt pirates" ("pirates" is the nickname of the school's sports teams) and "broomstick boys" (Kolker 2003; Wahl and Wertheim 2003). After learning of the attacks, school officials cancelled the football season and fired all five football coaches who were at the camp — including the revered head coach who had been coaching at the school since before some of his players were born. The incident, and the resulting actions, tore the community apart. While one group of parents put up green ribbons throughout the community to show their support for the victims (Tse 2003) others who spoke publicly about the sexual assault received threatening letters indicating that they would also "be sodomized with broomsticks unless they stopped speaking about the case" (ESPN.com 2003; Wahl and Wertheim 2003).

The coaches repeatedly insisted they had no knowledge that hazing had taken place at the school in the past and they had properly supervised the athletes during the entire training camp (Martinez 2003). A Pennsylvania Grand Jury arrived at a very different conclusion, however, when it issued a scathing report accusing the coaches of being "more concerned with being coaches of a football team than interested in the well-being of the players" and "these assaults appear to have grown out of a custom or history of hazing at both the football camp and at [this particular] High School" [Healy 2004].

Does this sound like an "innocent sport tradition that helps a team bond?" Do any of us truly believe our athletes or our children should have to endure this kind of treatment just to be part of an athletic team? Obviously, this was a particularly heinous case, but hazing in sport — even in its mildest forms — is purposely designed to humiliate, degrade, or harm another person — and ironically, a *teammate* at that. Coaches, parents, and administrators are duty-bound to educate themselves and others about what hazing really is — and what it isn't — so they can prevent events like this from happening to the athletes they have been entrusted to protect.

Busting the 10 Myths of Hazing

The main reason hazing is such a serious problem in sport today is that coaches administrators, and parents, like us, tend to buy into the myths and misconceptions that are used to rationalize these hazardous and hurtful activities. Here are the Top 10 hazing myths that continue to put our athletes at risk. As you read through the following myths, think about how many times you've heard something like this. Perhaps even more to the point, ask yourself how many of these myths you actually believe.

Myth #1: Hazing is an innocent rite of passage. One thing that confuses a lot of us and something that can lead to the common misconception that hazing is a relatively harmless activity, is that the term itself often means different things to different people. A personal definition of hazing could easily encompass everything from silly behaviors such as wearing mismatched articles of clothing and singing inane songs to, as we saw in the example of the high school football team, nothing short of violent — and potentially deadly — rape, torture and assault. The problem with even the mildest form of hazing is that it tends to escalate in intensity year-by-year as previously hazed victims finally "get their turn" to set the rules governing the initiation of the next group of newcomers (Lipkins 2006). Although it may appear difficult to determine what exactly is — and is not — hazing, here are a few simple guidelines that can serve as early warning signals to help coaches and athletes decide when things are getting out of control (adapted from Stop-Hazing.org 2005a). If you answer "yes" to any of the following questions, you have a potential hazing problem on your team:

- Is any alcohol, drug, or horrible-tasting concoction ingested?
- Would the active or current members of the group object to participating with the new members and doing exactly what they're required to do?
- Does the activity involve or risk any form of emotional or physical abuse?
- Is there any risk of injury or question of safety?
- Do the participants (or you) have any reservation about honestly describing every aspect of the initiation activity to parents or administrators?
- Would you object to the hazing activity being photographed for the school newspaper or filmed by a local TV news crew?

Myth #2: Hazing rarely happens at junior high or high schools. For many, the term "hazing" conjures up images of brutal treatment of young adults entering the military service, or attempting to join college fraternities or sororities. Although hazing has always played an important role in the initiation of military troops, street gangs, and college students (Nuwer 2004), it would be a terrible mistake to think similar barbaric traditions haven't filtered down into our high schools and — in some cases — even our junior high schools. In the wake of their own hazing scandal that resulted in season-long suspensions of six football players, and the forfeiting of a football game, researchers at Alfred University conducted the first national study to examine the frequency with which hazing occurs at the high school level (Hoover and Pollard 2000). Their findings were disturbing:

• Nearly half (48 percent) of high school kids who belonged to groups had been hazed. That translates into about 1.5 million high school students who are being hazed in the United States each year.
• Nearly all students who were hazed reported being subjected to humiliating activities and about 30 percent said they were expected to perform potentially illegal acts as part of their initiation.
• About one out of every ten high school students reported they decided not join a group because they were afraid they would be hazed and nearly that many (7 percent) said they left a group due to hazing.

Myth #3: Hazing is not that common in sports. Despite numerous reports of athletes intentionally humiliating, harassing, and otherwise hurting their teammates during initiation rituals, there are still plenty of coaches and administrators who have difficulty coming to grips with the fact that athletics is a hotbed of hazing activity. However, the Alfred University study (Hoover and Pollard 2000) found that the greatest number of high school students experience hazing in conjunction with their participation in sports (24 percent). Similarly, a study examining the hazing of athletes in suburban middle and high schools indicated nearly 18 percent of athletes at five high schools and three middle schools had been subjected to hazing (Gershel, et al. 2003). Shockingly, over 13 percent of sixth graders (kids usually about 11 or 12 years old) reported they had already been hazed in as a part of their athletic participation.

Myth #4: Hazing isn't a problem on girl's and women's teams. Those of us who primarily coach female athletes might be tempted to think there's no need for us to spend valuable time discussing the dangers of hazing with our team. We may believe that hazing is only — or at least primarily — a problem in male sports. According to the research evidence, that would be a mistake. In a survey of over 5,000 female college athletes, nearly half (48.5 percent) reported being hazed. In addition, over one-third (33.6 percent) admitted to hazing another athlete on her team (McGlone 2005). The Alfred University study of high school hazing (Hoover and Pollard 2000) also lends support to the notion that hazing is common among female athletes. Perhaps the most shocking real-life example that girls and women are subjecting their teammates to hazing blared across every television set in the country on May 5, 2003. Amateur video of dozens of senior girls "initiating" the junior girls at Glenbrook North High School in suburban Chicago was shown repeatedly on every network news program. The video depicted the junior girls huddled together on the ground while the seniors threw urine, feces, and animal guts on them. The alcohol-fueled seniors kick and beat their younger classmates with their fists, plastic buckets, and just about anything else they could get their hands on. By the time it finally ended nearly 100 girls were treated for minor injuries and five had to be taken to the hospital (CNN.com 2003).

Myth #5: Hazing doesn't happen in church-affiliated groups or teams. A major factor contributing to the prevalence of hazing is our natural tendency to think cruel behavior toward teammates — such as those depicted in the football hazing case at the beginning of this chapter — simply "can't happen here." This sense of "immunity" may be most pronounced in institutions and organizations that devote their entire existence to the moral and ethical development of their members. Even the Alfred University researchers did not fully anticipate the extent to which hazing was found to be present in "church-related" groups. In their final report they specifically noted that

> the level of hazing for church groups was surprising. Not only did a quarter of the students belonging to church groups report involvement in hazing behaviors, they were more apt to be involved with dangerous hazing activities than students in other groups, except gangs, fraternities, and cheerleaders [Hoover and Pollard 2000, 18].

Myth #6: It's not hazing if it's voluntary. There are several points where this myth falls apart and they all stem from a general misunderstanding of the meaning of the term "voluntary." First, for any behavior to be voluntary, it has to be agreed to without any pressure, force, or coercion. If athletes feel submitting — or refusing to submit — to a hazing ritual will change their status on the team in any way, their consent cannot be considered voluntary. Because athletes — particularly younger athletes — want desperately to be accepted into the group, it's usually pretty easy to get them go along with almost anything in order to become part of the team. Second, the term voluntary is totally meaningless if it does not include a full disclosure of everything a person is volunteering to do (or will be done to them). After all, how can someone truly volunteer for something if they don't even know what it is? Therefore, in order to give voluntary permission to be hazed, athletes must understand — in advance — everything that will happen during the hazing activity. Finally, in the unlikely event that: (1) athletes are in no way pressured or coerced to take part in the hazing and (2) they are completely aware of absolutely everything the hazing will entail, they still can't give their voluntary consent if they haven't reached the legal age of consent in their jurisdiction. The issue here is similar to that of "statutory rape" where consent to engage in sexual activity is given by a person who is too young to legally agree or consent to such activity. As you might well imagine, rarely (if ever) does hazing contain all three essential elements required of "voluntary, informed consent." Therefore, it's a false and misleading argument to portray hazing as ever being truly "voluntary."

Myth #7: My athletes (or children) would tell me if they were being hazed. We'd like to think that the athletes under our supervision would come to us if they were being abused by their teammates. After all, if they don't tell us, how would we ever find out? And that, of course, is the real problem. In almost every hazing case that comes to light, the coaches, parents, and administrators all say the exact same thing: "We had no idea this was going on—if we had, we would have put a stop to it." Now of course it's quite possible these authority figures are just pleading ignorance to avoid blame or legal liability but in most cases coaches and parents really weren't aware that the hazing was taking place—but they should have been. Like most of us, they probably didn't give hazing a second thought and simply assumed that if such a thing was happening, one of the athletes would tell them about it. Unfortunately, that's a faulty—and very dangerous—assumption. Think about it from our athletes' perspective. If the team is hazing one another, the whole point is to keep it a secret. Simply put, as coaches and parents we're not *supposed* to ever find out about it. And the truly frightening part is that the more dangerous the form of hazing taking place, the less likely it is we'll ever be told. Not surprisingly, research evidence strongly suggests that our kids often have no intention of ever telling us if hazing is occurring on their team. In the Alfred University study, for example (Hoover and Pollard 2000), high school athletes were asked if they would report an incident of hazing. About 40 percent of the athletes said they would not report hazing even if it occurred. Perhaps even more enlightening were the reasons the kids said they would not tell us if their team was hazing its members. Some simply didn't see it as a problem, "Sometimes accidents happen" (28 percent) but most indicated that either "There is no one to tell" (36 percent), "Adults wouldn't know how to handle it right" (27 percent), "Other kids would make my life miserable" (24 percent), or "I just wouldn't tell on my friends no matter what" (16 percent).

Myth #8: I was hazed, and it didn't hurt me. The part of this myth that needs debunking has nothing to do with whether or not someone can be hazed without suffering serious injury. That's certainly possible. The mistake is in assuming that our one specific experience can be generalized to accurately represent thousands of other cases. This type of illogical argument is so common, in fact, that those who study such things have a special name for it. It's called "the fallacy of hasty generalization" (Walton 1992) and here's an example that will clearly illustrate why it makes absolutely no sense: Suppose I told you I went out last night and had so much to drink that I was practically "falling down drunk" by the end of the evening. I staggered to my car, fumbled around for my keys, weaved myself in and out of traffic, and arrived home safely a few minutes later. Since neither I — nor anyone else — was injured would it therefore be reasonable and accurate to assume that, "driving while drunk is not a serious problem"? Of course not. Even though no one was hurt on this particular occasion, drunk driving can — and does — hurt lots of people. And so does hazing.

Myth #9: Hazing promotes team unity. The argument heard most often in defense of hazing is that it somehow helps a group come together by creating a close bond among teammates. What this overlooks, however, is that bonding — the mere attachment to others — can be positive or negative. In the case of hazing, the bond between victim and tormentor is created through fear, confusion, and stress. It's similar to what we sometimes call the "Stockholm Syndrome" where prisoners or hostages begin to identify with their captors. In dangerous or threatening situations, it seems our brains instinctively know that our best chance for survival rests in our ability to form a close psychological attachment to those who have complete control over our safety and welfare (Auerbach, et al. 1994; Barron 2000). And our brains aren't only wired for physical survival. They have also developed to protect us from ourselves. We've known for years, for example, that the more severe the hazing, the more victims feel attracted to the group (Aronson and Mills 1959). This might sound very strange but it is rather easy to explain if you consider that the brain of someone who has just endured a severe hazing is receiving mixed signals. The victims are, of course, well aware of the terrible price they have paid to become a member of this group. They also understand that "no one in their right mind" would agree to undergo such terrible treatment for a worthless cause. Therefore, the only way the severe hazing can make sense is if the "end justifies the means." In other words, they force themselves to conclude that, "Membership in this group must be very valuable or I wouldn't have been willing to subject myself to this kind of torture" (Festinger 1957). Although in a technical sense a grotesque form of "bonding" can take place between the victim and the group which is based on degradation and divisiveness. This, of course, is quite different from a positive bonding between teammates that has been built on mutual trust, concern, and respect.

Myth #10: If hazing was really that dangerous, it would be illegal. This actually isn't a myth at all — it's a mistake. It's absolutely true that when there is overwhelming evidence that a behavior puts enough people at risk for serious injury, society will generally step in to make the dangerous behavior illegal. And that's exactly why hazing *is* illegal! Laws specifically prohibiting hazing have been passed in 44 of the 50 states. Only Alaska, Hawaii, Montana, New Mexico, South Dakota, and Wyoming have, at this point, failed to pass laws designed to outlaw hazing (StopHazing.org 2005b). It's important to note that what we're talking about here are laws that have been specifically written to ban the act of hazing itself. In addition, behaviors that comprise most hazing incidents (e.g., kidnapping, intimidation, criminal sexual conduct, reckless endangerment, assault, battery, "hate crimes," extortion, underage drinking, etc.) are, of course, criminally punishable offenses in their own right.

The "Mother" of All Hazing Myths

Because so many coaches, parents, and administrators naively accept one or more of the previously described hazing myths, our children are at greater risk of being hazing. There's one other myth, however, that probably does as much to perpetuate the problem as all the others combined—"*There's not much I can do to prevent the kids on my team from hazing one another.*" Of all the myths related to hazing, this is the most damaging. Not only is it false, it is generally used as a convenient excuse to shirk our responsibilities to safeguard our athletes.

Accepting Responsibility for the Role We Play in Hazing

There is a natural tendency for coaches to minimize their role in hazing. Sometimes we simply fall prey to one or more of the common myths that make it easy to conclude that hazing is not that much of a problem. Sometimes we successfully convince ourselves that as long as we didn't actually suggest or take part in the hazing activity we aren't really responsible. After all, we may reason, if our players take it on themselves to secretly initiate their teammates in hazardous or humiliating ways, what can we do? The plain and simple answer is—plenty. And when we don't do everything in our power to stop hazing, we're probably more than a little to blame when our athletes end up hurting one another.

Instituting and reinforcing strong anti-hazing policies. The first step every coach can, and should, take to protect his or her athletes from hazing is to implement and enforce the strictest possible anti-hazing policies. Every team — regardless of age, gender, sport, or affiliation — should have a formal written policy that expressly prohibits *all* forms of "secret group initiation." It is important that everyone associated with the team understands that hazing activities: (1) are illegal, (2) undermine team unity and trust, (3) are emotionally and physically dangerous, and (4) will not be tolerated. These team rules — and the serious penalties for breaking them — should be clearly and forcefully explained to all athletes, parents, coaches, and administrators prior to every season.

Modeling non-abusive behavior. The way we act sets the tone for the entire team. Think about the not-so-subtle signals we're sending every time we deliberately and publicly intimidate, humiliate, embarrass, or ridicule our athletes. Whether we intend to or not, we are clearly showing everyone involved that the culture of this team is such that as long as you're bigger, stronger, or hold a position of authority, it is acceptable — even your privilege and prerogative — to disrespect and degrade other members of the team. When that message is sent by members of the coaching staff dozens of times over the course of a season, it's not difficult to see how athletes can come away with the impression that cruelty and abuse toward others is a normal, natural, and expected part of being a member of this team.

Forming anti-hazing relationships with others. As important as our role is when it comes to eliminating hazing, we can't do it alone. We need to enlist the support of parents, administrators, other coaches, and well-regarded athletes on our team if we have any hope of protecting our players from suffering the insult and injury of hazing. Much of the time and effort we spend trying to combat hazing will be wasted if it's not reinforced by everyone in a position of authority. Every time a parent, administrator or coach minimizes a hazing incident by referring to it as "innocent horseplay that got out of hand" or dismisses the potential seriousness of these crimes with the mocking assertion that "boys will be boys," the less likely it is we'll ever be able to successfully address this hurtful behavior. As respected leaders in the community it's our job, as coaches, to educate ourselves and others about the true hazards associated with hazing.

Paying attention to the "warning signs" of hazing. Whenever and wherever a serious hazing incident becomes public, you can bet that the reactions of the coaches and sport administrators involved will be pretty much the same: "I had no idea this was happening on my team." We began this chapter by posing the question of how you would ever know if your athletes were hazing one another. Keep in mind that hazing is an illicit, and often illegal, behavior. Therefore, from the perspective of our athletes, the whole point is to do whatever is necessary to keep us from finding out about it in the first place. The good news is that like most illicit activities, hazing will often leave clues that can help us determine if we have a potential problem. First and foremost, we need to acknowledge and accept the fact that hazing might actually be occurring on our team. As uncomfortable as this admission may be, any reluctance to consider this possibility will only keep us from recognizing the early warning signs of its existence — even if they present themselves. If you've developed a trusting, caring relationship with your athletes, it's possible that someone might tell you straight out that the members of your team are hazing one another. If they do, you have to take these allegations seriously — regardless of how difficult or disturbing it will be. But these direct reports of hazing are rare. More often, we have to be on the lookout for strange or unusual behavior. Even in the high school football example that we examined earlier, there were clear signals that something was wrong. Recall that "some of the younger boys were beaten so severely with plastic garbage bags filled with ice that it left welts and bruises on their faces, chests, arms, and legs." Wouldn't an observant coach notice these unusual injuries? Wouldn't it be even more curious if several athletes had this same pattern of bruising? And wouldn't it seem stranger still if you didn't recall these athletes sustaining their injuries during practice? And finally, wouldn't it be odd that only the younger members of the team seem to be injured in this way? The head coach of this team even testified that one of the young victims frequently came to him asking for a drink. A psychologist who heard the testimony said that "As the coach told this story, it seemed he was aware that the boy was trying to make contact" (Lipkins 2006, 51). Instead of trying to understand what was bothering the boy, the coach ignored the warning signs and simply ridiculed him further by giving him a new nickname — "Gatorade."

Establishing positive team bonding experiences. Perhaps the most frequent justification given for hazing is that it builds a close bond between the members of a team (Myth #9). Although learning that you can trust and depend on the members of your team is an important part of athletics, the distorted bonding that comes from degrading and demeaning teammates is not the type of bonding that most teams are looking for. It's up to us, then, to make certain that new members are welcomed into our group — not with frightening secret initiations — but with public induction ceremonies designed to emphasize the genuine respect members should have for one another. There are a number of excellent positive team building experiences we can offer as a replacement to hazing. A couple of good books that might give us some ideas are *101 Teambuilding Activities: Ideas Every Coach Can Use to Enhance Teamwork, Communication, and Trust* coauthored by Greg Dale, professor of sport psychology and sport ethics at Duke University and the director of the Sport Psychology and Leadership Programs for Duke athletics (Dale and Conant 2004) and *101 Positive Athletic Traditions: Building Positive Team Legacies* by longtime teacher, coach, administrator, and author Bruce Brown (Brown 2004).

Preventing the "second hazing." In the same way rape victims are often required to endure a "second raping"—by the legal system, the media, and the community—when their cases become public, hazing victims are also forced to relive the embarrassing, humiliating, and degrading details surrounding their assault (Lipkins 2006). Another, perhaps even more upsetting, way this "second hazing" resembles a "second raping" is in the contempt and hostility the community often shows toward the victims of the crime. In fact, hazing victims are likely to receive even harsher treatment from their "friends and neighbors" because those accused of direct or indirect involvement in the cruelty are often well-known, respected members of the community. The natural tendency for the locals to "circle the wagons" around anyone being implicated in such horrible acts leads to the common assertion that the victim is either grossly exaggerating or outright lying about the events that took place—or was even in some way responsible for what happened. To see a clear example of the "second hazing" and intimidation that can surface after a hazing incident, let's reexamine the specifics surrounding the football camp hazing described earlier:

> Upon their return to school the victims ... were subjected to verbal taunts of being "football faggots," "butt pirates," and "broomstick boys".... While one group of parents put up green ribbons throughout the community to show their support for the victims others who spoke publicly about the sexual assault received threatening letters indicating that they would also "be sodomized with broomsticks unless they stopped speaking about the case."

As coaches we must take all accusations of hazing seriously. We also have to support and protect anyone who has the courage to file a hazing complaint.

Becoming Part of the Hazing Solution

The adage "If you're not part of the solution, you're part of the problem" is never more apt than in the case of hazing. As uncomfortable as it is, we have to accept the fact that when we don't take decisive actions to eliminate and prevent hazing from taking place on our team, we are deliberately choosing to be part of the problem. If we fail to educate ourselves, our athletes, and our community about the dangers of hazing, we are deliberately choosing to be part of the problem. If we refuse to develop and enforce strong anti-hazing policies we are deliberately choosing to be part of the problem. If we allow ourselves or others to simply dismiss hazing as "isolated incidents" or "innocent horseplay" we are deliberately choosing to be part of the problem. And if we fail to provide respect and compassion to those who have suffered the indignities of hazing we are deliberately choosing to be part of the problem.

Fortunately, being a coach also puts us in the unique position to play an important role in the hazing solution. As coaches, we all know our primary responsibility is to provide protection and support to every member of our team. If we ever need an easy way to remind ourselves of our obligation to do everything in our power to eliminate and prevent hazing, we need only think of the courageous and proactive stance against hazing Dallas Cowboy Head Coach Jason Garrett has taken with his quote at the beginning of this chapter: "The young guys are part of our football team. They certainly need to get themselves acclimated in a lot of different ways, and our veteran players are in charge of welcoming them to the NFL in a real positive way.... There's not going to be anything that's demeaning in any way that a rookie has to do. We just don't believe in that (MacMahon 2011). And we shouldn't either.

Notes

Preface

1. Suzuki, S. 1983. *Zen mind, beginner's mind: Informal talks on Zen meditation and practice.* Weatherhill: New York.

2. Wooden, J. (with S. Jamison). 2004. *My personal best: Life lessons from an All-American journey.* McGraw-Hill: New York.

3. Even Coach Bryant would eventually renounce these harsh coaching methods and apologized to his players for exposing them to such dangerous and degrading conditions.

Myth No. 1

1. Walsh, B. (with S. Jamison and C. Walsh). 2009. *The score takes care of itself: My philosophy of leadership.* New York: Portfolio.

Myth No. 2

1. Coach Izzo has made this and similar statements throughout his coaching career. Most notably, he said these exact words at the post-game press conference after his Spartans had beaten the University of Connecticut 82-73 in the 2009 NCAA Final Four to advance to the national title game against North Carolina.

2. Data were collected on 271 hockey players selected for the following National teams and Amateur Hockey Association of the United States (AHAUS) Selection Camps: 1984 Junior National Camp, 1984 Junior National Team, 1985 National Midget Camp, 1985 17-Select Camp, 1986 National Midget Team, 1986 17-Select Camp, and 1987 Junior National Team (Albrecht & Schultz, 1988).

3. *USA Hockey.* 2009. *2009–2010 Annual Guide.* Colorado Springs, CO: USA Hockey.

Myth No. 3

1. Krzyzewski, M. (with J. Spatola) 2006. *Beyond basketball: Coach K's keywords for success.* (2006). New York: Business Plus.

Myth No. 4

1. Stringer, C.V. (with L. Tucker). 2008. *Standing tall: A memoir of tragedy and triumph.* New York: Three Rivers Press.

Myth No. 5

1. Torre, J. (with H. Dreher). 1999. *Joe Torre's Ground Rules for Winners.* New York: Hyperion.

Myth No. 6

1. Wooden, J. (with S. Jamison). 2004. *My personal best: Life lessons from an All-American journey.* New York: McGraw-Hill.

Myth No. 7

1. Krzyzewski, M. (with D.T. Phillips). 2000. *Leading with the heart: Coach K's successful strategies for basketball, business, and life.* New York: Warner.

Myth No. 8

1. Smith, D. (with J. Kilgo and S. Jenkins). 2002. *A coach's life*. New York: Random House.

2. There are dozens of pre-printed practice plans specific to every sport imaginable. Some are available online by just typing your sport and the term "practice plans" into your search engine. Of course there are also a number of more traditional books available. One good source is Human Kinetics Publishers, http://www.human kinetics.com/.

Myth No. 9

1. Dungy, T. (with N. Whitaker). 2007. *Quiet strength: The principles, practices, and priorities of a winning life*. Carol Stream, IL: Tyndal House.

Myth No. 10

1. This quote from legendary coach Tom Landry appears at hundreds of locations on the internet including most sites devoted to famous quotations (such as Quotations-Book.com at http://quotationsbook.com/quote/38432/). It doesn't, however, appear to have appeared in print anywhere.

2. What we are calling the *"Adrenaline Rush"* theory is called "Drive Theory" in the scientific literature. Similarly, our *"Goldilocks"* Theory is typically presented as the "Inverted-U Hypothesis," and our *"What You Think Is What You Get"* theory is more formally referred to as "Reversal Theory."

Myth No. 11

1. Wooden, J. and S. Jamison. 2010. *Wooden on Leadership*. New York: McGraw-Hill.

2. It is commonly held that Baron Pierre de Coubertin, founder of the Modern Olympic Games, fashioned the current Olympic Creed (sometimes called the Olympic Code) after a speech given to the athletes during the 1908 London Olympic Games by Ethelbert Talbot, the bishop of Central Pennsylvania. However, it now seems more likely that de Coubertin's inspiration was drawn from his reading of the classic *Metamorphoses* by the ancient poet Ovid (Young 1994). The Olympic Creed, whatever its genesis, has been prominently displayed on the scoreboard at every Olympic Game since 1936, reminding all participants and spectators that "The most important thing in the Olympic Games is not to win but to take part, just as the most important thing in life is not the triumph but the struggle. The essential thing is not to have conquered but to have fought well" (Mallon and Buchanan 2006, 210).

3. Somewhat different versions of this story have appeared elsewhere. Kohn (1993), for example, relates a story in which the old man is verbally insulted by a group of kids every day when they pass his house on their way home from school. Another difference is that in Kohn's telling of the story, the old man gives the kids a dollar a piece on the first day, a quarter each on the second and third days and only a penny on the fourth — causing them to leave and never return.

Myth No. 12

1. This quote from Coach Pete Carroll appears in both written and video form on the Stack Magazine website, http://www.stack.com/video/1353518167/Pete-Carroll-on-MultiSport-Athletes/. It appears he is being interviewed about his views on sport specialization while on the field after a practice.

2. The image of Tiger Woods as a "well-rounded" family man took a serious hit on Thanksgiving day of 2009 when he and his wife, Elin, had a huge fight over his continual philandering. The domestic quarrel ended up in a car crash, a divorce, the release of embarrassing sexual escapades, treatment for a sex addiction, the loss of virtually every sponsor, and several years of mediocre golf on the PGA tour.

Myth No. 13

1. This quote from Coach Bylsma appears on page 131 of a book he wrote with

his father, Jay, in 2001, *So You Want to Play in the NHL: A Guide for Young Players.*

Myth No. 14

1. Wooden, J. and S. Jamison. 2010. *Wooden on Leadership.* New York: McGraw-Hill.

Myth No. 15

1. This quote from the new Head Coach of the Cowboys was undoubtedly an effort to eliminate distractions caused by hazing such as the media storm that occurred the previous year when Cowboys' rookie, and first-round draft pick, Dez Bryant refused to take part in the rookie ritual of carrying veterans' (Roy William's) shoulder pads to the locker room.

References

A&E Television Networks. 1999. *Basketball: The dream teams.* (The History Channel) Cat. No. AAE-42900.

Agassi, A. 2009. *Open: An autobiography.* New York: Vintage.

Albom, M. 2000. Magic to Mateen: A new era at MSU. *Detroit Free Press.* April 5.

Albrecht, R. 2007. Moral victories often the best kind. *The Grand Rapids Press*, February 7, C2.

Albrecht, R. 2009. Drop and give us 20, Seifried: A practical response to "Defending the use of punishment by coaches." *Quest* 61: 470–475.

Albrecht, R.R., and T.D. Schultz. 1988. *A biased selection of amateur hockey players to national-level teams based on month of birth.* Unpublished report to the Amateur Hockey Association of the United States (AHAUS).

Al Huang, C., and J. Lynch. 1992. *Thinking body, dancing mind.* New York: Bantam.

Allen, R. 2001. Planning for the season. In *Program for athletic coaches' education* (3rd ed.), ed. V. Seefeldt and, M.A. Clark, 245–252. Traverse City, MI: Cooper.

American Academy of Pediatrics. 2000. Intensive training and sports specialization in young athletes. (Committee on Sports Medicine and Fitness). *Pediatrics* 106: 154–157.

American Orthopaedic Society for Sports Medicine (2008). *AOSSM sports tips: Overuse injuries.* http://www.sportsmed.org/uploadedFiles/Content/Patient/Sports_Tips/ST%20Overuse%20Injuries%202008.pdf.

Amorose, A.J., and T.S. Horn. 2000. Intrinsic motivation: Relationships with collegiate athletes' gender, scholarship status, and perceptions of their coaches' behavior. *Journal of Sport and Exercise Psychology* 22: 63–84.

Anheuser-Busch. 2003. *Budweiser True* television commercial (Leon interview). http://www.youtube.com/watch?v=3BkIh1R5utY. Anheuser-Busch, Budweiser Beer: St. Louis, MO.

Apter, M.J. 1984. Reversal theory and personality: A review. *Journal of Research in Personality* 18: 265–288.

Aronson, E., and J. Mills. 1959. The effects of severity of initiation on liking for a group. *Journal of Abnormal and Social Psychology* 59: 177–181.

Auerbach, S. M., D.J. Kiesler, T. Strentz, J. Schmidt, and C. Serio. 1994. Interpersonal impacts and adjustment to the stress of simulated captivity: An empirical test of the Stockholm Syndrome. *Journal of Social and Clinical Psychology* 13: 207–221.

Bacon, J.U. 2012. *Three and out: Rich Rodriquez and the Michigan Wolverines in the crucible of college football.* New York: Picador.

Baker, J., J. Côté, and B. Abernethy. 2003. Sport-specific practice and the development of expert decision-making in team ball sports. *Journal of Applied Sport Psychology* 15: 12–25.

Balyi, I. 2001. Sport system building and long-term athlete development in Canada. The situation and the solutions. *Coaches report: The official publication of the Canadian Professional Coaches Association, Vol. 8*, 25–28.

Bandura, A. 1997. *Self-efficacy: The exercise of control.* New York: W.H. Freeman.

Barnsley, R.H., A.H. Thompson, and P.E. Barnsley. 1985. Hockey success and birthdate: The relative age effect. *Canadian Association for Health, Physical Education, and Recreation* 51: 23–28.

Baron, R.S. 2000. Arousal, capacity, and intense indoctrination. *Personality and Social Psychology Review* 4: 238–254.

Baume, N., I. Hellemans, and M. Saugy. 2007. Guide to over-the-counter sports supplements for athletes. *International SportMed Journal* 8:2–10.

Berra, Y. 1998. *The Yogi Berra book: I really didn't say everything I said.* New York: LTD Enterprises.

Berra, Y. (with D. Kaplin). 2008. *You can observe a lot by watching: What I've learned about teamwork from the Yankees and life.* Hoboken, NJ: John Wiley and Sons.

Bishop, J.B. (Ed.). 1919. *Theodore Roosevelt's Letters to his Children.* New York: Charles Scribner's Sons.

Boucher, J., and B. Mutimer. 1994. The relative age phenomenon in sport: A replication and extension with ice-hockey players. *Research Quarterly for Exercise and Sport* 65: 377–381.

Boucher, J., and W. Halliwell. 1991. The Novem System: A practical solution to age grouping. *Canadian Association for Health, Physical Education, and Recreation* 57: 16–20.

Brady, E. 1996. Nike's marketing images nearing the out-of-bounds line. *NCAA News.* http://fs.ncaa.org/Docs/NCAA NewsArchive/1996/19960819/comment. html#3.

Brewer, B. W., J.L. VanRaalte, and D.E. Linder. 1993. Athletic Identity: Hercules' muscles or Achilles' heel? *International Journal of Sport Psychology* 24: 237–254.

Brewer, J., P. Balsom, and J. Davis. 1995. Seasonal birth distribution amongst European soccer players. *Sports Exercise and Injury* 1: 154–157.

Brewer, J., P. Balsom, J. Davis, and B. Ekblom. 1992. The influence of birth date and physical development on the selection of a male junior international soccer squad. *Journal of Sport Sciences* 10: 561–562.

Brown, B.E. 2004. *101 positive athletic traditions: Building positive team legacies.* Monterey, CA: Coaches Choice.

Burton, D. 1989. The impact of goal specificity and task complexity on basketball skill development. *The Sport Psychologist* 3: 34–47.

Burton, D. 1992. The Jekyll/Hyde nature of goals: Reconceptualizing goal setting in sport. In *Advances in sport psychology,* ed. T. Horn, 267–297. Champaign, IL: Human Kinetics.

Burton, D. 1993. Goal setting in sport. In *Handbook of research on sport psychology,* ed R.N. Singer, M. Murphey, and L.K. Tennant, 467–491. New York: Macmillan.

Butterfield, F. 2002. Fatal fight at rink nearly severed head, doctor testifies. *New York Times.* January 5.

Bylsma, D., and J. Bylsma. 1998. *So your son wants to play in the NHL.* Chelsea, MI: Sleeping Bear.

Bylsma, D. and J. Bylsma. 2001. *So you want to play in the NHL: A guide for young players.* Lincolnwood, IL: Contemporary.

Bylsma, J. M. 2000. We are burning out our babies... *The Grand Rapids Press,* January 7.

Cameron, J., and W.D. Pierce. 1994. Reinforcement, reward, and intrinsic motivation: A meta-analysis. *Review of Educational Research* 64: 363–423.

Cary, P. (2004). Fixing kids' sports. *U.S. News and World Report,* July 7, 44–48; 50; 52–53.

Casady, M. 1974. The tricky business of giving rewards. *Psychology Today* 8, no. 4: 52.

CBSInteractive.com. 2012. *Official site of the University of Nevada Athletics.* http://www.nevadawolfpack.com/trads/unv-trads.html.

Centers for Disease Control and Prevention. 1997. Guidelines for school and community programs to promote lifelong physical activity among young people. *Morbidity and Mortality Weekly Report, 46* (no. RR-6), 1–36.

ChampionshipCoachesNetwork. 2011. *Duke men's basketball coach Mike Krzyzewski on coaching.* http://www.championship coachesnetwork.com/public/249.cfm.

Chandler, V. 2011. The NFL's good guys: Tony Dungy and nine other class acts in pro football. *Bleacher Report.* http://bleacherreport.com/articles/646231-the-nfls-good-guys-tony-dungy-and-nine-other-class-acts-in-pro-football March 28.

Chaplin, J.P. 1975. *Dictionary of psychology.* New York: Dell.

CNN.com. 2003. *Initiation turned hazing investigated.* http://www.cnn.com/2003/US/Midwest/05/07/hs.hazing/index.html.

Coakley, J. 1992. Burnout among adolescent athletes: A personal failure or social problem? *Sociology of Sport Journal* 9: 271–285.

Cobley, S., J. Baker, N. Wattie, and J. McKenna. 2009. Annual age-grouping and athlete development: A meta-analytic review of relative age effects in sport. *Sports Medicine* 39: 235–256.

Cotten, D.J., and T.J. Wilde. 1997. *Sport law for sport managers.* Dubuque, IA: Kendall/Hunt.

Covey, S.R. 2004. *The seven habits of highly effective people.* New York: Free.

Cox, R.H. 2012. *Sport psychology: Concepts and applications,* 7th ed. New York: McGraw-Hill.

Crain, W. 2003. *Reclaiming childhood: Letting children be children in our achievement-oriented society.* New York: Henry Holt.

Csikszentmihalyi, M. 1975. *Beyond boredom and anxiety.* San Francisco: Jossey-Bass.

Csikszentmihalyi, M. 1990. *Flow: The psychology of optimal experience.* New York: Harper and Row.

Csikszentmihalyi, M. 1997. *Finding flow: The psychology of engagement with everyday life.* New York: Basic.

Dale, G., and S. Conant. 2004. *101 team building activities: Ideas every coach can use to enhance teamwork, communication and trust.* Durham, NC: Excellence in Performance.

D'Alessio, J. 2009. Sporting News' 50 greatest coaches of all time. SportingNews.com, *July 29. http://www.sportingnews.com/college-basketball/article/2009-07-29/sporting-news-50-greatest-coaches-all-time.*

Davis, S. 2003. Player-of-the-year race is wide open. *Sports Illustrated, SI.com.* http://sportsillustrated.cnn.com/inside_game/seth_davis/news/2003/02/25/hoop_thoughts/ (February 25).

Deci, E. L., R.M. Ryan, and R. Koestner. 2001. The pervasive negative effects of reward on intrinsic motivation: Response to Cameron (2001). *Review of Educational Research* 71: 43–51.

Dent, J. 1999. *The Junction Boys: How ten days in hell with Bear Bryant forged a championship team.* New York: St. Martin's.

Doran, G.T. 1981. There's a S.M.A.R.T. way to write management goals and objectives. *Management Review* 70: 35–36.

Dudink, A. 1994. Birth date and sporting success. *Nature* 368: 592.

Dungy, T. (with N. Whitaker). 2007. *Quiet strength: The principles, practices, and priorities of a winning life.* Carol Stream, IL: Tyndale.

Duran, R. (with R. Lipsey). 2002. *In every kid there lurks a Tiger.* New York: Hyperion.

Easterbrook, J. A. 1959. The effect of emotion on cue utilization and the organization of behavior. *Psychological Review* 66: 183–201.

Ebling, J. 2002. Ex-Spartan Morris Peterson has become a go-to player in his second season in Toronto. *Lansing State Journal.com.* http://www.greenandwhite.com/basketball/p_020427_morris_peterson.html. (April 27).

Elkind, D. 2001. *The hurried child: Growing up too fast too soon,* 3rd ed. Cambridge, MA: Perseus.

Elliott, S. 1996. After $5 billion is bet, marketers are racing to be noticed amidst the clutter of the Summer Games. *The New York Times,* D6. July 16.

Epstein, J. 1988. Effective schools or effective students? Dealing with diversity. In *Policies for America's public schools,* ed. R. Haskins and B. MacRae, 89–126. Norwood, NJ: Ablex.

Epstein, J. 1989. Family structures and student motivation: A developmental perspective. In *Research on motivation in education,* Vol. 3, ed. C. Ames and

R. Ames, 259–295. New York: Academic.

Ericsson, K.A., K. Nandagopal, and R.W. Roring. 2009. Toward a science of exceptional achievement: Attaining superior performance through deliberate practice. *Annals of the New York Academy of Sciences* 1172: 199–217.

Ericsson, K.A., R. Krampe, and C. Tesch-Romer. 1993. The role of deliberate practice in the acquisition of expert performance. *Psychological Review* 100: 363–406.

ESPN. 2003. *Sunday NFL Countdown*, November 9.

ESPN.com. 2002. Sale, Pelletier share gold with Russian pair. *ESPN.com* http://sports.espn.go.com/oly/winter02/figure/news?id=1333280

ESPN.com. 2003. *Outspoken parents told to keep quiet*. http://espn.go.com/otherfb/news/2003/1011/1635729.html (October 11).

Ewing, M.E., and V. Seefeldt. 2002. Patterns of participation in American agency-sponsored youth sports. In *Children and Youth in Sport. A Biopsychosocial Perspective*, ed. F.L Smoll and R.E. Smith, 39–60. Dubuque, IA: Kendall Hunt.

Farrey, T. 2008. *Game on: The All-American race to make champions of our children*. New York: ESPN.

Feltz, D.L. 2007. Self-confidence and sports performance. In *Essential readings in sport and exercise psychology*, ed. D. Smith and M. Bar-Eli, 278–294. Champaign, IL: Human Kinetics.

Feltz, D.L., and D.M. Landers. 1983. Effects of mental practice on motor skill learning and performance: A meta-analysis. *Journal of Sport Psychology* 5: 25–57.

Feltz, D.L., S.E. Short, and P.J. Sullivan. 2007. *Self-efficacy in sport*. Champaign, IL: Human Kinetics.

Festinger, L. 1957. *A theory of cognitive dissonance*. Evanston, IL: Row Peterson.

Fitts, P.M., and M.I. Posner. 1967. *Human performance*. Belmont CA: Brock-Cole.

Flegal, K.M. 2005. Epidemiologic aspects of overweight and obesity in the United States. *Physiology and Behavior* 86: 599–602.

Fleishman, E.A. 1975. Toward a taxonomy of human performance. *American Psychologist* 30: 1127–1149.

Fleser, D. 2008. *Sign didn't cause Camargo's injury*. http://www.govolsxtra.com/news/2008/mar/24/sign-didnt-cause-camargos-injury/.

Flint, F.A. 1999. Seeing helps believing: Modeling in injury rehabilitation. In *Psychological bases of sport injuries*, 2nd ed., ed. D. Pargman, 221–234. Morgantown, WV: Fitness Information Technology.

Gelin, D. 1996. Bound for Glory. *Sports Illustrated*, 100–104. December 2.

Gershel, J.C., R.J. Katz-Sidlow, E. Small, and S. Zandieh. 2003. Hazing of suburban middle school and high school athletes. *Journal of Adolescent Health* 32: 333–335.

Gladwell, M. 2008. *Outliers: The story of success*. New York: Little, Brown.

Gould, D., E. Udry, D. Bridges, and L. Beck. 1997. Coping with season-ending injuries. *The Sport Psychologist* 11: 379–399.

Greene, D., and M.R. Lepper. 1974. Intrinsic motivation: How to turn play into work. *Psychology Today* 8, no. 4: 49–54.

Greene, J. 1999. When Carr speaks, players listen. *Orlando Sentinel*. January 1.

Gretzky, W., and J. Taylor. 1984. *Gretzky: From the backyard rink to the Stanley Cup*. Toronto: McClelland and Stewart.

Griffith, C.R. 1926. *Psychology of coaching: A study of coaching methods from the point of view of psychology*. New York: Charles Scribner's Sons.

Grinczel, S. 2002. Torbert glad for ankle sprain since it revealed bone chip that caused problems last season. *MLive.com*. November 27.

Havel, C. 2003. Coach Knight focuses on Packers' minds. *Texas Tech: The official website of Texas Tech Athletics*. http://www.texastech.com/sports/m-baskbl/spec-rel/082003aaa.html.

Hayes, N. 2003. *When the game stands tall: The story of the De La Salle Spartans and football's longest winning streak*. Berkeley, CA: Frog

Healy, P. 2004. Report says hazing culture led to attacks on 3 athletes. *New York*

Times.com http://www.nytimes.com/ 2004/03/11/nyregion/report-says-hazing-culture-led-to-attacks-on-3-athletes.html (March 11).

Hecimovich, M. 2004. Sport specialization in youth: A literature review. *Journal of the American Chiropractic Association* 41: 32–41.

Hellstedt, J.C. 1987. The coach/parent/athlete relationship. *The Sport Psychologist* 1: 151–160.

Hockey Canada. 2002. *Relax, it's just a game.* Public service announcement 2002 advertising campaign. http://www.hockeycanada.ca/multimedia/kids/games/videos.php.

Hockey Canada. 2003. *Relax, it's just a game.* Public Service Announcement 2003 advertising campaign. http://www.hockeycanada.ca/multimedia/kids/games/videos.php.

Hollembeak, J., and A.J. Amorose. 2005. Perceived coaching behaviors and college athletes' intrinsic motivation: A test of self-determination theory. *Journal of Applied Sport Psychology* 17: 20–36.

Honore, C. 2008. *Under pressure: Rescuing our children from the culture of hyper-parenting.* New York: HarperCollins.

Hoover, N.C., and N.J. Pollard. (2000). *Initiation rites in American high schools: A national survey (final report),* (Alfred University, Alfred NY). http://www.alfred.edu/hs_hazing/.

Horne, T.S. 2002. Coaching effectiveness in the sport domain. In *Advances in sport psychology,* ed. T.S. Horne, 151–200. Champaign, IL: Human Kinetics.

Hosick, M.B. 2012. Multiyear scholarship rule narrowly upheld: Vote to override legislation falls just short of required mark. *NCAA.com.* http://www.ncaa.com/news/ncaa/article/2012-02-17/multiyear-scholarships-be-allowed.

Jackson, P. (with H. Delehanty). 1995. *Sacred hoops: Spiritual lessons of a hardwood warrior.* New York: Hyperion.

Jackson, S., and M. Csikszentmihalyi. 1999. *Flow in sports.* Champaign, IL: Human Kinetics.

Karau, S.J., and K.D. Williams. 1993. Social loafing: A meta-analytic review and the-oretical integration. *Journal of Personality and Social Psychology* 65: 681–706.

Katz, A. 2007. Spartan's performance stacks up against anyone. ESPN.com. http://sports.espn.go.com/ncb/columns/story?columnist=katz_andy&id=2862538 May 7.

Kerr, J.H. 1985. The experience of arousal: A new basis for studying arousal effects in sport. *Journal of Sport Sciences* 3: 169–179.

Kingston, K.M., and L. Hardy. 1997. Effects of different types of goals on processes that support performance. *The Sport Psychologist* 11: 277–293.

Kipling, R. 1895. *The second jungle book.* New York: Century.

Klein, H.J., M.J. Wesson, J.R. Hollenbeck, and B.J. Alge. 1999. Goal commitment and the goal setting process: Conceptual clarification and empirical synthesis. *Journal of Applied Psychology* 84: 885–896.

Kohn, A. 1993. *Punished by rewards: The trouble with gold stars, incentive plans, A's, praise, and other bribes.* New York: Houghton Mifflin.

Kolker, R. 2003. Out of bounds. *New York Magazine.* October 27. http://nymag.com/nymetro/news/features/n_9391/

Krug, M. 1999. Playing tennis in the zone. *Athletic Insight: The Online Journal of Sport Psychology* 1: 13–20.

Krzyzewski, M. (with D.T. Phillips). 2000. *Leading with the heart: Coach K's successful strategies for basketball, business, and life.* New York: Warner.

Krzyzewski, M. (with J.K. Spatola). 2006. *Beyond basketball: Coach K's keywords for success.* New York: Business Plus.

Landers, D.M., and S.M. Arent. 2010. Arousal-performance relationships. In *Applied sport psychology: Personal growth to peak performance,* 6th ed., ed. J.M. Williams, 221–246. New York: McGraw-Hill.

LansingStateJournal.com. 2008. *Izzo: "Responsibility falls on my shoulders" coach has tempered reaction to MSU's loss at Penn State.* February 5. http://www.lansingstatejournal.com/article/20080205/GW0201/802050335/Izzo-Responsibility-falls-my-shoulders.

Latané, B., K. Williams, and S. Harkins. 1979. Many hands make light the work: The causes and consequences of social loafing. *Journal of Personality and Social Psychology* 37: 822–832.

Launder, A. 2001. *Play practice: The Games Approach to teaching and coaching sports.* Champaign, IL: Human Kinetics.

Lemyre, F., P. Trudel, and N. Durand-Bush. 2007. How youth-sport coaches learn to coach. *The Sport Psychologist,* 21: 191–209.

Lepper, M.R., D. Greene, and R. Nisbet. 1973. Undermining children's intrinsic interest with extrinsic reward: A test of the "overjustification" hypothesis. *Journal of Personality and Social Psychology* 28: 29–137.

Lepper, M. R., and J. Henderlong. 2000. Turning "play" into "work" and "work" into "play": 25 years of research on intrinsic versus extrinsic motivation. In *Intrinsic and extrinsic motivation: The search for optimal motivation and performance,* eds. C. Sansone and J.M. Harackiewicz , 257–307. San Diego: Academic.

Lipkins, S. 2006. *Preventing hazing: How parents, teachers, and coaches can stop the violence, harassment, and humiliation.* San Francisco: Jossey-Bass.

Lloyd, J., and K. Fox. 1992. Achievement goals and motivation to exercise in adolescent girls: A preliminary intervention study. *British Journal of Physical Education Research Supplement* 11: 12–16.

Looney, D.S. 1988. Bred to be a superstar. *Sports Illustrated,* February 22.

MacMahon, T. 2011. Jason Garrett draws line for hazing. *ESPNDallas.com.* August 14.

Mah C.D., K.E. Mah, E.J. Kezirian, and W.C. Dement. 2011. The effects of sleep extension on the athletic performance of collegiate basketball players. *Sleep* 34: 943–950.

Mallon, B., and I. Buchanan. 2006. *Historical dictionary of the Olympic movement,* 3rd ed. Lanham, MD: Scarecrow.

Martens, R. 1978. *Joy and sadness in children's sports.* Champaign, IL: Human Kinetics.

Martens, R. 2004. *Successful coaching,* 3rd ed. Champaign, IL: Human Kinetics.

Martens, R. 2012. *Successful coaching,* 4th ed. Champaign, IL: Human Kinetics.

Martens, R., and V. Seefeldt, eds. 1979. *Guidelines for children's sports.* Washington, D.C.: American Alliance for Health, Physical Education, Recreation, and Dance.

Martinez, J. 2003. L.I. head coach sorry for hazing. *NYDailyNews.com.* http://articles.nydailynews.com/2003-10-01/news/18236397_1_coaches-apology-mepham-high-school (October 1).

Mason, D. (2008). *Age of specialization: One sport vs. multiple sports.* Guiford Orthopaedic and Sports Medicine Center webpage, September. http://www.guilfordortho.com/age_of_specialization.htm.

McCarthy, M. 2003. Wake up consumers? Nike's brash CEO dares to just do it; Knight prepares to accept top Cannes Lions award. *USA Today,* p. B1. June 16.

McCarthy, M. 2012. Police: Dad attacks youth coach, then bites ear. *USA Today.com,* March 12.

McCombs, P. 2002. Wrestling coach has a featherweight problem. *The Washington Post,* C1. February 27.

McGlone, C.A. 2005. Hazing in N.C.A.A. Division I women's athletics: An exploratory analysis. PhD diss., University of New Mexico.

McPherson, B.D. 1978. The child in competitive sport: Influence of the social milieu. In *Children in sport: A contemporary anthology,* ed. R.A. Magill, M.J. Ash, and F.L. Smoll, 219–249. Champaign, IL: Human Kinetics.

Mercer, J. 1944. *Ac-Cent-Tchu-Ate the Positive.* Capitol Records.

Merron, J. (2003). Animals were harmed in the making of this list. *ESPN.com Page 2.* http://espn.go.com/page2/s/list/sportanimalcruelty.html.

Merton, R. K. 1948. The self-fulfilling prophecy. *Antioch Review* 8:193–210.

Mitchell, G.J. (2007). *Report to the Commissioner of Baseball of an independent investigation into the illegal use of steroids and other performance enhancing substances by players in Major League Baseball.* New York: Office of the Commissioner of Baseball.

Moceanu, D. (with P. Williams and T. Williams). 2012. *Off balance: A memoir.* New York: Simon and Schuster.

Moran, A.P. 2004. *Sport and exercise psychology: A critical introduction.* New York: Routledge.

Morris, G.S. 1977. Dynamic visual acuity: Implications for the physical educator and coach. *Motor Skills Theory into Practice* 2: 15–20.

Musch, J. 2002. Birthdate and success in youth soccer: Investigating the development of the relative age effect. *Sportonomics* 8: 22–28.

Musch, J., and R. Hay. 1999. The relative age effect in soccer: Cross-cultural evidence for a systematic discrimination against children born late in the competition year. *Sociology of Sport Journal* 16: 54–64.

Musch, J., and S. Grondin. 2001. Unequal competition as an impediment to personal development: A review of relative age effect in sport. *Developmental Review* 21: 147–167.

NASPE. 1995. *National standards for athletic coaches: Quality coaches, quality sports.* Dubuque, IA, Kendall/Hunt Publishing.

NASPE. 2006. *National standards for sport coaches: Quality coaches, quality sports.* Reston, VA: Author.

Nater. S., and R. Gallimore. 2006. *You haven't taught until they've learned: John Wooden's teaching principles and practices.* Morgantown, WV: Fitness Information Technology.

National Institutes of Health. 1998. *Clinical guidelines on the identification, evaluation, and treatment of overweight and obesity in adults: The evidence report.* NIH Publication No. 98–4083. Washington: U.S. Department of Health and Human Services.

NCAA. 2006. *Presidential Task Force on the Future of Division I Intercollegiate Athletics* (Student-Athlete Well-Being Subcommittee). January 18. http://www.ncaa.org/wps/wcm/connect/5be116004e0b865984c7f41ad6fc8b25/athletics_aid.doc?MOD=AJPERES&CACHEID=5be116004e0b865984c7f41ad6fc8b25.

NCAA. 2008. *NCAA presidential task force on the future of Division I Intercollegiate Athletics Student-athlete well-being subcommittee* (Supplement No. 10). August 19. http://fs.ncaa.org/Docs/DI_SA_Awards_Benefits_Fin_Aid_Cab/2008/September/S%2010.pdf.

NCAA. 2009. *Time commitments of NCAA student-athletes.* National Collegiate Athletic Association, Division I Academic Cabinet. http://fs.ncaa.org/Docs/Misc_Committees_DB/Academic%20Cabinet/02-02-09/Web/Supp%20No%2020a.pdf

NCAA. 2010. *University of Michigan public infractions report* http://www.ncaa.org/wps/wcm/connect/public/ncaa/pdfs/2010/20101104+univ+of+michigan+report .

NCAA. 2012. *Estimated probability of competing in athletics beyond the high school interscholastic level.* http://www.ncaa.org/wps/wcm/connect/public/ncaa/pdfs/2011/2011+probability+of+going+pro.

New Balance (2005a). *New Balance–zero.* (Television advertisement created by Boathouse, Needham, MA). http://adland.tv/commercials/new-balance-zero-2006-30-usa.

New Balance (2005b). *New Balance—for love or money—cross country.* (Television advertisement created by Boathouse, Needham, MA). http://adland.tv/commercials/new-balance-love-or-money-cross-country-2005-030-usa.

New Balance (2005c). *For love or money? coaches.* (Television advertisement created by Boathouse, Needham, MA). http://adland.tv/commercials/new-balance-love-or-money-coaches-2005-030-usa.

Nietzsche, F. 1997. *Twilight of the idols, or, how to philosophize with a hammer.* Trans. R. Polt. Indianapolis: Hackett. (Orig. pub. 1889).

Nolan, J.E., and G. Howell. 2010. Hockey success and birth date: The relative effect revisited. *International Review for the Sociology of Sport* 45: 507–512.

Nuwer, H. 2004. Introduction: Exterminating the frat rats. In *The hazing reader*, ed. H. Nuwer, xiii–xxvii. Bloomington: Indiana University Press.

Ommundsen, Y., and G.C. Roberts. 1999. Effect of motivational climate profiles on motivational indices in team sport. *Scan-*

dinavian *Journal of Medicine and Science in Sports* 9: 389–397.

Palmer, P.J. 1998. *The courage to teach: Exploring the inner landscape of a teacher's life.* San Francisco: Jossey-Bass.

Pargman, D. 2007. *Psychological bases of sport injuries,* 3rd ed., Morgantown, WV: Fitness Information Technology.

Petitpas, A., and S. Danish. 1995. Caring for injured athletes. In *Sport psychology interventions,* ed. S. Murphy, 255–281. Champaign, IL: Human Kinetics.

Podlog, L., and R.C. Eklund. 2006. A longitudinal investigation of competitive athletes' return to sport following serious injury. *Journal of Applied Sport Psychology* 18: 44–68.

PR Newswire Association. 2005. *New Balance debuts "For love or money?" advertising campaign for 2005; campaign celebrates amateur athletes and looks to stimulate dialogue on the values in sports today.* http://www.thefreelibrary.com/New+Balance+Debuts+%27For+Love+or+Money%3F%27+Advertising+Campaign+for...-a0129351450.

Prisco, P. 2009. Izzo's track record in March put Spartans in good spot. *CBSSports.com* http://www.cbssports.com/collegebasketball/story/11537767.

Radelet, M.A., S.M. Lephart, E.N. Rubinstein, and J.B. Myers. 2002. Survey of the injury rate for children in community sports. *Pediatrics* 110: e3.

Raedeke, T.D., and A.L. Smith. 2001. Development and preliminary validation of an athlete burnout measure. *Journal of Sport and Exercise Psychology* 23: 281–306.

Ravizza, K., and T. Hanson. 1994. *Heads-up baseball: Playing the game one pitch at a time.* Chicago: Masters.

Reger, J. 2002. *Quotable Wooden.* Lanham, MD: TowleHouse.

Reilly, R. 2002. Out of touch with my feminine side. *Sports Illustrated,* 102 (April 3).

Rice, G. 1941. Alumnus football (poem). In *Only the brave, and other poems* (p. 144). New York: Barnes.

Roberts, G.C. 1980. Children in competition: A theoretical perspective and recommendations for practice. *Motor Skills: Theory into Practice* 4: 37–50.

Roberts, G.C. 2001. Understanding the dynamics of motivation in physical activity: The influence of achievement goals on motivational processes. In *Advances in motivation in sport and exercise,* ed. G.C. Roberts, 1–50. Champaign, IL: Human Kinetics.

Robinson, T.T., and A.V. Carron. 1982. Personal and situational factors associated with dropping out versus maintaining participation in competitive sport. *Journal of Sport Psychology* 4: 364–378.

Rockne, K. 1924. Letter on psychology and motivation written to Coleman R. Griffith. Coleman Griffith Collection. University Archives, University of Illinois at Urbana-Champaign.

Rose, J., and R.F.J. Jevne. 1993. Psychosocial processes associated with athletic injuries. *The Sport Psychologist* 7: 309–328.

Rosenfeld, A., and N. Wise. 2000. *The over-scheduled child: Avoiding the hyper-parenting trap.* New York: St. Martin's.

Rosenthal, R., and L. Jacobson. 1968. *Pygmalion in the classroom: Teacher expectation and pupils' intellectual development.* New York: Rinehart and Winston.

Rothenberg, R. 1999. Ad age advertising century: The greatest icon. *Advertising Age.* March 29. Available online at: http://adage.com/article/special-report-the-advertising-century/ad-age-advertising-century-greatest-icon/140149/.

Russell, B., and T. Branch. 1979. *Second wind: The memoirs of an opinionated man.* New York: Random House.

Ryan, E.D. 1977. Attribution, intrinsic motivation, and athletics. In *Proceedings of the National Association for Physical Education of College Men/National Association for Physical Education of College Women National Conference,* eds. L.I. Gedvilas and M.E. Kneer, 346–353. Chicago: University of Illinois at Chicago Circle Press.

Ryan, E.D. 1980. Attribution, intrinsic motivation, and athletics: A replication and extension. In *Psychology of motor behavior and sport, 1979,* eds. C.H. Nadeau, W.R. Halliwell, K.M. Newell, and G.C. Roberts, 19–26. Champaign, IL: Human Kinetics.

Ryan, J. 2000. *Little girls in pretty boxes: The making and breaking of elite gymnasts and figure skaters.* New York: Warner.

Ryan, R.M., and E.L. Deci. 2000. Self-determination theory and the facilitation of intrinsic motivation, social development, and well-being. *American Psychologist* 55: 68–78.

Sanderson, F.H., and H.T.A. Whiting. 1974. Dynamic visual acuity and performance in a catching task. *Journal of Motor Behavior* 6: 87–94.

Sanderson, F.H., and H.T.A. Whiting. 1978. Dynamic visual acuity: A possible factor in catching performance. *Journal of Motor Behavior* 10: 7–14.

Santoliquito, J. 2006. Youth coach faced gun-toting parent. *ESPN.com,* Oct. 25

Schlabach, M. 2007. Rush's health a key for the Jayhawks' season. *ESPN.com.* http://sports.espn.go.com/ncb/columns/story?columnist=schlabach_mark&id=3060383

Schwartz, L. (1999). The Great One. *ESPN.com.* http://a.espncdn.com/sportscentury/features/00229711.html.

Scout.com. 2006. *Marinelli discontent after loss to Seattle.* September 11, 2006. http://det.scout.com/2/566996.html.

Seifriz, J., J.L. Duda, and L. Chi. 1992. The relationship of perceived motivational climate to intrinsic motivation and beliefs about success in basketball. *Journal of Sport and Exercise Psychology* 14: 375–391.

Shelley, G.A. 1999. Using qualitative case analysis in the study of athletic injury: A model for implementation. In *Psychological bases of sport injuries,* 2nd ed, ed. D. Pargman, 305–319. Morgantown, WV: Fitness Information Technology.

Sifton, E. 2003. *The serenity prayer: Faith and politics in times of peace and war.* New York: Norton.

Sink, M. 2002. Hockey youth game postponed after fight by parents. *New York Times.* Feb. 1.

Smith, G. 1998. Eyes of the storm. *Sports Illustrated.* March 2.

Smith, R.E. 1986. Toward a negative-affective model of athletic burnout. *Journal of Sport Psychology* 8: 36–50.

Sonner, S. 2008. *Romo says kids should play more than one sport.* Associated Press

Story. http://seattletimes.nwsource.com/html/sports/2009495737_apglftahoecelebsromo.html.

Spence, J.T., and K.W. Spence. 1966. The motivational components of manifest anxiety: Drive and drive stimuli. In *Anxiety and behavior,* ed. C.D. Spielberger, 291–326. New York: Academic.

Sperber, M. 1993. *Shake down the thunder: The creation of Notre Dame football.* Bloomington: Indiana University Press.

SportsIllustrated.com. 2012. Texas high school to open $60M football stadium. http://sportsillustrated.cnn.com/2012/highschool/08/30/allen-high-football-stadium.ap/index.html

Stack Magazine 2007. *Pete Carroll on multisport athletes* (video interview). http://www.stack.com/video/1353518167/Pete-Carroll-on-MultiSport-Athletes/.

Stallings, L.M. 1982. *Motor learning from theory to practice.* St. Louis: Mosby.

Starkes, J. L. 2000. The road to expertise: Is practice the only determinant? *International Journal of Sport Psychology* 31: 431–451.

Stenson, J. (2005). Keeping kids in the game: Too much emphasis on one sport can lead to lasting injuries. MSNBC.com. http://www.msnbc.msn.com/id/7288461/.

StopHazing.org. 2005a. Myths and facts about hazing. http://www.stophazing.org/mythsandfacts.html.

StopHazing.org. 2005b. State Anti-Hazing Laws. http://www.stophazing.org/laws.html.

Suzuki, S. 1970. *Zen mind, beginner's mind.* New York: Weatherhill.

Teel, D. 2004. J.J. and the picture perfect jump shot; Duke's shooting star taught himself the basics. *Newport News Daily Press.* p. C1. February 22.

Thompson, A., R. Barnsley, and G. Stebelsky. 1991. "Born to play ball": The relative age effect and major league baseball. *Sociology of Sport Journal* 8: 146–151.

Treasure, D.C. 1997. Perceptions of the motivational climate and elementary school children's cognitive and affective responses. *Journal of Sport and Exercise Psychology* 19: 278–290.

Treasure, D.C. 2001. Enhancing young people's motivation in youth sport: An achievement goal approach. In *Advances in motivation in sport and exercise*, ed. G.C. Roberts, 79–100. Champaign, IL: Human Kinetics.

Tse, T.M. 2003. *"Tough call" on Mepham coaches*. Newsday.com. (November 2). http://www.newsday.com/news/tough-call-on-coaches-1.333741.

Tucker, D. 2008. Knee injury may have been blessing for Brandon Rush, Kansas. *USAToday.com*. http://www.usatoday.com/sports/college/mensbasketball/2008-02-08-2497864919_x.htm

Twain, M. 1876. *The adventures of Tom Sawyer*. Hartford, CT: American.

Udry. E. 1999. The paradox of injuries: Unexpected positive consequences. In *Psychological bases of sport injuries,* 2nd ed., ed. D. Pargman, 79–88. Morgantown, WV: Fitness Information Technology.

Udry, E., D. Gould, D. Bridges, and L. Beck. 1997. Down but not out: Athlete responses to season-ending injury. *Journal of Sport and Exercise Psychology* 19: 229–248.

United States Department of Education. 2011. Office of Postsecondary Education Equity in Athletics Disclosure Website. http://www.ope.ed.gov/athletics.

USAToday.com. 2004. *Parent allegedly beats Little League coach with metal bat.* http://www.usatoday.com/news/nation/2004-04-14-baseball-fight_x.htm.

Vallerand, R.J. 1997. Toward a hierarchical model of intrinsic and extrinsic motivation. *Advances in Experimental Social Psychology* 29: 271–360.

Vallerand, R.J. 2001. A hierarchical model of intrinsic and extrinsic motivation in sport and exercise. In *Advances in motivation in sport and exercise*, ed. G.C. Roberts, 263–319. Champaign, IL: Human Kinetics.

Verhulst, J. 1992. Seasonal birth distribution of West European soccer players: A possible explanation. *Medical Hypotheses* 38: 346–348.

Wahl, G., and L.J. Wertheim. 2003. A rite gone terribly wrong. *Sports Illustrated*, December 22, pp. 68–77.

Walsh, B. (with S. Jamison and C. Walsh). 2009. *The score takes care of itself: My philosophy of leadership*. New York: Portfolio.

Walton, D. 1992. *The place of emotion in argument*. University Park: Pennsylvania State University Press.

Weber, J. 2002. Wolverines guided by mental toughness. *Detroit Free Press*. May 23.

Weinberg, R.S., and D. Gould. 2003. *Foundations of Sport & Exercise Psychology*, 3rd ed. Champaign, IL: Human Kinetics.

Weinberg, R.S., and D. Gould. 2007. *Foundations of sport and exercise psychology,* 4th ed. Champaign, IL: Human Kinetics.

Weinberg, R.S., and D. Gould. 2011. *Foundations of sport and exercise psychology,* 5th ed. Champaign, IL: Human Kinetics.

Weiss, M.R., and A.J. Amarose. 2008. Motivational orientations and sport behavior. In *Advances in sport psychology,* 3rd ed., ed. T.S. Horn, 115–154. Champaign, IL: Human Kinetics.

Weiss, W.M., and M.R. Weiss. 2003. Attraction- and entrapment-based commitment among competitive female gymnasts. *Journal of Sport and Exercise Psychology* 25: 229–247.

Wieberg, S. 2004. Millions of dollars pour into high school football. *USAToday.com*. http://www.usatoday.com/sports/preps/football/2004-10-05-spending-cover-x.htm.

Wiese-Bjornst, D.M., A.M. Smith, S.M. Shaffer, and M.A. Morrey. 1998. An integrated model of response to sport injury: Psychological and sociological dynamics. *Journal of Applied Sport Psychology* 10: 46–69.

Witz, B. 2008. Soccer as N.B.A. building block. *NewYorkTimes.com*. (May). http://www.nytimes.com/2008/05/18/sports/basketball/18lakers.html.

Wooden, J., and S. Jamison. 2010. *The wisdom of Wooden: My century on and off the court*. New York: McGraw-Hill.

Wooden, J. (with S. Jamison). 1997. *Wooden: A lifetime of observations and reflections on and off the court*. Chicago: Contemporary.

Wooden, J. (with S. Jamison). 2004. *My personal best: Life lessons from an All-American journey*. New York: McGraw-Hill.

Wooden, J. (with S. Jamison), 2005. *Wooden on leadership.* New York: McGraw-Hill.

Woods, E. (with P. McDaniel). 1997. *Training a Tiger: A father's guide to raising a winner in both golf and life.* New York: HarperCollins.

Wrisberg, C.A., and L.A. Fisher. 2004. The benefits of injury. *Athletic Therapy Today* 9 no.6: 50–51.

Young, D.C. 1994. On the source of the Olympic Credo. *OLYMPIKA: The International Journal of Olympic Studies* 3: 17–25.

Ziglar, Z. 2000. *See you at the top: 25th Anniversary Edition,* 2d rev. ed. Gretna, LA: Pelican.

Index